RACE TALK AND THE CONSPIRACY OF SILENCE

Understanding and Facilitating Difficult Dialogues on Race

DERALD WING SUE

WILEY

Library of Congress Cataloging-in-Publication Data

Sue, Derald Wing.
    Race talk and the conspiracy of silence : understanding and facilitating difficult dialogues on race / Derald Wing Sue. — 1
        pages cm
    Includes index.
    ISBN 978-1-118-95872-8 (hardback : alk. paper)
    ISBN 978-1-119-24198-0 (paper)
    ISBN 978-1-118-95965-7 (ePub)
    ISBN 978-1-118-95966-4 (ePDF)
    1. Social psychology. 2. Racism in education. 3. Multicultural education. I. Title.
    HM1019.S84 2015
    370.117—dc23
                                                                        2014031894

Printed in the United States of America

10 9 8 7 6 5 4 3 2 1

*I would like to dedicate this book to my wife, Paulina Wee;
my son, Derald Paul; my daughter, Marissa Catherine;
my daughter-in-law, Claire Iris; and my granddaughters,
Carolyn Riley and Juliette Daisy.
I have been truly blessed in having such a loving
and supportive family, and they bring such joy to my life.*

Contents

Preface

Race Talk and the Conspiracy of Silence is a sequel to the highly successful book *Microaggressions in Everyday Life: Race, Gender, and Sexual Orientation* (Sue, 2010). It was developed over a 10-year period of research and observation of participants engaged in difficult conversations on race, racism, Whiteness, and White privilege. Our research team, for example, discovered that almost all difficult dialogues on race were triggered by racial microaggressions that were often invisible to the perpetrators during race talk. We found that difficult dialogues on race are most likely to occur when interpersonal encounters (a) highlight major differences in worldviews, personalities, and perspectives; (b) are challenged publicly; (c) are found to be offensive to others; (d) may reveal uncomfortable personal racial biases and prejudices; (e) arouse or trigger intense emotional responses; (f) are more difficult when they involve an unequal status relationship of power and privilege between the participants; and (g) contain a hidden disparaging message to people of color (racial microaggression) who find these interactions offensive, triggering intense emotional responses. The explosive nature of race talk makes it hard for participants to understand one another's points of view. Any individual or group engaged in a difficult dialogue feels at risk for potentially disclosing intimate thoughts, beliefs, or feelings related to the topic of race.

It goes without saying that race talk between individuals from different racial/cultural groups is often filled with strong powerful emotions, misunderstandings, accusations, and negative outcomes. How our society perceives race is centuries old and is filled with ambivalence, confusion, misunderstanding, conflict, and intensely powerful feelings. The way we engage in race talk is reenacted daily in worksites, community forums, media, neighborhoods, churches, and classrooms. As classrooms become increasingly diverse, for example, difficult dialogues on race have often served to polarize students and teachers alike, rather than to clarify and increase mutual understanding about race and race relations. Our studies suggest that most well-intentioned teachers, trainers, and facilitators of race talk find themselves ill prepared to deal with the often explosive race-related emotions that manifest themselves in the classroom and places of employment. Poorly handled by teachers and trainers, such dialogues may result in disastrous consequences (anger, hostility, silence, complaints, misunderstandings, blockages of the learning process, etc.); skillfully handled, they present an opportunity for growth, improved communication, and learning.

The primary purpose of writing this book is fivefold: (1) to uncover the reasons that race talk is difficult, (2) to expose the explicit and hidden rules that govern how race is discussed in U.S. society, (3) to illuminate the detrimental consequences of a failure to honestly dialogue about race, (4) to outline the benefits of successful conversations on race, and (5) to propose solutions in overcoming obstacles to honest racial dialogues. In essence, this book is about the psychology of racial dialogues and the meaning, importance, and benefits they have for our society. It is written for educators who teach and work in academic and school settings; trainers and facilitators in business, industry, governmental agencies, and health settings concerned with improving race relations through honest conversations on race; and parents who must help their children (White and children of color) navigate the contradictions and hidden messages of racial prejudice, bias, and discrimination. These objectives are extremely important for several reasons.

First, it has been shown that honest race talk is one of the most powerful means to dispel stereotypes and biases, to increase racial literacy and critical consciousness about race issues, to decrease fear of differences, to broaden one's horizons, to increase compassion and empathy, to increase appreciation of all colors and cultures, and to enhance a greater sense of belonging and connectedness.

Second, research suggests that the inability of teachers, trainers, and parents to facilitate a successful dialogue on race has major consequences for persons of color because being unheard and silenced (a) assails their mental health, (b) creates a hostile and invalidating campus, work, or societal climate, (c) perpetuates stereotype threat, (d) creates physical health problems, (e) saturates the broader society with cues that signal devaluation of social group identities, and (f) lowers classroom and work productivity and problem solving abilities.

Third, a failure of successful race talk has negative effects on White Americans as well. The inability or reluctance to dialogue openly and honestly with people of color on topics of race and racism leads to a lack of checks and balances to their worldviews. It (a) lowers empathic ability, (b) dims perceptual awareness and accuracy, (c) lessens compassion for others, (d) leads to self-denigration and a sense of failure, and (e) allows many to live in a world of false deception about the nature and operation of racism and their complicity in the perpetuation of silence.

ORGANIZATION

Race Talk and the Conspiracy of Silence is divided into five sections.

Section I: The Characteristics, Dynamics, and Meaning of Race Talk is composed of three chapters.

Chapter 1: What Is Race Talk?
Chapter 2: The Characteristics and Dynamics of Race Talk
Chapter 3: The Stories We Tell: White Talk Versus Back Talk

All three chapters introduce readers to the manifestation, dynamics, meaning, and impact of race talk for both White Americans and people of color. One of the primary goals of these chapters is to help readers recognize when a difficult dialogue on race is occurring, the psychological and societal barriers preventing honest dialogue, and more importantly the hidden meanings (oftentimes disparaging) being transmitted between different individuals and groups. Race talk is truly a clash of different racial realities in which people of color and Whites perceive race issues in opposition to one another.

Section II: The Constraining Ground Rules for Race Talk is composed of two chapters.

Chapter 4: "The Entire World's a Stage!"
Chapter 5: Color-Blind Means Color-Mute

These chapters bring to light the hidden ground rules embedded in society, in academia, and in ourselves that serve as barriers to honest race talk. The politeness protocol, a powerful ground rule in race talk, is exacerbated because of impression management strategies we all use. In academia, the academic protocol reveals Western European norms (how we learn and ask/answer questions about the human condition) that allow educators to avoid and/or dilute the meaning and importance of race talk. More importantly is the discussion and analysis of color blindness and how it silences race talk. Color blindness, rather than enhancing race relations, seems to be harmful and detrimental to those who profess it and to those who experience it.

Section III: Why Is It Difficult for People of Color to Honestly Talk About Race? is composed of two chapters.

Chapter 6: "What Are the Consequences for Saying What I Mean?"
Chapter 7: "To Speak or How to Speak, That Is the Question"

These chapters are unique in that they discuss the fears, constraints, and concerns from people of color about honest race talk. In this case, issues of power and oppression, forced compliance, fear of the consequences for honestly saying what they mean, and concern whether their communication styles will make them misunderstood are the central issues covered in these chapters. In addition to the effects power inequalities have on race talk, these chapters explore the damaging consequences they have on people of color.

Section IV: Why Is It Difficult for White People to Honestly Talk About Race? contains two chapters.

Chapter 8: "I'm Not Racist!"
Chapter 9: "I'm Not White; I'm Italian!"

Complementing the last section on why people of color find race talk difficult, these chapters explore why Whites find honest racial dialogues anxiety provoking. These chapters explore in depth why Whites find race talk frightening. As a result, they use many forms of denial to keep from concluding that they possess racist attitudes and biases and that they ultimately benefit from White privilege. Race talk threatens to unmask the hidden secrets of racism and potentially forces Whites to consider their responsibility in the perpetuation of racism.

Section V: Race Talk and Special Group Considerations contains two chapters.

Chapter 10: Interracial/Interethnic Race Talk: Difficult Dialogues Between Groups of Color
Chapter 11: Race Talk and White Racial Identity Development: For Whites Only

These two chapters discuss unique race talk issues specific to people of color and Whites. Few scholarly works address the issue of interracial/interethnic relationships and the difficult racial dialogues that ensue from them. Chapter 10 specifically deals with the hot-button issues of bias and prejudice among groups of color, and the difficulty they have talking about them with one another. The chapter makes a distinction between race talk between groups of color and of that between Whites and people of color. This distinction can be a subject of a difficult dialogue as well. Chapter 11 has the subheading "For Whites Only" and is meant to alert White Americans to two things: (1) the need to develop a nonracist and antiracist White identity, and (2) how White awareness is related to race talk. Both chapters cover topics usually avoided in racial discourse.

Section VI: Guidelines, Conditions, and Solutions for Having Honest Racial Dialogues includes two last chapters.

Chapter 12: Being an Agent of Change: Guidelines for Educators, Parents, and Trainers

Chapter 13: Helping People Talk About Race: Facilitation Skills for Educators and Trainers

These chapters pull together lessons learned from the previous ones to derive implications as to how educators, facilitators, and parents can break the silence of race, to help trainees, students, and children not fear discussions of race, and to point out that parents and educators are in unique and vital roles to help their charges understand issues of race and racism. It outlines specific actions and experiences both trainers and trainees must undergo in order to benefit from race talk. The last chapter was especially written for teachers and trainers who are concerned with how to facilitate difficult dialogues on race.

FINAL THOUGHTS

Although this book is on the psychology of race talk, it is really more than that. The attitudes, beliefs, and fears inherent in race talk symbolize our society's resistance to unmasking the embedded inequities and basic unfairness imposed on citizens of color. We avoid honest racial dialogues because innocence and naïveté could no longer serve as excuses for inaction. Race talk potentially makes the "invisible" visible and opens gateways to view the world of oppression through realistic eyes. It has the possibility of helping us becoming nonracist and antiracist. But silence and inaction only serve to perpetuate the status quo of race relations. Will we, as a nation, choose the path we have always traveled, a journey of silence that has benefited only a select group and oppressed others, or will we show courage and choose the road less traveled, a journey of racial reality that may be full of discomfort and pain, but offers benefits to all groups in our society? It would be unfortunate, indeed, to look back one day and echo the words of poet John Greenleaf Whittier, who wrote, "For of all sad words of tongue or pen, the saddest are these: It might have been!"

Preface to the Paperback Edition

In the nine months since release of the hardcover version of this book, we have been given more and more reasons to become aware of the conspiracy of silence surrounding issues of race and racism. Even when forced to confront matters of bigotry and discrimination, the implications of these dialogues have been resisted, avoided, dismissed, and/or minimized by politicians, civic leaders, many concerned citizens, and even well-intentioned educators. Knowingly or unknowingly, our society has colluded in a conspiracy of silence about race that allows those in power to live in comfort, naiveté and innocence, while people of color continue to live quiet lives of desperation, attempting to speak, but having their voices unheard or silenced.

For many years I have watched with disappointment and sadness as Americans have wrestled with issues of race and racism in apparent futility. From shooting deaths of unarmed Black men such as Trayvon Martin, Michael Brown and Tamir Rice (12-year old youth), the unwarranted federal charges of espionage against Chinese Americans such as Professor Xi Xianoxing of Temple University and hydrologist Sherry Chen of the National Weather Service, and the recent school suspension and police detention of 14-year old Ahmed Mohamed because he was suspected of building a suspicious device (a clock as a science project) pose difficult questions concerning the role racial bias plays in these heartbreaking incidents.

Did race have anything to do with the shooting deaths of these three African American males? Did the arrest of Dr. Xi and Mrs. Chen have anything to do with their Chinese ancestry, and our current soured relations with China? Did anti-Muslim sentiment or terrorist stereotypes of Middle Easterners play a role in the arrest of teenager Ahmed Mohamed? From the perspective of many people of color, the answer is a resounding "Yes!" People of color also assert that these overt incidents represent only the tip of the iceberg, and that they also experience less visible but equally harmful forms of constant and continual racial microaggressions that serve to denigrate, insult, invalidate and disempower them.

The continual media reports of African Americans being unjustly profiled, arrested and killed has led to the "Black Lives Matter" movement in an attempt to bring attention to the plight of Black people. The movement has challenged White society's false assumption that race plays a minor or insignificant role in the actions taken by law enforcement agencies, and societal disparities that exist between Blacks and Whites in living standards. Rather than listen and engage in open dialogue, many White Americans have countered the phrase "Black lives matter" with "White lives matter," or "All lives matter;" thereby diluting or diminishing the legitimacy of racial concerns. The fact that African American men are 21% more likely to be killed by the police than White men and that African Americans as a group have a significantly lower standard of living in employment, healthcare, and education are silenced or unspoken secrets. Many in our society simply ignore these disparities, diminish their importance, offer more benign explanations for their existence, or simply do not believe these disparities are due to racism.

Interestingly, when incidents of "racial misunderstanding occur," however, the most common solution offered by educators, political pundits, news commentators and business leaders is the need to engage in racial dialogues. Americans need to talk more about race in order to increase mutual understanding and racial harmony. But instead of bridging racial divides, much of the recent discussion of race and racism in mainstream and social media seems to have increased antagonism between racial groups and led to a hardening of biased views.

Why do attempts at racial dialogue fail so miserably? I have found that simply encouraging people to discuss race issues without understanding what it entails can actually prove detrimental and harmful. Unless one understands the dynamics and meaning of racial conversations, and unless it is carefully planned, racial dialogues can actually backfire and create greater chasms between groups.

Racial dialogues represent a clash of racial realities. In many respects race talk is grounded in the stories we tell to ourselves and others about our values, beliefs and opinions on race. For many White Americans who engage in racial conversations they are expressing honest beliefs that racism is a thing of the past, that they personally do not harbor racist beliefs, that anyone who works hard in this society can succeed, and that they treat everyone with respect and dignity.

The stories from people of color contain different themes that are akin to "telling on racism." Race talk from people of color challenges the racial reality of White Americans: "We do not live in a post-racial era, racism is alive and well, meritocracy is a myth, and White people are unknowingly responsible for creating many of the hardships experienced by people of color."

Herein lay one of the major obstacles to honest and meaningful racial conversations. Many well-intentioned citizens harbor deep-seated fears about possessing unconscious racial biases that assail their images of being good, moral and decent human beings who would never intentionally discriminate. Race talk threatens to unmask the ugly secrets of personal prejudices. Ironically, successful racial dialogues as a means to increase awareness and compassion can only come about when we acknowledge and take responsibility for our implicit biases and behaviors.

None of us is immune from inheriting the racial biases of our society. We were not born into this world freely choosing to be bigoted and biased! We took this on through a painful process of social and cultural conditioning. Until we are honest with ourselves can we be open and honest with one another.

In closing, I am reminded of a statement by Dallas Mavericks owner Mark Cuban when he publicly stated: "know I'm prejudiced, and I know I'm bigoted in a lot of different ways . . . If I see a black kid in a hoodie on my side of the street, I'll move to the other side of the street. If I see a white guy with a shaved head and tattoo, I'll move back to the other side of the street. None of us have pure thoughts; we all live in glass houses."

Cuban's point was that everyone is prejudiced. Acknowledgement is the first step to successful racial dialogues and to overcoming our biases.

Learning to talk about race is crucial if we hope to achieve the equal society that has long been part of the American mythos. Each one of us, through our everyday interactions with each other and the example we provide for the next generation, can contribute to this hallmark of social justice. In *Race Talk and the Conspiracy of Silence*, a concrete set of guidelines and solutions for engaging in honest racial dialogue will help policy makers, politicians, law enforcement officials, educators, parents, and trainers become agents of change by bringing the issue of race to light in a positive manner.

Derald Wing Sue

Acknowledgments

Writing this book has been another labor of love, and finishing it has provided me with a deep sense of accomplishment and satisfaction. Ironically, as I experience the sense of happiness and fulfillment, I am also deeply saddened by the passing of Maya Angelou. Her life, how she lived it, and her powerful voice in the face of oppression helped many of us to find the courage to speak against bias, bigotry, and racism. She was a true inspiration and I (we) will all miss her. But the legacy and writings she has left behind assure us she will not be forgotten, and she will continue to impact many generations to come. It is people like Maya Angelou, who, despite my never having known them personally, have been responsible for helping me write this book. In mind and spirit, she will always be with me (us). So thank you, Maya.

About the Author

Derald Wing Sue is Professor of Psychology and Education in the Department of Counseling and Clinical Psychology at Teachers College, Columbia University. He also has a courtesy appointment with the Columbia University School of Social Work. He served as president of the Society for the Psychological Study of Ethnic Minority Issues, the Society of Counseling Psychology, and the Asian American Psychological Association. Dr. Sue has served and continues to serve as consulting editor for numerous publications. He is author of over 160 publications, including 18 books, and is well-known for his work on racism/antiracism, cultural competence, multicultural counseling and therapy, and social justice advocacy. Three of his books, *Counseling the Culturally Diverse: Theory and Practice*; *Microaggressions in Everyday Life: Race, Gender, and Sexual Orientation*; and *Overcoming Our Racism: The Journey to Liberation*, are considered classics in the field. Dr. Sue's research on racial, gender, and sexual orientation microaggressions provided a major breakthrough in understanding how everyday slights, insults, and invalidations toward marginalized groups create psychological harm to their mental and physical health, and create disparities for them in education, employment, and health care. His most recent research on the psychology of racial dialogues represents breakthroughs in identifying why race talk elicits so much anxiety among participants. Two national surveys have identified Derald Wing Sue as "the most influential multicultural scholar in the United States," and his works are among the most frequently cited.

The Characteristics, Dynamics, and Meaning of Race Talk

CHAPTER ONE

What Is Race Talk?

It gets so tiring, you know. It sucks you dry. People don't trust you. From the moment I [African American male] wake up, I know stepping out the door, that it will be the same, day after day. The bus can be packed, but no one will sit next to you.... I guess it may be a good thing because you always get more room, no one crowds you. You get served last...when they serve you, they have this phony smile and just want to get rid of you...you have to show more ID to cash a check, you turn on the TV and there you always see someone like you, being handcuffed and jailed. They look like you and sometimes you begin to think it is you! You are a plague! You try to hold it in, but sometimes you lose it. Explaining doesn't help. They don't want to hear. Even when they ask, "Why do you have a chip on your shoulder?" Shit...I just walk away now. It doesn't do any good explaining. (Sue, 2010, p. 87)

Questions: Is life as hard as this Black man describes? Is he exaggerating or misreading the action of others? Is he oversensitive or paranoid? Is he right in concluding that others don't want to listen to his explanations? Why is he so angry and resentful? Do you believe him or not? If not, what are your reasons?

Thomas Lee was a Chinese American award-winning journalist for the *Star Tribune* who went to interview the president of a large manufacturing company. He arrived a few minutes late and informed the receptionist at the front desk that he was looking for the president's executive assistant. She responded by asking whether he was delivering food from a local Chinese restaurant. Lee recounts that this wasn't the first time he had been mistaken for a Chinese food delivery person. In college he had similar experiences when he would arrive at his girlfriend's dorm with dinner and the attendant would assume just that. Embarrassed by such encounters, he generally let them go, but it consistently left him feeling like a second-class citizen. Writing about this experience in the *Star Tribune*, he provides insights into the internal dilemma of Chinese Americans who are frequently stereotyped as service workers. The experience was even more stunning to him because he was wearing a dress shirt, black slacks, and black dress shoes. True, he also wore sunglasses and was sporting a backpack, but Lee asked how many food delivery guys carry kung pao chicken in a Gap bag? When the receptionist realized her error, Lee said she offered a clumsy explanation and said her boss always ordered food for lunch. He sarcastically wrote that he was grateful she didn't speak extra slowly to him, or offer a tip (Lee, 2009).

Questions: Have you ever mistaken a person of color for a service worker? Or, as a White person, have you ever been mistaken for a service worker? What were your reactions? How did you handle the situation? Did you make up an excuse? Were you offended? Why is it such a big deal? Is there a difference between being mistaken for a service worker as a White person or a person of color? What are the differences?

Discussing race issues in class is one of my greatest fears as a teacher [White female professor]. Nothing good ever seems to come from it. Last week, we discussed the intersection of race and law. New York City's "stop and frisk" policy came up. Some of the students of color called it "racial profiling" but one White student indirectly implied it was warranted because of crime statistics. He [White student] stated that most crimes were committed by Blacks, especially in Harlem. It was an incendiary moment, and the exchanges were explosive! Students of color accused certain classmates of being racially biased. Most of the White students were scared to death and refused to participate. One White female student began to cry. I tried my best to comfort her and admonished students to respect one another. When that didn't work, I tabled the discussion. For the rest of the semester whenever the topic of race arose we avoided it. I knew I was failing my role as the teacher, but I didn't know what to do. When the semester ended, we were all relieved. (Anonymous workshop participant's story)

Questions: What makes talking about race such a hot-button issue? What do you think was going on with the White students? What do you think was going on with the students of color? What makes racial dialogues so difficult? Can you picture yourself in this situation? What fears would you have as a White person? What fears would you have as a person of color?

You see, the subjects I [White psychologist] am about to discuss—ethnocentrism and racism, including my own racism—are topics that most Whites tend to avoid. We shy away from discussing these issues for many reasons: We are racked with guilt over the way people of color have been treated in our nation; we fear that we will be accused of mistreating others; we particularly fear being called the "R" word—racist—so we grow uneasy whenever issues of race emerge; and we tend to back away, change the subject, respond defensively, assert our innocence and our "color blindness," denying that we could possibly be ethnocentric or racist. (Kiselica, 1999, p. 14)

Questions: Is Kiselica admitting to us that he is a racist? Is he a bad person or an honest person? What does the word *racist* mean to you? Is it possible for anyone born and raised in the United States not to have inherited the racial biases, prejudices, and stereotypes of our ancestors? Is it difficult for you to entertain this notion? How accurate is Kiselica's description of the strategies used to avoid talking about race?

These four vignettes introduce us to the psychology of racial dialogues, conversations that touch upon topics of race, racism, Whiteness, and White privilege (Sue, 2013). The purpose of writing this book is fivefold: (1) to uncover the reasons that make race talk difficult, (2) to expose the explicit and hidden rules that govern how race is discussed in U.S. society, (3) to illuminate the detrimental consequences of a failure to honestly dialogue about race, (4) to outline the benefits of successful conversations on race, and (5) to propose solutions in overcoming obstacles to honest racial dialogues. In essence, this book is about the psychology of racial dialogues, and the meaning, importance, and benefits they have for our society.

How our society perceives race is centuries old and is filled with ambivalence, confusion, misunderstanding, conflict, and intense, powerful feelings.

The ways that we perceive and talk about race are reenacted daily in worksites, community forums, media, neighborhoods, churches, and classrooms. Current events in our society remind us that the election of the first African American president, Barack Obama, did not signal the beginning of a post-racial era and that racism would become a thing of the past. The killing of Trayvon Martin, an African American teenager, on February 26, 2012, and the subsequent acquittal of George Zimmerman on July 13, 2013, have created a national uproar on the role of race and racism in our society and, especially, the law. This high-profile event was followed on August 9, 2014, in Ferguson, Missouri, with the killing of Michael Brown, an unarmed African American 18-year-old, by a White police officer. The incident set off riots in Ferguson, allegations of racism and a local police cover-up, and calls for an independent investigation by the Justice Department and the FBI. Once again, as in many times in the past, calls for a national dialogue on race were echoed by many people of color and White allies. Once again, however, it was met by counter-arguments that race had nothing to do with the shooting of Michael Brown or Trayvon Martin or the outcome of the George Zimmerman verdict (CNN Staff, 2014; Eligon, 2013; Keita, 2013; Yankah, 2013). Once again, our nation witnessed angry debates that served to divide and confuse rather than bridge, clarify, and heal.

These two opposing viewpoints represent divisions much deeper than just a difference of opinion, but point to why dialogues on race are so difficult to bridge; they inevitably evoke a clash of racial realities (Sue et al., 2007). The four narratives presented at the beginning give us some idea of the manifestation, dynamics, and impact of race talk. Discussions of race between people with differing racial realities (Bell, 2002; Bonilla-Silva, 2006; Sue, 2010) are likely to engender strong feelings of discomfort, anger, and anxiety; most people prefer to avoid the topic of race, to remain silent, to minimize its importance or impact, or to pretend not to notice it. It is not far-fetched to say that talking about race is one of the most difficult conversations to undertake as it is potentially filled with accusations and/or possible unpleasant revelations about oneself and others. But, we are still left with the nagging question: Why are honest conversations about race such a difficult undertaking? The opening four quotes provide clues to the psychology of racial dialogues. Let us briefly use them to analyze some of the dynamics and principles that underlie race talk that I hope to cover in this book.

RACE TALK REPRESENTS A POTENTIAL CLASH OF RACIAL REALITIES

First, quotes from the African American and Asian American men in our opening narratives represent a racial reality that Whites seldom experience. In the former, the Black American is telling a story of a life filled with incidents of racial microaggressions that deem him "a dangerous Black male," "up to no good," a potentially violent criminal, untrustworthy, and someone to be avoided. In the latter case, the Asian American journalist is lamenting the fact that well-intentioned Whites continue to perceive him as a service worker (delivery boy) and that such stereotypes follow him everywhere and are constant and continuing across situations. Sue et al. (2007) have labeled these as "racial microaggressions"—the everyday slights, insults, indignities, and invalidations delivered toward people of color because of their visible racial/ethnic minority characteristics.

In a historic moment in American politics, President Barack Obama in an impromptu speech on July 19, 2013, made the following statement in the aftermath of the Zimmerman verdict:

> There are very few African American men in this country who haven't had the experience of being followed when they were shopping in a department store. That includes me. There are very few African American men who haven't had the experience of walking across the street and hearing the locks click on the doors of cars. That happens to me—at least before I was a senator. There are very few African Americans who haven't had the experience of getting on an elevator and a woman clutching her purse nervously and holding her breath until she had a chance to get off. That happens often. (Obama, 2013)

President Obama is describing three manifestations of microaggressive behaviors that communicate a common theme directed at Black Americans: They are criminals and potentially dangerous. Being served last, asking for more identification, and mistaking a person of color for a service worker are all racial microaggressions because they contain a hidden message to targets: "You are a second-class citizen," "You are up to no good," and "You are a lesser human being." Studies show that racial microaggressions may appear harmless and trivial, but they are detrimental to mental and physical health, and create disparities in employment, education, and health care (American Psychological Association [APA] Presidential Task Force on

Preventing Discrimination and Promoting Diversity, 2012; Sue, 2010). Yet, despite personal experiences of oppression and discrimination described by people of color, despite President Obama's own reflections of the reality of racism, and despite accumulating evidence in the social-psychological literature that well-intentioned White Americans may harbor unconscious biases (APA Presidential Task Force, 2012), many White Americans continue to deny or to minimize its existence and impact. Here are some responses on the Internet to President Obama's remarks:

> "I thought the President of the United States was president for everyone, not just Black Americans."
>
> "My mother was attacked by three Black men and beaten and kicked. The injuries stayed with her until the day she died. She was scared of Black men not because they were Black, but because she was nearly killed by 3 Black men."
>
> "The President is wrong! This is not a race thing. If I am not mistaken Zimmerman is Hispanic 'n' White."
>
> "The President cannot presume to be a spokesperson for all minorities. My Black friend says these examples are exaggerated. So, Mr. President, control your paranoid self."
>
> "Why would/should/could there be separate versions of laws based on skin color? What specific thing about stand your ground don't you understand? It's for everyone. Separate but equal was a failure, remember?"
>
> "Let's see, Blacks get arrested more and people of other races are weary because statistics prove that Blacks are more likely to commit violent crimes. Don't tell me to turn the other cheek and not be vigilant."

Most of these posted responses were taken from the National Journal Staff (2013), and the overwhelming numbers were negative reactions to President Obama's racial narrative and excoriated him for making what they considered biased statements. In essence, they denied his racial reality and appeared to only consider race issues from their own ethnocentric lens. Each of these reactions may seem logical from a White perspective, but when their basic assumptions are unmasked they reveal a one-sided view of the situation. For example, the second quote suggests that the mother's fear of Black men was not prejudice, but the result of being nearly beaten to death by three African American men. It begs the following question: If the mother had been nearly beaten to death by three White men, would she fear all White males? The belief by respondent 3 that Zimmerman was a person of color contains two erroneous beliefs: (1) persons of color cannot be biased against one another, and (2) a failure of critical consciousness that Latinos/as/Hispanics are an ethnic group and not a racial one. In fact, Latinos/as can be of any racial group (Black, Native American, White, etc.) depending on geographical origin and/or cultural immersion. All the reactions made to Obama's comments represent racial microinvalidations. They are commonly experienced by people of color when they try to tell their stories of discrimination, prejudice, and suffering, oftentimes at the hands of well-intentioned White Americans.

Returning to the story of the Asian American journalist who was mistaken for a Chinese delivery person, Thomas Lee describes telling the story to his friends and colleagues, expecting them to share in the humor, to laugh and to sympathize. He was stunned, however, that they seemed to imply his interpretation was incorrect and that he was oversensitive. Instead of what seemed obvious to Lee (that it was a stereotype), they offered several alternative explanations: It was his backpack; it was his sunglasses; it was his age. Even worse was colleagues' offering Lee tips on how he could avoid these problems in the future. They suggested he wear a jacket, carry a briefcase, or behave differently. One suggestion was for Lee to even walk differently. Lee incredulously responds: "Walk differently? I wasn't aware that I walked like a deliveryman. I'm not even sure how a deliveryman walks. Just to be safe, maybe I should don a tuxedo, speak in a faux British accent, and goose-step my way to the front desk." He did find solace in the words of a close friend who offered a meaningful insight. White people, according to his friend, don't view things in terms of race, while people of color normally do (Lee, 2009).

Should, however, more liberated White people entertain the possibility of bias in their actions or the behavior of others, it is generally dismissed as unintentional and a minor offense: "Both the African American and Asian American (including President Obama) should just 'get over it.'" In other words, racial microaggressions are oftentimes considered by perpetrators to be relatively insignificant slights and that the person of color is overreacting. "Mistaking the Chinese American journalist for a service worker may be insulting and offensive, but what great harm has been done?"

Research, however, shows that while racial microaggressions might seem to be micro acts or small slights, they oftentimes have devastating macro harmful consequences (Sue et al., 2007; Zou & Dickter, 2013). For example, believing Black males are prone to violence and a menace to society can result in situations of racial profiling, more severe or greater likelihood of death sentences given to Black defendants than to White ones, and greater inclination to shoot Black suspects (Correll, 2009; Correll, Park, Judd, & Wittenbrink, 2007; Eberhardt, Davies, Purdie-Vaughns, & Johnson, 2006; J. M. Jones, 2013a, 2013b). In the case of Trayvon Martin and Michael Brown, sadly to say, it may have resulted in their deaths.

Second, it goes without saying that the racial reality of people of color is different than that of White Americans. Dialogues on race seldom bridge these worldviews as they are often antagonistic to one another. The racial reality of most White Americans is of a nation that has conquered racism, that we now live in a postracial era, that racism is a thing of the past, that equal access and opportunity are available to everyone, and that we should be a color-blind society (Bell, 2002, 2003; Bolgatz, 2005; Neville, Awad, Brooks, Flores, & Bluemel, 2013; Pollock, 2004). Herein lays one of the major dilemmas attributed to the invisibility of Whiteness and the racial reality embedded in it. In the George Zimmerman trial, the judge ruled that the phrase *racial profiling* could not be used, but the word *profiling*, without *racial*, was allowable; both the prosecution and defense emphasized that this was not a race issue throughout the trial and in their summations; and finally one of the five White jurors (B-37) said that "race" never arose in the jury deliberations. Nevertheless, it is clear that race was the 800-pound gorilla in the room that everyone pretended not to see.

In other words, considering race was taboo and bringing it into the conversation was playing the race card. The result was that all the key White players (the judge, defense, jurors, and even the prosecution) cooperated in a conspiracy of silence. As the earlier quote from the Chinese American journalist indicates, Whites "don't initially view things in terms of race, while people of color normally do." Even this statement, however, belies the real truth; Whites do view race issues through the prism of their own race and culture (Whiteness), and thus race is always a factor. Whiteness in terms of race is just invisible to them because it represents a default standard from which to compare everything else.

When teachers complain that students of color should not bring their cultural baggage into the classroom, they are unaware that is precisely what they, themselves, are doing (bringing in their cultural baggage and perspectives—White Euro-American norms related to education and teaching, curriculum, history, etc.). Whites view race as residing in others, but not themselves. They may not realize that Whiteness is the background from which the figure of difference emerges. The fact is that race is a function of each and every one of us. As long as Whiteness is invisible, it can be imposed innocently upon people of color with harmful consequences.

> Because White culture is the dominant cultural norm in the United States, it acts as an invisible veil that limits many people from seeing it as a cultural system.... Often, it is easier for many Whites to identify and acknowledge the different cultures of minorities than accept their own racial identity.... The difficulty of accepting such a view is that White culture is omnipresent. It is so interwoven in the fabric of everyday living that Whites cannot step outside and see their beliefs, values, and behaviors as creating a distinct cultural group. (Katz, 1985, pp. 616–617)

RACE TALK PUSHES EMOTIONAL HOT BUTTONS

When in mixed company, race talk often pushes powerful emotional hot buttons in people. The dialogue can become quite heated, evoking personal attacks, and in some cases participants may feel threatened by physical retaliation (Sue, 2013). The feelings and emotions may run the gamut of defensiveness, anxiety, anger, guilt, helplessness, blame, embarrassment, hurt feelings, and invalidation (Utsey, Gernat, & Hammar, 2005; Willow, 2008). These feelings are experienced by both Whites and persons of color, albeit the reasons may be quite different. Returning to the four opening case narratives, let's identify the types of emotions being experienced by the players in these four situations.

First, the Black man expresses strong **anger** and **resentment** toward Whites for how he perceives they are treating him. In interracial dialogues, these feelings are likely to form much of his interactions with others. His daily experiences of racial slights have made him believe that trying to explain to White Americans about these indignities would do little good. In fact, he expresses **pessimism**, rightly or wrongly, that Whites simply do not understand, and worst yet, they do not care to hear his thoughts and feelings about race and racism. He feels **hopeless** and **frustrated** about making White Americans understand and states, "Shit...I just walk away now. It doesn't do any good explaining." In an interracial dialogue, he is likely to have little patience in race talk and likely to have a short fuse and could be quite emotionally explosive in such encounters. Although he does not directly mention it, one can surmise that he is also **tired** and drained at having to constantly deal with the never ending onslaught of microaggressions.

Second, the Chinese American journalist feels **embarrassed** and **insulted** for being mistaken as a Chinese delivery person by the dormitory attendant and the receptionist, and tries to make light of being treated as a second-class citizen. But his narrative indicates that he is deeply **disturbed** by these continual microaggressions as expressed through his **sarcasm** that at least the receptionist did not speak extra slow to him or offer a tip. What seemed to bother him greatly was the attribution that he did something wrong; that he walked like a delivery person, should not have carried a backpack, and so forth. He is **surprised** and **angered** by the fact that even his friends did not understand and seemed to imply that he was to **blame** for these insults. In his interracial dialogues with the receptionist when confronted with her mistake, she chose to cover up (make up an excuse) rather than recover (apologize) from the mistaken assumption. In his attempt to share his experience with friends, they minimized the events and implied the fault lay with the journalist (blaming the victim). His experience in interracial encounters is that **Whites just don't get it!**

The third example of race talk has major implications for conversations on race in the classroom and other public forums. If, as we have indicated, racial dialogues among students are a necessity for developing critical racial consciousness and improving race relations, then this scenario is discouraging. As can be seen, the interaction of the White teacher, White students, and students of color can **trigger intense and overwhelming emotions**. Indeed, the intensity of the interactions resulted in one student **crying** (generally a sign of becoming overcome with emotions). White students often feel unjustly **accused of racism** and become **defensive**. The female teacher also openly admits that discussing race in her classroom is one of her **greatest fears** and characterizes exchanges between White and Black students as incendiary, with the combination of both **anger** and **fear**. Her apprehension about discussing race and racism also appears linked to her feelings of **inadequacy** in facilitating a dialogue on race. The teacher appears **confused** about what was occurring in her classroom and **helpless** about how to manage the dialogue that threatens to get out of control. Thus, rather than facilitate a difficult dialogue on race and making the incident a learning opportunity, she avoids the topic. In interracial dialogues, Whites may choose to opt out or avoid any of the discussions.

Last, it is important to note Mark Kiselica's open admission to racist thoughts, feelings, and behaviors. As a White psychologist, he offers insights into the reasons why many Whites **fear** open dialogues on race; they may ultimately reveal unpleasant secrets about themselves. In his own racial/cultural awakening, he realizes that discussing race and racism is so difficult for many Whites because they are racked with **guilt** about how people of color have been treated in the United States, **fearful** that they will be accused of being a racist, and **blamed** for the oppression of others. Maintaining one's innocence by avoiding racial topics is a major strategy used to hold on to one's self-image as a good, moral, and decent human being who is innocent of racial bias and discrimination. Kiselica's reflection is a powerful statement that addresses a major question: Can anyone born and raised in our society not inherit the racial biases of our ancestors and institutions? When I pose this question to my students, surprisingly an overwhelming number say no. In other words, on an intellectual level they admit that we are products of our social conditioning and escaping internalizing biases and prejudices is impossible. Yet, when racial biases are discussed, they have great difficulty entertaining the notion that they have personally inherited racial biases; "racism resides in others, but not me!"

Thus, it is clear that race talk triggers intense emotions in people and the feelings expressed by participants are multiple and often confusing. These feelings and emotions can be overwhelming and painful, resulting in defensive strategies among participants to avoid, dilute, or sideline race talk. In a series of studies, Sue and colleagues (Sue, Lin, Torino, Capodilupo, & Rivera, 2009; Sue, Rivera, Capodilupo, Lin, & Torino, 2010; Sue et al., 2011; Sue, Torino, Capodilupo, Rivera, & Lin, 2009) found that nested or embedded feelings during race talk often hide the true reasons for these reactions, and that unmasking them can be painful to participants. We will return to this conclusion and discuss their implications and meanings in future chapters.

RACE TALK EVOKES AVOIDANCE STRATEGIES

As mentioned earlier, most people prefer to avoid discussing race for many different reasons. White Americans are fearful that whatever they say or do in a racial dialogue might make them appear biased and racist. Thus, as observed by Kiselica (1999), they may enter a conversation on race with great trepidation, be very careful about what and how they say things, remain silent and guarded, minimize or dilute the importance of the racial issues, profess color blindness, and voice their thoughts and opinions in politically correct language (Bryan, Wilson, Lewis, & Wills, 2012; Ford, 2012; Zou & Dickter, 2013). By these avoidance maneuvers, Whites are likely to present an inauthentic self, to be less than honest, and to be guarded in how much they disclose to others. In their attempts to appear free of bias, their communications often become convoluted and constricted (Bolgatz, 2005; Utsey et al., 2005) and contrary to their intentions, research indicates they have directly the opposite impact on people of color. In other words, these avoidance strategies actually make them appear *more* biased and prejudiced (Shelton, Richeson, Salvatore, & Trawalter, 2005; Vorauer & Turpie, 2004).

Although people of color are generally more willing than their White counterparts to engage in race talk, they are often prevented from doing so for a number of different reasons. Primarily, their experience has been that many White Americans are unprepared or unable to acknowledge race as an intimate factor in interpersonal interactions. In attempting to talk race, they are likely to be met with many resistances and/or punished for bringing up the topic. They may be accused of playing the race card, others may profess color blindness, or their racial realities may be assailed ("Race had nothing to do with it," "There is only once race, the human race," or "Why does everything have to do with race?"). For both the African American and Asian American males in the opening narratives, these are the complaints they are describing. As a result, many persons of color are placed in a situation where bringing up the topic of race may result in denial, interpersonal conflict, or isolation from coworkers, neighbors, or fellow students. In some respects, people of color are very aware how most White Americans are likely to react to racial topics so they may also minimize differences in order to assure acceptance from fellow White Americans. They must walk a tightrope between being true to oneself and at the same time not risk offending others. Let us use an example of this strategy.

In 2004, a young candidate for the U.S. Senate in Illinois, Barack Obama, stood before a national audience at the Democratic National Convention and delivered an eloquent and inspiring speech that catapulted him to political stardom and ultimately the presidency of the United States. The phrase most remembered and cited was when he declared, "There is not a Black America and a White America and Latino America and Asian America; there's the United States of America." The speech, however, that has won him critical acclaim was the one he delivered in 2008, "A More Perfect Union," in response to his relationship to the Reverend Jeremiah Wright, who made what many White Americans claimed to be highly inflammatory racist comments against Whites. As a candidate for the highest office in the land, Obama tried to reassure the American public with two important messages: (1) that being a product of a Black father and White mother "has seared into my genetic makeup the idea that this nation is more than the sum of its parts—that out of many, we are truly one" and (2) that race is an issue that the nation cannot afford to ignore.

On the one hand, in both speeches he downplayed differences and stressed the commonality and unity of the human condition, and on the other hand, he pointed to the need to discuss and educate one another about race. Ironically, as president of the United States, Obama has largely been silent about race except during ceremonial occasions or when a highly visible racial incident makes avoiding the topic difficult. The unwarranted arrest of a well-respected Harvard Black scholar, Henry Louis Gates, by a White police officer who mistook Gates for a burglar breaking into his own home is such an example. And the 2013 not guilty verdict for George Zimmerman in the killing of Black teenager Trayvon Martin has compelled President Obama to address the issue of race. Up until the death of Trayvon Martin, however, Obama seldom initiated discussions of race on his own.

In many respects, President Obama would probably lose his credibility and be marginalized were he to directly address or initiate discussions of race. He would be accused of being a president for Black America rather than president of everyone (as we saw in one of the blog comments). To maintain his credibility, he has to dilute acknowledging differences, stress commonalities, and play the role of a unifier rather than a divider. Avoiding direct discussions of race and attempting to transcend race has been a strategy he has used to maintain his authority as president. Unfortunately, these maneuvers tend to have a major downside: They maintain the superficiality of race talk and implicitly suggest that racial discussions are divisive and deviant.

In summary, racial dialogues are very difficult for White people. They are often overwhelmed with powerful emotions such as anxiety, fear, anger, betrayal, or defensiveness. They are fearful that they will be misunderstood and unjustly accused of being biased. They are ambivalent about engaging the topic and employ avoidance maneuvers (remaining silent, actively diluting, dismissing, or negating its importance in conversations that touch upon race). Nervousness, fear, and discomfort are frequently manifested in telltale behavioral signs: White people increase their personal space between themselves and people of color, become fidgety, avoid eye contact, and blink excessively (Trawalter & Richeson, 2008). On the other hand, people of color in race talk often experience a denial and invalidation of their racial realities, feeling that their racial integrities are being assailed, and frustrated that their White counterparts are so unaware of their biases and privileges. This discomfort is likewise indicated by impatience, disinclination to believe what the White person says, and fidgety behaviors (Trawalter & Richeson, 2008).

Why Is Successful Race Talk Important?

In the past, Bill Clinton's Presidential Initiative on Race (1998) encouraged a "national dialogue on race" and indicated that constructive conversations have the potential to heal racial and ethnic divides, reduce prejudice and misinformation, and foster improved race relations. Unfortunately, his initiative promised much, but failed to materialize when it was sidetracked by the Monica Lewinsky scandal. Nevertheless, an overwhelming body of literature suggests that, under the right conditions, interracial and intergroup interactions and dialogues have positive benefits and evoke constructive changes among participants (APA Presidential Task Force, 2012; Ford, 2012; Sorensen, Nagda, Gurin, & Maxwell, 2009; Valentine, Prentice, Torres, & Arellano, 2012). This has been acknowledged by the U.S. Supreme Court in its 2003 ruling of the University of Michigan's use of affirmative action in their admissions process (Grutter v. Bollinger, 539 U.S. 306 [2003]). Speaking on behalf of the majority, Supreme Court Justice Sandra Day O'Connor wrote about the positive benefits of the affirmative action program used by the law school:

> The . . . claim is further bolstered by numerous expert studies and reports showing that such diversity promotes learning outcomes and prepares students better for an increasingly diverse workforce, for society, and for the legal profession. Major American businesses have made clear that the skills needed in today's increasingly global marketplace can only be developed through exposure to widely diverse people, cultures, ideas, and viewpoints.

But exposure is not enough, especially if diversity does not lead to interracial contact and dialogue (APA Presidential Task Force, 2012; Sorensen et al., 2009). For example, it has been found that interracial contact as a means to dispel stereotypes and biases is one condition that must prevail to have a positive effect (Allport, 1954; Pettigrew & Tropp, 2006). But in spite of being a diverse society, we are not an integrated one despite living and working next to one another. I frequently ask students in my classes on race, for example, the following question: "How many of you live in an integrated neighborhood?" Because Columbia University is in Harlem and because apartments and housing are less expensive than in other parts of Manhattan, a good percentage of students raise their hands eagerly to show that they practice nondiscrimination. I generally respond with this statement: "There is a difference between living in Harlem and *how you live in Harlem*." When I explore the meaning of this statement with them, the following facts about their lived experiences arise. First, although students live in the Harlem neighborhood, they seldom participate in community events, seldom shop in the local retail outlets or grocery stores, seldom attend the Black churches, seldom socialize with their Black neighbors, and only engage in the most casual and superficial conversations about race. So, although they live near African American neighbors, their whole orientation is toward the Columbia University campus, Midtown, Downtown, and the Village. So, although we may live next to people who differ from us in terms of race, culture, and ethnicity; work side-by-side with one another; or go to school with classmates of color, sadly, we do not engage in meaningful racial dialogues with one another.

A whole body of literature supports the belief that encountering diverse racial points of view, being able to engage in racial conversations, and successfully acknowledging and integrating differing perspectives lead to an expansion of critical consciousness (Gurin, Dey, Hurtado, & Gurin, 2002; Jayakumar, 2008). On a cognitive level, many have observed that cross-racial interactions and dialogues are a necessity to increase racial literacy, expand the ability to critically analyze racial ideologies, and dispel stereotypes and misinformation about other groups (Bolgatz, 2005; Ford, 2012; Pollock, 2004; Stevens, Plaut, & Sanchez-Burks, 2008). On an emotive level, participants of successful racial dialogues report less intimidation and fear of differences, an increased compassion for others, a broadening of their horizons, appreciation of people of all colors and cultures, and a greater sense of belonging and connectedness with all groups (APA Presidential Task Force, 2012; Bell, 2002; President's Initiative on Race, 1999; Sue, 2003).

Yet it is ironic that race talk is often silenced, ignored, diluted, and/or discussed in very superficial ways for fear of offending others or creating potentially explosive situations. In future chapters, we will have more to say about the educational benefits of race talk and how educators, trainers, and parents are uniquely situated to create learning opportunities that facilitate difficult dialogues on race.

CHAPTER TWO

The Characteristics and Dynamics of Race Talk

Teaching a class in urban education, I was analyzing brief biographical sketches of Black Americans who described how race impacted their lives and the special hardships they encountered. Contrary to the usual class involvement, the responses were brief, tepid, and guarded. It was like "pulling teeth" to get any type of response. Finally, a White female student observed that it was not a "race" issue and that being a woman she had also experienced low expectations.... Immediately, a White male student chimed in and asked, "Isn't it a social class issue?" Another White female student agreed, and went into a long monologue concerning how class issues are always neglected in discussions of social justice. She asked, "Why is everything always about race?"

I could sense the energy in the classroom rise when one of the few Black female students angrily confronted the White female with these words: "You have no idea what it's like to be Black! I don't care if you are poor or not, but you have White skin. Do you know what that means? Don't tell me that being Black isn't different from being White." A Latina student also added

This chapter was previously published in the *American Psychologist* as "Race Talk: The Psychology of Racial Dialogues," by D. W. Sue, 2013, *American Psychologist, 68*, pp. 663–672. Copyright 2013 by the American Psychological Association. Adapted and reprinted with permission.

to the rejoinder by stating "You will never understand. Whites don't have to understand. Why are White people so scared to talk about race?"

The two White female students seemed baffled and became defensive. After an attempt to clarify their points, both seemed to only inflame the debate. One of the female students began to cry, and the second student indignantly got up, stated she was not going to be insulted, and left the classroom. At that point, many of the students tried to comfort the crying student while the few students of color appeared unmoved.

As a White male professor, I felt overwhelmed with anxiety and paralyzed. I was fearful of losing control of the classroom...and didn't know what to do. Finally, I told everyone to calm down, not to let their emotions interfere with their learning, and to respect one another. I suggested that we table the discussion and go on to another topic. (adapted from Sue, 2010, pp. 231–232)

Questions: What do you think is happening in this dialogue between White students and students of color? How would you describe the actions of the White students? How would you describe the actions of the students of color? What do you believe is behind their reactions? Why are the students so upset? It is obvious that the professor is trying to act as a mediator between the students. How successful is he? How would you handle the situation if you were the teacher?

Although this vignette occurs in a classroom setting, it has characteristics and dynamics representative of almost any racial dialogue that occurs in the media, governmental institutions, workplaces, community forums, neighborhood events, sports, and even among friends (Sue, Lin, et al., 2009). Three recent examples bring home the inflammatory and explosive nature of race talk across national settings.

First, Cliven Bundy, a White Nevada rancher refused to pay for grazing his cattle on federal land, thwarted authorities in an armed standoff, and became a folk hero to conservative groups who rushed to his side in the fight against Big Government. On April 19, 2014, he spoke freely about his views on African Americans in public housing projects: "They didn't have nothing to do...they were basically on government subsidy, so now what do they do? They abort their young children, they put their young men in jail, because they never learned how to pick cotton. And I've often wondered, are they better off as slaves, picking cotton and having a family life and doing things, or are they better off under government subsidy? They didn't get no more freedom. They got less freedom."

Second, on April 25, 2014, it became known that Donald Sterling, owner of the NBA Los Angeles Clippers, made highly inflammatory racist statements that were recorded by a female friend and subsequently released to the public. The owner was irritated over an Instagram picture of the girlfriend with basketball hall of fame player Magic Johnson. Sterling stated to her, "It bothers me a lot that you want to broadcast that you're associating with Black people," and, "You can sleep with [Black people]. You can bring them in, you can do whatever you want," but "the little I ask you is ... not to bring them to my games." As a result of these remarks and the ensuing public outcry, the NBA commissioner banned Sterling from the league for life, fined him $2.5 million, and requested he immediately sell the team.

Third, Dallas Mavericks owner Mark Cuban in an interview on May 21, 2014, spoke freely about his own thoughts concerning Donald Sterling: "I know I'm prejudiced, and I know I'm bigoted in a lot of different ways.... If I see a black kid in a hoodie on my side of the street, I'll move to the other side of the street. If I see a white guy with a shaved head and tattoo, I'll move back to the other side of the street. None of us have pure thoughts; we all live in glass houses." Cuban's point was that everyone is prejudiced and that he works against his own biases, and everyone should do likewise. Despite this point, Cuban issued an apology on Twitter to the Trayvon Martin family for his reference to a hoodie.

These three statements have set off a firestorm of anger and condemnation with political pundits taking various positions. Although most condemned Bundy and Sterling, others came to the defense of Cuban, indicating that he was simply being honest and that dealing with racism must allow people to confront their own biases openly and publicly. Although none of us would support racist statements and racism, public condemnation, ironically, may work against honest race talk and the eradication of bigotry. The lesson people learn in watching these events is "Don't express your true thoughts and feelings about race in public, because bad things will happen to you." This is one of the issues we address in this book.

Race talk, or dialogues and conversations that touch upon topics of race, racism, Whiteness, and White privilege, can prove explosive (Sue, Rivera, Capodilupo, Lin, & Torino, 2010; Watt, 2007; Young, 2003). Race talk is generally filled with intense and powerful emotions (Bell, 2003), creates a threatening environment for participants (Sue et al., 2011), reveals major differences in worldviews or perspectives (Bryan, Wilson, Lewis, & Wills, 2012; Young, 2003), and often results in disastrous consequences such as a hardening of biased racial views (Zou & Dickter, 2013). Unless instigated in some manner, the majority of people in interracial settings would prefer to avoid such topical discussions and/or to minimize and dilute their importance and meaning (Valentine et al., 2012).

But, what exactly is race talk? What characteristics form the basis of a difficult dialogue on race? What makes it so difficult for people to honestly dialogue about race? If racial dialogues are an important means to combat racism and discrimination, how can we make people more comfortable and willing to explore racial topics? Answering these questions is especially urgent as difficult dialogues on race become unavoidable, and well-intentioned people of all races find themselves unprepared to deal with the explosive emotions that result in polarization and hard feelings (Valentine et al., 2012). Poorly handled, race talk can result in increased antagonism among students, misunderstandings, and blockages in learning. Skillfully handled, however, race talk can improve communication and learning, enhance racial harmony, increase racial literacy, and expand critical consciousness of one's racial/cultural identity (Pasque, Chesler, Charbeneau, & Carlson, 2013).

This chapter provides a summary of the content and issues that will be expanded in forthcoming chapters. My intent here is to give readers an overview or a broad picture of the psychology of racial dialogues first, and then to cover each section in this chapter in a more systematic and in-depth manner. In other words, see the forest first, and then the trees will enhance our understanding of race talk.

WHAT ARE CHARACTERISTICS OF RACE TALK?

Over a 5-year period, my colleagues and I have conducted a series of studies to explore the psychology of racial dialogues or race talk in higher education as an attempt to answer this question (Sue, Lin, et al., 2009; Sue et al., 2010; Sue et al., 2011; Sue, Torino, et al., 2009). Although our focus has been in an educational context, I believe the findings are equally applicable to all racial dialogues whether they occur in education, employment, health care, or the media. We specifically focused on (a) the characteristics of race talk, (b) ground rules or guidelines that explicitly and implicitly dictate how and when race is discussed, (c) whether people of color and Whites perceive them differently from one another, (d) the impact of race talk on participants, and (e) how educators could create conditions conducive to successful outcomes.

In our four studies, we ran focus groups and conducted individual interviews on four different populations—(1) students of color, (2) White students, (3) faculty of color, and (4) White faculty—in order to ascertain the convergence and divergence of perspectives on racial dialogues in the classroom. We found a nearly uniform agreement among participants as to the characteristics of race talk, but major differences in how it was experienced by Whites and persons of color. Our opening vignette is a prime example of some common themes that were extracted.

First, when a racial topic is broached in a mixed racial group, there is a disinclination to participate, and the dialogue in the classroom may be brewed in silence (Young, 2003). As indicated in Chapter 1, race talk is often characterized by extreme tension and anxiety. Oftentimes, the responses by students become tentative, obtuse, abstract, and filled with nonsensical utterances (Bolgatz, 2005). They may become guarded in expressing directly their beliefs and feelings, fearful that they may be misinterpreted. The apprehension about a racial dialogue can result in *rhetorical incoherence*, a term coined by Bonilla-Silva (2006) in reference to difficulty in articulation, barely audible speech, voice constriction, trembling voices, and mispronunciation of common words associated with race.

Second, once race talk begins, it triggers and heightens powerful uncomfortable emotions such as defensiveness, anxiety, anger, helplessness, blame, and invalidation (Utsey et al., 2005; Willow, 2008). The dialogue can become quite heated, evoking personal attacks, and in rare cases participants may feel threatened by physical retaliation. It is clear, for example, that students of color felt insulted by the remarks of a few White students. Likewise, it is obvious that the two White female students felt falsely accused of being biased and they became very defensive.

Third, participants in race talk often feel that their perspectives or worldviews are being challenged and invalidated (Bell, 2002, 2003); the result is that they feel compelled to defend their positions. Rather than a dialogue (listening and exchanging ideas), race talk becomes a monologue where the participants simply state and restate their initial positions, oftentimes with greater intensity and conviction.

Fourth, as race talk becomes increasingly uncomfortable and threatening, there are attempts to dilute, diminish, change, mystify, or terminate the topic

(Pasque et al., 2013). The White students, for example, avoided acknowledging race as a legitimate topic by equating the issue with gender and/or social class, one student walked out, and the professor invoked his authority to "table the discussion," thus ending further debate on the topic.

Fifth, because race is such an important aspect of their identities, students of color may find the avoidant behavior of Whites offensive and interpret them as racial microaggressions (Sue, 2010; Sue et al., 2007) that negate their racial identities and assail their integrities. On the other hand, when confronted with their avoidant behaviors, White students may feel equally offended, misunderstood, insulted, and unjustly accused of being racist.

Sixth, when the situation threatens to get out of control, the professor (although well intentioned) colluded with the White students by admonishing them to "respect one another" and "calm down" (indirectly suggesting that emotions had no role in the classroom), and moved on to another topic, thus reinforcing a conspiracy of silence (Sue, 2005).

Last, the greater authority and power of the professor to determine appropriate dialogue behavior in the classroom supported and reinforced the White students' ability to define racial reality (Sue, 2010), and allowed them to determine the manner by which race talk could be addressed and processed in the classroom.

In summary, our findings suggest that difficult dialogues on race (a) are potentially threatening conversations or interactions between members of different racial and ethnic groups, (b) reveal major differences in worldviews that are challenged publically, (c) are found to be offensive to participants, (d) arouse intense emotions such as dread and anxiety (for Whites) and anger and frustration (for people of color) that disrupt communication and behaviors, (e) are often instigated by racial microaggressions, and (f) involve an unequal status relationship of power and privilege among participants (Sue, Lin, et al., 2009; Young, 2003; Young & Davis-Russell, 2002).

How Do Societal Ground Rules (Norms) Impede Race Talk?

Many scholars have likened race talk to storytelling in which a master narrative (White talk) depicts historical and cultural themes of racial progress, of a fair and just society, of equal access and opportunity, of meritocracy, and of color blindness (Bell, 2002, 2003; Bolgatz, 2005; Pollock, 2004). For people of color, however, their own tales represent a counter-narrative or back talk in which their stories challenge and dispute the ones told by Whites. Their stories contain themes of past and continuing discrimination, the pain of oppression from well-intentioned Whites, power and privilege of the dominant group, and the myth of meritocracy (Accapadi, 2007; Bell, 2003; Bryan et al., 2012; Sue, 2005). In describing the master narrative, Feagin (2001) uses the term *sincere fictions* to describe the sincere beliefs of Whites that they are fair, moral, and decent human beings who are not responsible for inequities in the lives of people of color, that racism is no longer a detrimental force in society, and that our nation should be color-blind. They are fictions in that White talk ignores and denies the realities of racism and its harmful consequences to marginalized groups. Race talk is not only a clash of racial realities, but reenacts the differential power relationship between a dominant group master narrative (Whites) and the less powerful socially devalued group counter-narrative (persons of color; Sue et al., 2007).

The counter-narratives of race talk are extremely threatening to Whites and to our society because they may unmask the secrets of power and privilege, and how the public transcript of a master narrative justifies the continued subordination of people of color (Bell, 2003; Sue, 2005). If racism is a thing of the past and no longer a force in the lives of people of color, for example, it allows Whites to maintain their innocence and naïveté while absolving them from taking personal responsibility to rectify injustices (Accapadi, 2007; Feagin, 2001; Frankenberg, 1997; Sue, 2005). Thus, our society implicitly and explicitly discourages race talk through normative ground rules that ignore and silence honest discussions about race and its impact on the lives of people of color. Three of these are the politeness protocol, the academic protocol, and the color-blind protocol (APA Presidential Task Force, 2012; Sue, 2010; Young, 2003).

Race Talk Violates the Politeness Protocol

When and how we talk about race is often dictated by the politeness protocol whose ground rule states that potentially offensive or uncomfortable topics should be (a) avoided, ignored, and silenced or (b) spoken about in a very light, casual, and superficial manner. Addressing topics of race, racism, Whiteness, and White privilege are discouraged in favor of friendly and noncontroversial topics. In mixed company (social gatherings, public forums, classrooms, and neighborhood events), race talk is seen as improper and impolite and potentially divisive, creating disagreements, offending participants, and working against social harmony (APA Presidential Task Force, 2012;

Zou & Dickster, 2013). In social interactions, the focus is generally on small talk and pleasantries that do not result in conflicting opinions/beliefs. In their extreme form, race topics are considered socially taboo and are generally avoided by participants, even when they are considered relevant and important to the dialogue.

If race enters the public discourse, however, explorations of the topic remain on a very superficial level. The taboo against race talk and how it is discussed is often enforced through social means: being told that the topic is not a proper one, having people excuse themselves from the conversation, being labeled as socially insensitive, and being isolated socially. Violating these conversation conventions can have very negative consequences as to how one is perceived (rude or complaining) and treated in future interactions (dismissed and retaliated against; Rasinki & Czopp, 2010; Zou & Dickter, 2013). Depending on the stance they take, Whites who violate the politeness protocol may be accused of being "racist" or a "bleeding heart liberal." Although people of color appear more comfortable and willing to dialogue on topics of race, it is important to note that social pressures to follow the politeness protocol are placed on them as well. Depending on their stance, people of color may be accused of being an Uncle Tom—playing along to get along—or playing the race card.

Race Talk Violates the Academic Protocol

Race talk along with the expressions of strong and intense emotions is often discouraged in the classroom. In academia, intellectual inquiry is characterized by objectivity, detachment, and rational discourse; empirical reality is valued over experiential reality (hooks, 1994). In the social sciences, the Western tradition of mind-body dualism operates from several assumptions: (a) reality consists of what is observed and measured through the five senses; (b) science operates from universal principles and, until recently, cultural influences were minimized; and (c) reductionism, separation, and isolation of variables (objects or elements) allow for determining cause–effect relationships—the ultimate means of asking and answering questions about the human condition (Highlen, 1996; Sue & Sue, 2013; Walsh & Shapiro, 2006). In many respects, these assumptions elevate the mind over the body (spirit and emotions) and dictate that classrooms should be conducted in a sterile, objective decorum devoid of feelings. Many educators, thus, view emotions as antagonistic to reason and conduct their classes according to the academic protocol.

Race talk violates the academic protocol for several reasons. First is the implicit assumption that expressing and discussing emotions is not in the realm of legitimate academic inquiry and advancement. When race issues are discussed in the classroom, however, they may push hot buttons in participants and evoke strong and powerful feelings that become very heated. When this happens, students are often admonished to calm down, to respect one another, and to discuss the topic in a manner consistent with objective and rational discourse (APA Presidential Task Force, 2012). There is a belief that dialogues on race are purely intellectual exercises, thereby minimizing the expression of emotions in race talk and losing an opportunity to explore their meanings. Second, race talk on the part of people of color is about *bearing witness* to their lived realities, their personal and collective experiences of subordination, and their stories of racism. The academic protocol discourages these sources of information and considers such anecdotal materials as opinions and less legitimate data (facts) to be explored (Bell, 2003; Bryan et al., 2012). Last, race talk is seldom simply a disagreement over facts or content. A dispute over whether women are as oppressed as people of color, whether race issues are more important than social class, or whether we now live in a postracial society masks the true hidden dialogue occurring between the students: fears of disclosing intimate thoughts and beliefs related to race/racism and the personal meaning it has for them (Sue, Lin, et al., 2009; Sue et al., 2010).

Race Talk Violates the Color-Blind Protocol

A powerful social norm in our society is the belief that race does not matter, that we should be a color-blind society, and that people should be judged on the basis of their internal attributes and not the color of their skin (Apfelbaum, Sommers, & Norton, 2008; Neville, Lily, Duran, Lee, & Browne, 2000; Plaut, Thomas, & Goren, 2009). For Whites, to acknowledge or *see race* is to risk the possibility of being perceived as racist, so great effort is expended to avoid talking about race in order to appear fair and unprejudiced. Apfelbaum and associates (2008) have coined the phrase *strategic color blindness* to describe the pattern of behaviors used by Whites toward people of color to minimize differences, to appear unbiased, to appear friendly, to avoid interactions with people of color, to not acknowledge race-related topics, and even to pretend not seeing the person's race. Statements such as "When I look at you, I don't see you as Asian American; I just see you as an individual," or "We are all the same under the skin, just human beings," or "There is only one race, the human race" exemplify this stance. In essence, race talk violates the color-blind protocol.

Ironically, color blindness was originally meant to combat institutional prejudice and discrimination and to portray the person as being free of bias, but paradoxically, it seems to have the opposite effect. Social psychological research reveals that a color-blind orientation (ignoring or minimizing differences) and a multicultural one (recognizing and valuing diversity) have different institutional and personal consequences (Plaut et al., 2009). Organizations, for example, that profess a color-blind philosophy actually promote interpersonal discrimination among employees, use discriminatory policies and practices, and justify inequality (Apfelbaum et al., 2008; Saguy, Dovidio, & Pratto, 2008); a multicultural philosophy, however, promotes inclusive behaviors and policies (Purdie-Vaughns, Steele, Davies, Ditlmann, & Crosby, 2008). Further, strategic color blindness on a personal level seems to make those utilizing it appear more biased to people of color (APA Presidential Task Force, 2012; Zou & Dickter, 2013). Others have concluded that the pretense of not seeing color and avoiding critical consciousness of race lowers empathic ability, dims perceptual awareness, maintains false illusions, and allow Whites to live in a world of false deception (Bell, 2002; Kawakami, Dunn, Karmali, & Dovidio, 2009; Spanierman, Poteat, Beer, & Armstrong, 2006; Sue, 2005).

Why Is Race Talk So Difficult and Uncomfortable for Participants?

Our studies on racial dialogues in the classroom point to different reasons for why students/faculty of color and White students/faculty find them problematic. In general, persons of color are more willing to discuss topics of race than their White counterparts (Sue, Lin, et al., 2009; Sue et al., 2010). To them, the actual avoidance of race talk in a situation where it is deemed important and appropriate tends to make them feel silenced and invalidated. On the other hand, Whites express apprehensions about *opening up a can of worms*, whose contents are not entirely clear to them.

The Impact of Race Talk on Students and Faculty of Color

Students (Sue et al., 2010) and faculty of color (Sue et al., 2011) were unanimous in describing that difficult racial dialogues were often triggered by racial microaggressions in the classroom. Racial microaggressions are the everyday and common verbal, behavioral, or environmental indignities and slights directed toward people of color by well-intentioned Whites who are unaware that they have committed a transgression against a target group

(Sue et al., 2007). Students of color described frequent microaggressive themes related to ascription of intelligence, criminality, alien in one's own land, and denial of racial reality. For example, Black students often reported being asked how they were admitted into an Ivy League institution (implying that affirmative action and not merit was the reason); Asian American students reported how they were perceived as foreigners by classmates, who would speak extra slow to them; and some students of color described curricular content that implicitly portrayed them in stereotypical fashion. In general, the informants in these studies were able to report multiple instances of frequent and common microaggressions directed toward them by White classmates and occasionally a White professor. These racial microaggressions often triggered a difficult racial dialogue.

When microaggressions occur, students of color reported emotional, cognitive, and behavioral reactions related to the impact of the slights. Emotionally, many felt incensed when they believed their integrity was being attacked, and experienced strong feelings varying from annoyance and frustration to anger. Cognitively, many reported an internal conflict whether *to speak or not to speak*, attempted to ascertain the level of emotional support they were likely to receive in the dialogue, and more importantly, attempted to determine the consequences of their potential actions. Behaviorally, some reported *losing it* and would retaliate with anger and blame. Others, however, struggled with making sure that their actions would be received in the *right way* and worked hard to control their emotions and alter their communication styles (speak with less passion in order not to be labeled the *angry Black woman or man*). Ironically, this tactic made them feel less authentic and resulted in a nagging sense that they had sold out their integrity.

Faculty of color described very similar perceptions and dynamics as students of color: (a) microaggressions were often precipitators of race talk; (b) when they witnessed a microaggression in the classroom directed at a student of color or at them, it also evoked powerful emotional reactions; (c) they struggled with whether or how to address the racial topic in the classroom; and (d) they worried about the consequences and reactions from both White students and those of color (Sue et al., 2011). The microaggressions they were most likely to experience were having their scholarship and research devalued, experiencing the campus climate as hostile and invalidating, and having White students question their qualifications to hold the status of professor (Harlow, 2003; Stanley, 2006; Turner, Gonzalez, & Wood, 2008).

Adding to the pressure for professors of color was the unique role they played as the person in charge of the classroom. All expressed a great internal struggle between balancing personal values and beliefs with attempting to be an objective educator, and *not taking sides* between White students and those of color. They described this conflict as exhausting and overwhelming as they attempted to balance the flood of feelings and anger they experienced with helping students process the difficult dialogues. All struggled with a desire to correct racial misinformation while not taking sides with students of color. Interestingly, maintaining neutrality often enraged students of color, who looked to the professor of color for support and validation.

Additionally, people of color described how race talk is filtered through the lens of Western European norms that preside strongly in institutions of higher education and specifically in classrooms and that place them at a significant disadvantage. This latter effect is perhaps the most insidious and damaging of the outcomes. As an example, let us return to the opening vignette, where the outcome of a heated exchange resulted in a White female student crying, followed by attempts from classmates to console her. It appears that the student felt hurt and misunderstood, and was pained by *false* accusations. Her anguish was felt by the entire class, and fellow students rushed in to comfort her, to reassure and support her, and to make her feel better.

In an insightful article titled "When White Women Cry: How White Women's Tears Oppress Women of Color," Accapadi (2007) asserts that White standards of humanity often make their presence felt in racial and gender dialogues. These norms and standards work to the advantage of Whites and the disadvantage of people of color when racial conflicts emerge. She contends that historically, White women were depicted as purity, chastity, virtue, and goodness—the embodiment of womanhood. Along with these positive qualities, helplessness, vulnerability, and emotional fragility call for protection. Contrast this picture with the ones portraying women of color: tough and aggressive for Black women, unfeeling for Asian American females, and the many other stereotypes associated with Latinas and Indigenous women.

The moment that the female student started to cry, she revealed gender-based vulnerability and pain: the norms of humanity pulled for protection and consolation from others. Although not intentional or conscious, the impact on the dynamics of the racial dialogue changed in focus and outcome. First, the actual issue involved in the dialogue was sidetracked and no longer the center of attention. In most cases, such diversions ultimately prevent a return to the topic because of the discomfort that may again ensue. Second, the remainder of the class meeting was spent on consoling the female student and by default, suggested she was not at fault or wrong. In other words, she was the one being supported and validated. Third, the outcome of the debate is likely to place responsibility and blame on students of color. They were *so antagonistic that they made someone cry*. And, by sitting at their desks being *unmoved and unfeeling*, they lacked humanity and compassion for others.

The Impact of Race Talk on White Students and Faculty

One of the major findings from our studies on White students (Sue et al., 2010) and faculty (Sue, Torino, et al., 2009) was their inability to clearly identify and deconstruct racial microaggressions in the classrooms. They seemed oblivious to offensive microaggressive conduct in themselves and others, although they could sense the tension in the classroom and knew something was wrong. Unlike people of color, who could readily name and identify the offensive behavior, the White informants had great difficulty recognizing them. This was true for both White students and White professors, although the latter felt greater responsibility for pursuing and clarifying the topic. As indicated earlier, when race talk for Whites is instigated in the classroom, it is accompanied by extreme anxiety and dread, and followed by attempts to avoid further discussion. Our studies indicate a number of different ways in which race talk is discouraged: (a) remaining silent and refusing to participate, (b) diverting the conversation to a safer topic, (c) diluting or dismissing the importance of the topic, (d) instituting restrictive rules for how the dialogue should take place, (e) speaking about race from a global perspective or as a bystander and not an active participant, or (f) *tabling the discussion*.

This last ploy was most often used by professors who feared that such dialogues would produce unnecessary antagonisms between participants, result in a loss of classroom control, and reveal how unprepared they were to facilitate such heated exchanges (Pasque et al., 2013). They frankly admitted that they felt paralyzed and helpless, and feared having the incident become *the classroom from hell*. Ironically, by leaving racial offenses unspoken and untouched, they created an *elephant in the room* that interfered with learning and perpetuated a hostile, invalidating, and racially charged classroom climate for students of color (Solórzano, Ceja, & Yasso, 2000). Our studies and those of other scholars suggest four types of intersecting layers of fears that many White Americans possess when it comes to engaging in race talk

(Bell, 2002, 2003; Frankenberg, 1997; Neville, Spanierman, & Doan, 2006; Spanierman et al., 2006).

Fear of Appearing Racist

Earlier, I indicated how many Whites pretend not to notice differences in an attempt to appear nonracist. One of their greatest fears is that whatever is said or done during a race conversation may be misunderstood and deemed racist. Thus, when a race topic arises, they are likely to become quite guarded and deliberate in their responses. The verbal exchanges are likely to be superficial and noncommittal as they engage in strategic color blindness and other maneuvers to prevent the commission of unintended racial blunders. When topics of race or racism arise, they become anxious, constricted, and cautious in what they say. Remaining silent or consciously screening and censoring out anything they consider to be racially offensive become the hallmark of their communications. Unfortunately, research shows that such strategies are often unsuccessful and may have directly the opposite effect (Shelton, Richeson, Salvatore, & Trawalter, 2005; Vorauer & Turpie, 2004). In a laboratory experiment between Black and White volunteers, for example, Shelton and colleagues (2005) found that those who engaged in attempts to appear unbiased often made their stance very unclear and distorted, appeared inauthentic, and were perceived as being more racist. It appears that people who expend considerable energy to appear nonprejudiced make very poor conversational partners, resulting in behaviors that communicate distance and *phony friendliness*.

Fear of Realizing Their Racism

Below the fear of appearing racist lies an even more dreaded one: the realization that Whites harbor biased and prejudicial attitudes, albeit unknowingly (Sue, 2005). Although it can be debated whether anyone born and raised in the United States is immune from inheriting the racial biases of their forebears, research on aversive racism and implicit bias support the notion that most, if not all, have internalized prejudicial attitudes and behaviors (Dovidio, Gaertner, Kawakami, & Hodson, 2002; J. M. Jones, 1997). These implicit biases are extremely resistant to change as they operate outside the level of conscious awareness and make their appearance in subtle ways (i.e., racial microaggressions; Boysen & Vogel, 2008). Because most Whites experience themselves as good, moral, and fair-minded human beings who actively stand against overt acts of discrimination (hate crimes and obvious discriminatory acts), it is disturbing for them to realize that they possess racial biases. Race talk has the potential to open the can of worms by moving beyond the fear of appearing racist to being one. The teachings of democracy, equity, and equal access and opportunity that Whites profess to hold can be seriously challenged in race talk. The realization that one holds biased beliefs and attitudes, and has acted in discriminatory ways toward people of color, shatters a self-image of goodness many Whites hold about themselves. To accept this fact is truly alarming because it means acknowledging responsibility for the pain and suffering of others. This realization is likely to be strongly resisted and the feelings of anxiety, defensiveness, and anger during race talk are indicative of this realization.

Fear of Confronting White Privilege

To confront issues of race and racism is to confront Whiteness and White privilege (Spanierman et al., 2006; Sue & Sue, 2013; Watt, 2007). McIntosh (2002) has indicated that Whiteness is an invisible veil and represents a default standard by which differences are seen and judged. She further defines White privilege as the unearned benefits and advantages that accrue to Whites by virtue of their skin color (not necessarily due to their own efforts). The following statement is often used to illustrate privilege on the part of George W. Bush when he first ran for president of the United States: "George W. Bush was born on third base but believes he hit a triple." Like many White males who have attained positions of power and influence, the former president believes that he sacrificed and worked hard to attain the presidency. Invisible to him and many White Americans are two facts: (1) Many persons of color and women have worked equally hard if not harder but don't even make it to the batter's box, and (2) Bush benefited from White privilege, male privilege, and economic privilege.

Confronting White privilege in race talk means entertaining the possibility that meritocracy is a myth, that Whites did not attain their positions in life solely through their own efforts, that they have benefited from the historical and current racist arrangements and practices of society, and that they have been advantaged in society to the detriment of people of color. As J. M. Jones (1997) indicates, White privilege cannot exist outside the confines of White supremacy. Race talk threatens to unmask the hidden secret that the superior positions of many Whites were attained through the oppression of people of color and through current inequitable arrangements.

Fear of Taking Personal Responsibility to End Racism

Working through fears of appearing racist, acknowledging biased social conditioning, owning up to racist attitudes and beliefs, and realizing that one has benefited from White privilege are important changes, but they are not enough. Race talk ultimately asks White Americans a moral question that moves beyond these fears. If denying one's role in the perpetuation of inequities can no longer be placed on lack of awareness or naïveté, and if one realizes that silence and inaction are to collude in the oppressions of others, we must ask, How is it possible to allow situations of oppression and injustice to continue without taking personal responsibility to end them?

In a study aimed at participants' actual and anticipated response to a Black racial slur, experimenters found that White participants who predicted they would be upset with witnessing a racist act and would reject the racist actually experienced little emotional distress and did little to change their behaviors toward the perpetrator (Kawakami et al., 2009). In other words, although White Americans are well intentioned and honestly believe that in the face of racism they would act to end it, the tendency by most to do nothing is more the norm. Someone once said that the ultimate White privilege is the ability to acknowledge one's privilege, but do nothing about it. And frankly, this is where I believe the last battle must be waged. Race talk reminds Whites that they have both the responsibility and power to take action against racism and oppression. Accepting the existence of personal bias and utilizing this awareness to rectify injustices, however, is not an easy task.

Conclusions

In general, studies indicate that factors working against race talk for people of color are significantly different than for their White counterparts. Although White participants were disinclined to engage in race talk and/or addressed race issues superficially, people of color appear more willing to bear witness to their racial thoughts and experiences because they are such an intimate part of their identities. They feel shut off from discussing how race impacts their daily lives in society by the reactions and perceived consequences of doing so. Furthermore, the contextual norms of our society can hinder race talk by setting the parameters to how it is discussed and interpreted, thereby placing people of color at risk for negative outcomes.

For people of color race talk is difficult because they are placed in an unenviable position of (a) determining how to talk about the elephant in the room when Whites avoid acknowledging it; (b) dealing with the denial, defensiveness, and anxiety emanating from their White counterparts; (c) managing their intense anger at the continual denial; and (d) needing to constantly ascertain how much to open up, given the differential power dynamics that often exists between the majority and minority group.

For White Americans, the greatest obstacle to honest racial discourse is to make the invisible visible: how silence allows them to maintain a false belief in their own racial innocence, avoid personal blame for the oppression of others, and dodge responsibility to combat racism and oppression. Race talk threatens to unmask unpleasant and unflattering secrets about their roles in the perpetuation of oppression. Avoiding racial dialogues seems to have basic functions related to denial. The denial of color is really a denial of differences. The denial of differences is really a denial of power and privilege. The denial of power and privilege is really a denial of personal benefits that accrue to Whites by virtue of racial inequities. The denial that they profit from racism is really a denial of responsibility for their racism. Lastly, the denial of racism is really a denial of the necessity to take action against racism. Understanding the psychology of race talk from the perspective of White Americans and people of color has major implications for how educators and our society can use this knowledge to facilitate difficult dialogues on race.

CHAPTER THREE

The Stories We Tell: White Talk Versus Back Talk

In a workshop on racism, a racially mixed group of participants sat around discussing the topic of race. The following exchange took place between an African American man named Mal and a White male named Jack. After an especially intense discussion about what it means to be White, the following condensed and adapted version of the exchange took place. This dialogue represents an example of race talk.

Jack: I know this may sound racist, but we have been tiptoeing around being honest for too long. I don't like to feel like everything I say has to be politically correct. I know I'm White ... but what is the big deal about that? I don't like how minorities seem to be blaming all their problems on us [Whites]. My parents and grandparents weren't responsible for slavery! We didn't own slaves! We treat everyone the same, like human beings. What's so big about being a color? I'm White, isn't that a color? Didn't Martin Luther King say that we shouldn't be concerned about a person's color? You're not the only one [reference to people of color in the group] that has experienced discrimination. My father told me stories about how we Irish were discriminated against when we came to America. My great-grandparents sacrificed and worked 24 hours a day to provide a good living for their kids. No one gave them any handouts. But they adjusted and did what it took to succeed. They came over to this country, made a home for their family, and never whined about hard work.

Mal (visibly angry): Are you implying that people of color are lazy and don't work equally hard as your family? Are you implying that being White is no different than being Black?

Jack (interrupting): I knew this would happen. You are misinterpreting what I am saying. I think that too many Blacks believe White men are obstacles to them ... because, because we're not! I haven't placed any limits to what you can do in this society. You may be blocking your own progress by clinging to those false beliefs.

Mal (incredulous): I block my own progress?

Jack: Yes, by believing that you are not equal to me. You are stuck in the belief that Whites are the obstacles to your progress. Yes, racism happened in the past, but it's a small thing now. It's a different world we live in. You don't realize that the world is wide open to you. Don't we have a Black president now? Look at Asian Americans, for example. They have made it in our society by hard work and their dedication to their families. Look at my great-grandfather. He stood on his own ground, settled it, and made something of his life in the face of much prejudice. Every man can stand on his own ground. Why do you people [people of color] always have to fight being part of this country. What is that saying? Oh yeah, "When in Rome, do as the Romans do." Can't we all just be Americans?

Mal (obviously agitated and raising his voice): No, no, no, you listen.... Your great-grandfather and you are not standing on your own ground! You stand on the heads and bodies of Native Americans. America was a red nation, not a White one! Australia was a Black nation until Whites took it by force! Africa is a Black nation.... You enslaved the people and brought them to this country. And, yes, you say you did not enslave Africans and now you tell me that you didn't take the land of American Indians, but, you know what ... you still benefit from the actions of your ancestors! When you say that I block my own progress ... ha ... I think the police set limits on where I can go and do, I think society tells me what neighborhoods I can live in.... No, I don't block my own progress. [Shouting] That's what being White means ... to stand on someone else's ground, and then mystify it by saying you are not! . . . And, when you say that everything will be alright if we all just become Americans . . . that's a bunch of bullshit!

Jack: (sits in silence . . . appears uncomfortable and surprised by the outburst. Pushes his chair back and turns away from Mal.)

Questions: What do you see happening in this dialogue between Jack and Mal? How does this dialogue contain the characteristics of race talk? Can you list the contrasting beliefs and values each are expressing in the stories they are telling? How do they represent a clash of racial realities? Why do you think both are so upset with one another? What are points made by Jack that you agree and disagree with? What are points made by Mal that you agree and disagree with? Who do you think has a more accurate perception of the situation?

RACE TALK: NARRATIVES AND COUNTER-NARRATIVES

The dialogue between Jack and Mal represents race talk in its most intense and emotional form. As mentioned in the previous chapter, race talk may be conceptualized as a tale of two competing stories that clash with one another with regard to their cultural assumptions, values, and beliefs (Bell, 2003; van Dijk, 1993). Behind both Jack and Mal's dialogues are not only the individual experiences of each, but a symbolic reflection of a master narrative (White talk) that many Whites tell to one another and a counter-narrative (back talk) told by people of color that challenges themes told in the master narrative (Warren, 2000).

Indeed, it has been noted that race talk often reenacts the entire history of race relations in the United States (Cose, 1997). Through critical analysis of discourse, scholars have suggested that *White talk* can be likened to a public transcript (master narrative) that reinforces and legitimizes the position of the dominant group, implies it is the natural order of things, and suggests these arrangements were achieved through fairness (Warren, 2000). *Back talk*, however, voices a hidden transcript by people of color that contradicts those stories, and unearths ugly secrets of how Whites' advantaged positions are attained through oppression, power, and privilege (Bell, 2002; 2003; Cose, 1997; Scott, 1990). Back talk threatens to unmask the dirty lies or sincere fictions inherent in the stories told by many White Americans (Feagin, 2001). Not only does race talk represent a clash of racial realities, but it is also a sociopolitical act in which the dominant group attempts to impose their version upon less empowered groups in our society (Bell, 2002, 2003; Sue, 2013). When master narratives collide with counter-narratives, it reenacts and potentially unmasks the racial struggles of the past and present. That is why race talk can be characterized as an argument or battle over racial consciousness. Let us look at how the stories told by Jack and Mal contain clashing cultural themes and beliefs that bear upon race, racism, Whiteness, and White privilege.

TELLING ON RACISM: UNMASKING UGLY SECRETS

Because we are victims of our social conditioning, many stories we tell about ourselves, others, and our society transcend our idiosyncratic and unique development as racial/cultural beings. The master narrative of our culture tells us (a) that we are a democratic society; (b) that we are good, moral, and decent human beings; (c) that egalitarian relations are valued; (d) that truth and justice are important; (e) that equal access and opportunity are hallmarks of our society; (f) that prejudice and discrimination are bad; (g) that hard work and individual effort are the pathways to success; (h) that people should not be judged by the color of their skin; and (i) that although racism is abhorrent, it is now a thing of the past (Bell, 2002, 2003; Frankenberg, 1997; Sue, 2003, 2013). The channels that shape our racial realities are transmitted to us through schooling and education, the mass media, significant others, peers, and social groups (APA Presidential Task Force, 2012; Sue, 2003). This is the public transcript or conscious curriculum that White Americans are taught from the moment of birth. These values and beliefs become interwoven into their consciousness and worldview and are manifested in the stories they tell.

There is, however, a hidden curriculum (subsection of the master narrative), containing seeds of a counter-narrative, that emanates from these channels as well; through subtle and indirect ways (usually outside the level of conscious awareness), the hidden curriculum communicates that certain groups or individuals are less worthy and desirable than others and are deserving of their lesser treatment and status in life (Bell, 2003; Trawalter & Richeson, 2008; van Dijk, 1993). Back talk, according to Bell (2003), is akin to telling on racism. An example of this cultural conditioning is given here:

> It was a late summer afternoon. A group of white neighborhood mothers, obviously friends, had brought their 4- and 5-year-olds to the local McDonald's for a snack and to play on the swings and slides provided by the restaurant. They were all seated at a table watching their sons and daughters run about the play

area. In one corner of the yard sat a small black child pushing a red truck along the grass. One of the white girls from the group approached the black boy and they started a conversation. During that instant, the mother of the girl exchanged quick glances with the other mothers who nodded knowingly. She quickly rose from the table, walked over to the two, spoke to her daughter, and gently pulled her away to join her previous playmates. Within minutes, however, the girl again approached the black boy and both began to play with the truck. At that point, all the mothers rose from the table and loudly exclaimed to their children, "It's time to go now!" (Sue, 2003, pp. 89–90)

From the moment of birth, this hidden curriculum is taught to children and reinforced in many overt and subtle ways. Even the well-intentioned mothers in this scenario may be unaware that they are teaching their children that certain racial groups are inferior, dangerous, and to be avoided. To prevent this hidden curriculum from emerging into consciousness, the master narrative is rehearsed over and over by White Americans in the democratic stories they tell to themselves and others. The master narrative does several things for many White Americans: It (a) reassures them that they are good, moral, and fair people; (b) prevents them from being conscious of their biased cultural conditioning; (c) allows them to live in a world of false deception; (d) maintains their innocence and naïveté; (e) perpetuates the racial status quo; (f) acts as blinders that prevent White Americans from being conscious of inequities that exist for people of color; and (g) justifies inaction on their part (APA Presidential Task Force, 2012; Bell, 2002, 2003; van Dijk, 1999).

A Tale of Two Stories: Themes From White Talk and Back Talk

The personal stories and experiences told by both Jack and Mal exemplify the common cultural and historical themes that emerge from race talk. On the one hand, the stories told by Jack about race and racism are meant to reassure him and other Whites that they have no responsibility for inequities suffered by people of color; on the other hand, the counter-narratives told by Mal are likened to telling on racism (Bell, 2003) and meant to decode the racist assumptions of the master narrative. Race talk thus becomes a duel between two opposing belief systems (ideologies) of which much is at stake on personal, institutional, and societal levels.

Theme 1: We Live in a Meritocratic Society
In telling his story of race and racism, Jack insinuates that racism is no longer the reason that holds back the advancement of people of color. In fact,

he attributes the lack of progress to internal beliefs held by Mal and the erroneous assumption that Whites block their own paths to success. Jack implies that anyone can succeed in life through hard work and effort. He uses his great-grandfather as an example of the Horatio Alger story—the rags-to-riches theme achieved through hard work. Although the great-grandfather encountered discrimination, the tale told by Jack is that he stood strong and made himself a success through determination, individual effort, and perseverance. This is a common cultural and historical theme that is best exemplified in the many novels of Horatio Alger, who celebrated capitalist markets and romanticized the story that anyone, regardless of race or social class, can become a dazzling success. As such, these tales reinforce a cherished belief in America as a land of opportunity and the importance of rugged individualism.

The belief in hard work as the key to success is part of the Protestant ethic that implies a strong relationship between ability, effort, and success. People who succeed in our society work harder, have more skills, and are more competent. People who fail to achieve much in our society are seen as lazy, less capable, or less intelligent. Embedded in this ethos are democratic ideals repeated over and over in stories that portray the United States as being a land of opportunity. In one form or another, sayings such as "Everyone can make it in society if they work hard enough," "Justice and liberty apply to everyone," "God helps those who help themselves," and " Fulfill your personal destiny" are culturally conditioned into the thinking of White Americans.

Behind these phrases, however, lies one major flawed assumption: the erroneous belief that everyone operates on a level playing field. Mal's back talk indicates that meritocracy is a myth, that the system is rigged against people of color, that unfairness prevails, that he is not to blame for his lack of progress, and that systemic factors (individual and institutional racism) place obstacles in his path. For Jack to entertain this counter-narrative, he would have to conclude that life for people of color is not fair and that the playing field is tilted in such a way as to be an uphill journey for persons of color and a downhill one for Whites. The idea that you are the master of your own fate unfairly blames minority citizens for their inability to achieve more in this society. It fails to take into consideration the systemic forces of racism, prejudice, and discrimination and the operation of White privilege, a concept we will shortly discuss.

People of color who suffer in poverty and unemployment and who live in the ghettos or barrios are blamed or portrayed in the master narrative as suffering from deficiencies in their lifestyles or of possessing personal inadequacies (lack of intelligence, laziness, or dysfunctional cultural values). Our example of Cliven Bundy's 2014 statement about African Americans in Chapter 2 is a prime example of this thinking. These themes expressed in the dialogues of White Americans are insulting, offensive, and invalidating to the life experiences of persons of color. They are likely to touch hot buttons and result in highly emotional reactions from persons of color. In their attempt to counteract the false deception of Whites and the attribution of blame to them, people of color tell stories that contradict the notion of equal access and opportunities. Their back talk forces Whites to consider how they may unintentionally be the culprits in perpetuating racism, a potential realization they are disinclined to consider.

Theme 2: Racism Is a Thing of the Past

"You've come a long way baby" is a phrase used to indicate how much progress has been made by women in attaining equal access and opportunity in our society. The saying is intended to convey a sense of ongoing social progress in our society, and is appealing to many Whites because it reassures them that they live in a basically fair and just society that recognizes injustices and rectifies them over time (Bell, 2003; Cose, 1997; Feagin, 2001). Likewise, with respect to race and racism, many Whites express the fact that we live in a postracial era and point to the election of the first Black president as evidence of progressive change (Neville, Awad, Brooks, Flores, & Bluemel, 2013; Neville, Spanierman, & Doan, 2006).

White talk is filled with themes that depict racism as only a historical injustice, portray our society as transcending our racial past, and suggest that prejudice and discrimination are no longer major factors in the lives of people of color. Jack's story echoes these strong beliefs, which are shared by many White Americans. Mal's back talk tells another story, however, that directly contradicts the one told by Jack. He tells of a life of hardships where the police and society continue to place limits on what he can do and where he can travel. His stories and those of people of color tell of the constant and continuing forms of prejudice and discrimination that are visited upon them in their daily lives; that racism is far from dead, but alive and well; and that White Americans are oblivious to its existence.

Indeed, national polls on the existence and persistence of racism support these differing realities. Most African Americans, for example, believe racism is a constant and continuing reality in their lives, while most Whites seem to deny its existence or to minimize it (Astor, 1997; Babbington, 2008; Harris Poll,

1994; MTV, 2014; Pew Research Center, 2007). When asked how much discrimination still exists against Blacks, only 10% of Whites said "a lot" while 57% of Blacks said "a lot" (Babbington, 2008). Sixty-seven percent of Blacks described encountering discrimination and prejudice when applying for jobs, 50% reported incidents during shopping or dining out, and many stated it was a common occurrence to hear derogatory racial comments (Pew Research Center, 2007). Likewise, in a recent study of Asian American students, 78% reported experiencing racial microaggressions over a 2-week period (Ong, Burrow, Fuller-Rowell, Ja, & Sue, 2013) from well-intentioned White Americans. Despite these statistics, over 50% of Whites believe that people of color have achieved equality and that most are doing better than they really are, in contradiction to standard-of-living data (Harris Poll, 1994). Even among Millennials (ages 14 to 24), considered the most liberal generation to come along, 64% of nearly 2,000 White respondents believe having a Black president demonstrates that people of color have the same opportunities (MTV, 2014).

Theme 3: Color Blindness: Minimizing Differences or Pretending Not to See Them

There appears to be three aspects of this theme in White talk. First, there is an implicit assumption among many Whites that seeing race is an open admission of one's racism because it goes against the dictum that "Everyone should be treated the same" and "We are all the same under the skin." This has been referred to as a form of color-blind racial ideology that is an attempt to move beyond race and endorses the belief that race should not matter (Neville et al., 2013). When Jack says that color is not a big thing, that being White is a color, that Mal is equal to him, and that we should all just be Americans, he is minimizing and/or diluting the importance of race in the lives of people of color. In other words, Jack is attempting to blur the distinction between being a White man and a Black man and evokes the question from Mal, "Are you implying that being Black is no different than being White?" The implication here is that Mal is no different than Jack; they are simply human beings. For Mal to accept this equation means he would have to deny his racial experiences that form his racial/ethnic identity. It would also mean that he would have to deny his experiences of prejudice and discrimination and buy into the assumption that his ability to succeed in society as a Black man is no different than that of a White man (Zou & Dickter, 2013).

Second, the disinclination to see color (color-evasion) is often motivated by a belief that differences are divisive or deviant and we should stress similarities or sameness (Neville et al., 2013). One can surmise that the conversation about race in the opening scenario is filled with attempts by Jack to minimize differences between him and other people of color in the group. He prefers to stress commonalities by saying that we should all just be Americans. In this case, there is possible recognition of differences, but Jack and many White Americans prefer to stress commonalities or the universal level of identity—we are all members of the human race. This mentality suggests that stressing similarities leads to greater group cohesion (Sue & Sue, 2013). Although there is great merit in acknowledging and stressing commonalities of the human condition, the belief that pretending not to notice differences (race, culture, and ethnicity) contains a hidden message: There is something wrong with differences, and they ultimately lead to conflict. It has the unintended consequence of equating racial differences with being bad or deviant. Such a belief is often voiced in ways that attribute problems to groups in our society: the Black problem, the Asian problem, the Native American problem, the minority problem, or the problem of race. In other words, stories told by Whites often depict people of color as problem people. Rather than blackness being the problem, however, the problem is really society's perception of blackness. Thus, the locus of racial problems is not internal to the group, but resides in the social system (negative stereotypes and beliefs that justify unfair treatment of a whole group).

Third, another form of color blindness identified by Neville and colleagues (Neville et al., 2013) is power evasion (denial of racism by emphasizing equal opportunities) that cloaks inequities in sociopolitical relationships. Jack's story is filled with phrases that deny or radically minimize the existence of racism by implying that Mal (as a Black man) is no different than him. For him to acknowledge color would mean Jack could no longer ignore racism, ignore the discriminatory treatment faced by people of color, and ignore the power and privilege that Whites enjoy in America. This last point leads us to the topic of racial privilege and power, more specifically White privilege.

Theme 4: Invisibility of Power and Privilege

It is clear that Jack and many Whites perceive themselves as unbiased individuals who do not harbor racist thoughts and feelings: Their stories portray them as working toward social justice and as being good, moral, and decent individuals. They are not responsible for whatever happened in the past nor do they currently practice discrimination. Mal's comments in the dialogue challenge the assumptions made by Jack. Jack finds it hard to entertain the notion that being White means something far different than being Black or a person of color. In fact, he actively denies it by stating that Mal is equal to him. Mal, however, presses the point that the racial experiences of people of color are different from those of Whites, that Whites profit and benefit from the oppression of people of color, and that Whites have the power to impose their reality (stories) upon groups that are most disempowered in our society. Mal is frustrated, agitated, and angry that Jack seems oblivious and unaware of racism and his own biases. The outburst by Mal over the statement that "each man stands on his own ground" represents his reaction to what he views as White lies: (a) Whites tamed this country and settled the land in North America; (b) it was not taken from the indigenous people of this country; and (c) even if it were, Jack (and others like him) is not responsible for the actions of his ancestors. This defensive posture is heard often in the declarations of White Americans: "I didn't take land from the Native Americans." "My parents and I aren't responsible for slavery." "My family didn't incarcerate the Japanese Americans." "Why blame me? I'm innocent of those past actions." Mal's counter-narrative attempts to inform Jack that, yes, he may *not* have owned slaves or been responsible for other atrocities, but he and Whites continue *to benefit from the past injustices and inequities* created by their ancestors.

Much of the dilemma for Jack lies in his lack of critical racial consciousness. "What does it mean to be White?" would be a very difficult question for him to answer. He has seldom thought about being a White person because Whiteness is invisible to him. Strangely enough, Whiteness is most visible to people of color when it is denied, when it evokes puzzlement or negative reactions, and when it is equated with normality. For Jack, Whiteness is transparent precisely because of its everyday occurrence, its institutionalized normative features in the culture, and the fact that Whites are taught to think of their lives as morally neutral, average, and ideal (Sue, 2003).

When Jack asks why we can't all just be Americans and states, "When in Rome, do as the Romans do," his naïveté and obliviousness to the dynamic meaning of those quotes is obvious. Here are samples of statements by Whites that often find their way into racial dialogues and express themes of assimilation and acculturation:

"We should all learn to blend in."
"If you immigrate to this country, you should assimilate and acculturate."
"When in Rome, do as the Romans do."
"We are a melting pot."

The implicit assumption with these melting pot statements is that people of color would not encounter problems if they would simply assimilate and acculturate. They are constantly told that if they only become westernized, they will bear the fruits of the society like their White counterparts. When Jack asks, "Why can't we all just be Americans?" he is expressing this sentiment. There are two very invalid assumptions that anger people of color. First, let us for the moment assume that assimilation is desirable and that people who immigrate to this country should become Americans. If that is the case, shouldn't we all be Native Americans? This represents a back talk question voiced by Mal that undermines the justification used by many White Americans about other groups accommodating to a host culture. The answer to this question is very revealing. Seen from this perspective, the melting pot (a seemingly harmless and neutral concept) is in actuality a justification for political oppression and imposition—historical European colonization toward the Americas. The melting pot concept is a demand for forced compliance to the norms and standards of a dominant group who impose their power over other groups.

Second, although early White immigrants encountered prejudice and discrimination when arriving in this country, they were seen as not American enough. It took several generations, but when the children of immigrants became westernized, they could usually be expected to be accepted by other Whites. Thus early ethnic immigrants of largely Protestant and Anglo-Saxon background from countries such as Britain, Germany, Ireland, and Italy could expect to melt in and be accepted if they were White. Despite assimilating and acculturating, however, people of color are told in no uncertain terms that they continue to be unwelcome, undesirable, and inferior because of their visible racial ethnic differences. They can never be "true Americans." Thus, people of color conclude and are aware that the melting pot seems to have been meant for White Euro-Americans only.

In summary, the stories told by Whites in race talk attempt to mask the power and privilege they hold over disempowered groups in our society. White talk perpetuates an imbalance of economic, social, and political power; controls the gateways to power and privilege; and determines which groups will be allowed access to the benefits, privileges, and opportunities of the society.

Theme 5: Denial of Individual Racism
Oftentimes, dialogues on race are filled with White talk that denies individual prejudice and discrimination, racial bias, and responsibility for racism.

One of the greatest fears by many Whites is to be perceived as being racist. As Jack enters the racial dialogue, for example, he cautions that what he is about to say may appear racist, and bemoans political correctness as an obstacle to truthful conversation. In other words, he is denying that he harbors any racial animosity and implying that his beliefs and opinions represent honesty and not racism. Throughout his dialogue with Mal, Jack states that he and his family did not own slaves and are not responsible for slavery, that his great grandfather also experienced discrimination, and that he is not responsible for blocking Mal's path to success. Racial dialogues are filled with defensive statements that may be seen as denial of individual racism: "I don't discriminate; I treat everyone the same." "I have many Black friends." "I have nothing against interracial marriages, but I worry about the children." "Racists are only the skinheads, the Klan, and White supremacists—I am not like them." When people of color hear such statements, they immediately become vigilant and, rightly or wrongly, perceive the speaker as attempting to hide personal biases or as telling sincere fictions.

Again, the questions we can ask are these: Is it possible for anyone born and raised in the United States not to inherit the racial biases of his or her forebears? Is it unfair for people of color to assume that most White Americans harbor biases and prejudices in a racial dialogue? Or are they generally correct in this assumption? Answers to these questions seem to be present in the social psychological literature on race and racism (DeVos & Banaji, 2005; Dovidio, Gaertner, Kawakami, & Hodson, 2002; J. M. Jones, 1997) and on racial microaggressions (Sue, 2010; Sue, Capodilupo, & Holder, 2008). These findings seem to indicate that it is nearly impossible not to inherit the racial biases of our ancestors (Sue, 2003, 2004). People of color are wary of the tales Whites tell about being free of prejudice and bias because of the frequent racial microaggressions people of color receive from well-intentioned White colleagues, neighbors, and friends (Sue et al., 2007). The wariness is consistent with research findings that White Americans who consciously endorse egalitarian principles, profess to be fair-minded, deny that they possess racial bias, and would never deliberately discriminate engage in unintentional acts of discrimination (APA Presidential Task Force, 2012; Dovidio et al., 2002; J. M. Jones, 1997). Thus, when Whites tell stories that contain themes of denial of individual racial prejudice, their credibility and trustworthiness becomes questioned; the story teller is perceived as inauthentic.

Which Is the True Story?

The underlying assumptions and beliefs expressed in race talk between Whites and people of color have very different outcomes and implications depending on which version is accepted by society (Bell, 2002, 2003; Roy, 1999). Accepting White talk as accurate and true maintains the status quo and the current social arrangements of society, minimizes the effects of racism, and absolves responsibility for Whites to take action. Accepting the validity of back talk, however, means realizing that power, privilege, and political imposition have led to current social hierarchies, that Whites have been complicit in facilitating inequities, and that they are responsible to change the system. One can reasonably ask, Which is the true story?

We have repeatedly indicated in the previous chapters that race talk represents a clash of racial realities. Despite the voluminous research studies we have referred to in our description of the storytelling themes, especially as they support the perception of people of color, many Whites are disinclined to alter their way of viewing themselves and the world they live in. Why this is so will be discussed in a later chapter. While asking White folks about their Whiteness may prove beneficial at some levels, accepting their answers as truth is unlikely to elicit a deeper understanding of racial reality. This is not meant as a put-down of White Americans but acknowledges the invisibility of Whiteness and all that accompanies it. To get at the issue of Whiteness, it may be best to seek answers from persons of color. After all, if you want to understand oppression, should you ask the oppressor or the oppressed? If you want to learn about sexism, do you ask men or women? If you want to learn about racism, do you ask Whites or persons of color? Studies support the contention that the most accurate assessment of bias comes not from those who enjoy the privilege of power, but from those who are most disempowered (Hanna, Talley, & Guindon, 2000; J. M. Jones, 1997).

Common sense, for example, would lead us to conclude that people of color understand White people better than White folks understand persons of color. People of color operate within a White world and are forced to operate within that context. They are taught White ways, the English language, White Western European history and culture, and the thoughts and feelings of White Americans from the moment of birth or from the time they arrive in the United States. They attend all-White schools, are exposed to a Euro-American curriculum, work for White-controlled places of employment, and are subjected to a White justice system (Sue, 2003). They are also exposed to the beliefs, attitudes, values, biases, and prejudices of the dominant society. White Americans, however, seldom have much experience with people of color. While Whites may claim to have friends of color, they do not socialize together nor have much intimate contact with persons of color once they leave their places of employment. Although they may attend ethnic celebrations, dine in community restaurants to sample ethnic foods, or participate in fundraising for good causes related to ethnic arts and/or humanitarian goals, they often remain on the outskirts of the groups they hope to help or understand. Whites are acquainted with only the most superficial cosmetic workings of ethnic minority groups.

Thus the knowledge base of racial minorities comes primarily from a distorted picture of persons of color picked up from the media and an educational system that teaches them falsely with stories about how Columbus discovered America, the pioneers settled and tamed the West, and Christians civilized the heathens. Unlike people of color, White social, psychological, and economic survival is not based upon the ability to understand people of color. They have the privilege of disengaging from ethnic minority communities or individuals should they feel uncomfortable or tire of those associations. People of color do not enjoy that luxury.

This statement leads to a tongue-in-cheek story of what Robert Terry calls "The Parable of Ups and Downs." The Ups (a) are in power and control, (b) seldom worry about the Downs, (c) are willing to allow some token Downs to occupy moderate positions of influence, (d) associate primarily with one another, and (e) define the Downs as less intelligent and capable. The Downs (a) spend time trying to explain their Downness to the Ups, who find it difficult to believe; (b) are forced to justify their existence to the Ups; and (c) are constantly vigilant to the thoughts and actions of the Ups. Terry (1972) expresses this counter-narrative in a parable of what it means to occupy a dominant or subordinate position:

> The bad news is that when we're UP it often makes us stupid. We call that "DUMB-UPNESS." It's not because UPS are not smart. It's that UPS don't have to pay attention to DOWNS the way DOWNS have to pay attention to UPS. DOWNS always have to figure out what UPS are UP to. The only time UPS worry about DOWNS is when DOWNS get uppity, at which time they're put DOWN by the UPS. The UPS' perception is that DOWNS are overly sensitive; they have an attitude problem. It is never understood that UPS are underly sensitive and have an attitude problem. (pp. 2–3)

Hearing the Meaning of Back Talk

White talk and back talk contain two contrasting racial realities and their manifestations come out in the multiple themes of stories told through racial dialogues between Whites and people of color. Five of them—the myth of meritocracy, belief that racism is a thing of the past, color blindness, invisibility of power and privilege, and denial of individual racism—are recurrent themes in many of stories. Many other themes such as *blaming the victim, pathologizing the communication styles of people of color, being a human being, delegitimizing the issue by derogating the communicator, projecting an innocence and naïveté of racism,* and many others frequently make their appearance in race talk as well. These other themes will be more fully discussed in later chapters.

It takes considerable effort by Whites to hear and consider the legitimacy of back talk (Ford, 2012). Analysis of racial discourse between Whites and people of color may provide clues for how to break through the sincere fictions of White Americans (Bolgatz, 2005). Once race talk moves from an external public struggle to an internal personal struggle of conscience, it becomes frighteningly unpleasant for many White Americans. In an especially insightful analysis, Gene Robinson in a blog for the *Washington Post* (July 19, 2013) made the following observation of Chris Matthews, a TV host of the program *Hardball,* as he struggled to understand the racial reality of African American colleagues he interviewed:

> Is anyone noticing the remarkable journey Chris Matthews (host of MSNBC's *Hardball*) is on?...I write this not to embarrass him, but to honor him. On Thursday evening, July 18, right before our very eyes, we witness a transformation about race going on in the mind and heart of an already-liberal, racially-accepting human being. Throughout this evening's edition of Hardball, Matthews appears genuinely disturbed. In an effort to better understand what happened to Trayvon Martin and why, he interviews Val Nicholas (Vice President of NBC News) and Michael Steele (former chair of the Republican National Committee), both African American Professionals. He can't believe what he's hearing. He struggles to listen to their truth about what it's like to grow up and live as a black man in America.
>
> Nicholas describes finding himself staring down the barrel of a gun pointed at him by police having no reason for suspicion and confrontation other than the black color of his skin. Mr. Steele nods knowingly, and then offers his own experiences of being targeted because of his race alone. They both laugh about the "five block follow" in which a police cruiser follows them in their cars for five or so blocks, just because the color of their skin makes them suspicious.

Matthews listens in stunned disbelief knowing that he has never had such experiences, and the discomfort in his face worsens as he tastes his own white privilege.

And in the wake of the Zimmerman trial verdict, we have heard many black men (including the Attorney General of the United States) recounting about how, when they were young, their fathers had conversations with them about how to navigate such pervasive racial bias, and how these black men, now fathers themselves, are having these same conversations with their sons. Recalling the warnings from his dad, Nicholas recounts that his father told him that arguing with police will land him in jail, the hospital or the morgue not because of what he has or has not done, but because of the color of his skin. Steele adds that it's not "if" they get stopped, but "when."

This is not news to black men. But it is news to those of us who are white in this society and have never known such systemic racism. And what is remarkable, as Chris Matthews tries to absorb this subtle and endemic racism from which he unwittingly benefits, is his willingness to allow us, the viewers, to witness the dawning of knowledge and the change that is going on in his consciousness and understanding.

Matthews' public journey is modeling for white America how we can all learn from the tragedy of Trayvon Martin's death. Look at what he's doing, and see in it a way forward for greater racial understanding in this country:

1. He is willing to talk about race, to talk openly about what he knows (and what he does NOT know) about how race works in America.
2. He asks questions of people of color who do know about the experience of racism (without being embarrassed by his need to ask) and then he listens to them and believes their truth, shaking his head in acknowledgment of the fact that all of this has been going on under his own white radar screen.
3. He begins to make connections and analyze situations he once thought he understood.
4. And then, seemingly coming to the end of what he can absorb, he vulnerably and almost naively, mutters "All I can say right now is, I am so sorry."
5. And then he says, in a way that makes you think he means it, "We have to keep talking about this, publicly and on TV. I want to have those conversations."

Chris Matthews has modeled for us the way to bring redemption and healing from the disease and sin of racism highlighted by the Trayvon Martin killing. We can't bring Trayvon back from the dead. But those of us who are white can begin to have these conversations with people of color about what life is like in "colored" America. And it is profoundly relevant as we consider immigration reform, limits on voter rights, and relentless attempts to balance our budgets on the backs of the most vulnerable all of which have subtexts of systemic racism

We don't often think of political pundits as leading the way in moral behavior. But Chris Matthews, in his vulnerable act of allowing us to witness his own personal journey, is doing just that. It's a journey toward a more just America. It's a journey I want to be on with him. Don't you?

The Constraining Ground Rules for Race Talk

.

CHAPTER FOUR

"The Entire World's a Stage!"

Several years ago, I was at a political fundraiser to "get out the vote" in New York City. Although I am a Democrat, many of those attending were Republicans who supported either Mitt Romney or John McCain. As someone who has studied issues of race, ethnicity, and gender in psychology, I was excited about the prospect of electing either the first female (Hillary Clinton) or Black (Barack Obama) president. I remember a series of conversations I had during the cocktail hour with those in attendance. Most of them felt extremely superficial and I could not shake the feeling of being ignored or invalidated about my thoughts on race and gender. Most of the guests seemed to dance around the topic with tepid responses and niceties. I felt constrained in what could be discussed and how they were discussed.

One conversation in particular stood out. My wife and I had just joined a group who were speculating about the most likely Democratic or Republican candidates to run in the fall. When I observed that our nation had an opportunity to make history in the upcoming election, most in the group remained silent. After some period of time, one male guest flatly stated that race and gender were no longer hindrances in our society, that it would be much better to be colorblind, and that we should simply vote for the most qualified candidate. I countered by saying that race and gender were always factors, although at times not obvious. I gave the example of former Los Angeles mayor Tom Bradley (African American) who lost the California governor's race some time back. I mentioned that studies suggested race was a determining factor in his loss.

As we were dialoguing about the issue, I was aware that several of the group members politely excused themselves, while others appeared uncomfortable and remained silent. As I tried to press the point about the importance of race, I suddenly felt my wife's elbow jabbing me in the side. To me it was an obvious signal to discontinue the conversation. She quickly stated to the group that it was so nice to meet everyone, and wondered aloud whether I could get her a glass of Perrier. Later that evening, she took me aside and admonished me that race was not a topic that was appropriate to discuss in this setting, that I was embarrassing her, and that I should speak calmly and politely to others (which I thought I had done), even though she generally agrees with my opinions on these topics. Heeding my wife's warning, I made certain that my comments for the rest of the evening were "noncontroversial." Race and gender as a topic never arose again in any of my conversations. (APA Presidential Task Force, 2012, pp. 38–39)

Questions: What do you see happening in this social situation among the participants? Applying the principles of White talk versus back talk, can you distill the two competing messages being sent by both parties? What made dialogue about the race or gender of the political candidates uncomfortable for many of the attendees? Was the storyteller insensitive to the feelings of others? What social norms were being broken? Is talking about race or gender a taboo topic in social situations? When would it be appropriate to discuss these issues or express one's feelings and opinions? What are social ground rules for discussing race? How may they either hinder or facilitate open and honest racial dialogues?

> All the world's a stage,
> And all the men and women merely players.
> They have their exits and their entrances;
> And one man in his time plays many parts.
>
> William Shakespeare (1623), *As You Like It*, Act II, Scene 7

William Shakespeare's famous quote aptly describes the interactions of the players in our opening vignette. To many social scientists who have studied theories of social interaction and communication, the roles we play in life are many and varied and can be compared to a theatrical drama (Bolino & Turnley, 2003; Pin & Turndorg, 2009). The world is the stage from which we perform, and each act represents different settings that mold and shape our roles. Indeed, our performances (how we behave toward one another) are dictated by our internal need (a) to have others (the audience) perceive us favorably or in the manner we desire, (b) to control the definition of the situation (the script), and (c) to conform to the rules of the production, which may or may not be obvious to the participants (actors). At a social gathering such as a reception, cocktail hour, or fund-raiser, the people attending can all be likened to actors and actresses playing certain roles dictated by implicit and explicit situational norms and standards of conduct. These social, cultural, and political rules further interact with the communication styles of the participants and their impression management strategies (Johnson-Cartee, 2010; Pin & Turndorg, 2009).

THE POLITENESS PROTOCOL AND RACE TALK

It is generally acknowledged that sociologist Erving Goffman's seminal book (1959) *The Presentation of Self in Everyday Life* was among the first to propose an impression management theory in social interactions. Although Goffman did not apply his symbolic interaction theory to racial interactions and dialogues, increasing numbers of social scientists believe it has applicability to race talk in almost all settings (APA Presidential Task Force, 2012; Berbrier, 1999; Shih, Young, & Bucher, 2013; Sue, 2013; van Dijk, 1992). According to impression management theory, people have an inherent interest in how they are perceived and evaluated by others in nearly all situations, whether at home, school, work, or other public and social situations. We play many different roles dictated by those situations. In interracial interactions or when conversations touch upon topics of race or racism, powerful rules of conduct or norms place limits on how deeply the topic is explored and the manner in which it is discussed. Let us use the opening scenario to illustrate the intersecting social and political ground rules of racial dialogues and their effect on the behavior of the guests during the event.

The Staging

First, it is important to consider the context of the event and the definition of the situation. The fund-raiser was a nonpartisan political event intended to increase voter turnout by encouraging people to register for the upcoming primaries. All attendees had a shared mutual goal and the organizers of the event stressed that increasing voter turnout in a democratic society was for the good of our nation. That evening was about cooperation, group cohesion, consensus building, and working for the mutual good of everyone, regardless of political affiliation. The event was attended by local politicians, community leaders, academics, and neighborhood representatives who donated time or monetary contributions to a worthy cause. The affair was set in a large hall where wine, appetizers, and small snacks were provided. The occasion brought together many strangers and casual acquaintances making pleasant and polite conversation with one another. We might even go so far as to state that these guests represented very influential people in the community; they were relatively affluent, held important positions, and were generally active in a political and social sense. On the surface, the gathering was like any splendid social function with men and women nicely attired in their finest suits and fancy dresses, smiling and laughing at one another's jokes or comments, and clustered in small conversational groups. Occasionally, an individual or couple would break from one group to join another as they made the rounds to acquaint themselves with other guests. Implicit social norms embedded in the script called for avoidance of conflict and downplaying differences.

In retrospect, the hall, glittering lights, small dining stations, open bar, and musical ensemble can be likened to stage props, and the beautiful people as actors performing parts that they played in their social, cultural, and political scripts. From a distance the conversations and interactions appeared smooth, harmonious, and flowing with a social rhythm that spoke of mutuality, cooperation, and synchrony. Below this seemingly symphonic exterior, however, lay major differences in political persuasions, beliefs, attitudes, and even negative feelings toward certain groups or one another. What accounts for this harmonious scene despite the deep differences guests might possess? Given that for the first time in any presidential election two very viable and visible candidates for the highest office in the land (a Black man and a White woman) could break major racial and gender barriers, what accounts for its nearly total absence in conversations and/or very superficial discussions among attendees (except for the one incident described earlier), or the lack of acrimony among the guests when the topic arose?

Contextually, the answers seem to lie in what has been labeled the rules of the politeness protocol explicitly and implicitly embedded in the social norms inherent in social interactions. In the opening vignette to this section, the man at the fund-raiser experienced a very common social situation that has been described as the "politeness protocol" (Young, 2003). This protocol dictates that people should be nice and polite; take care not to offend others; keep conversations light, friendly, and noncontroversial; and avoid potential interpersonal conflict. It is often considered improper and impolite to discuss certain topics such as race, gender, and sexual orientation at social events, in public forums, and in many private functions for fear they will bring out differences of opinion that lead to disagreements, heated exchanges, and conflict (Sue, 2005). During the cocktail reception, for example, those in attendance tended to engage in pleasantries, small talk, and superficial dialogue. When the author of the vignette expressed his views on race and gender, he had violated the politeness protocol; certain topics or issues are considered taboo, but when brought up in a conversation, they are to be treated in a superficial and fleeting manner. Even his wife, whose thoughts and opinions probably matched his own, was sensitive to the violation. Race and deep discussions of it are taboo, and a code of silence reinforces avoidance of such dialogues.

Managing Impressions: The Roles Played by Actors

Research on impression management, or the tendency of people to present themselves to others in the most favorable light possible, offers clues as to other ground rules that prevent honest discussions of hot topics such as race (Roberts, 2005; Rosenfeld, Giacalone, & Riordan, 1995). When in mixed company, especially casual acquaintances or strangers, people attempt to manage and influence the images that others have of them. Social psychologists believe that there are three types of selves that we try to project to others using self-presentation techniques or tactics (Bolino & Turnley, 1999): *the authentic self, the ideal self,* and the *tactical self*. The authentic self is the image we project that is real and consistent with the way we view ourselves. This image is known and usually shared with close friends and family members, and contains what we believe to be our honest beliefs, attitudes, and feelings. These may contain personal secrets that others may misunderstand and may even create problems for us if known by them. For example, not wanting your son or daughter to marry outside of one's race or having racial biases against other groups are acknowledged only to people who share those beliefs and values.

The ideal self is the public image of ourselves that is consistent with the way we wish we were. In the case of the psychologist in the earlier scenario, he may have perceived himself as an expert on the psychology of racism, a knowledgeable professor of psychology, and someone whose observations and opinions on race and racism would carry weight and authority with the guests. This image was important for him to project to others. The tactical self, however, is the image that we hope to portray that is both positive and favorable to either our authentic or ideal self through the use of self-presentation techniques. Depending upon the situation, social setting, public forum, or classroom, any of these roles and their countless variations may be played. As indicated by Shakespeare, we play many different roles in our lifetime dictated by personal and public scripts upon a world stage.

In our society, general norms and values supported by the law condemn and prohibit racial prejudice and discrimination (van Dijk, 1992). From the moment of birth we are taught the values of democracy and nondiscrimination, and most of us perceive ourselves as good and moral individuals who would never consciously discriminate. To be called or labeled a racist is to be accused of being a hateful, irrational, and potentially violent individual who should be shunned and silenced. Such is the case of Donald Sterling, owner of the Los Angeles Clippers, when he made recorded racist comments in 2014 that became known to the public. The label *racist* is a socially horrendous label, and an abhorrent and vile stigma to most ordinary White citizens. Thus, we are motivated to have others perceive us as people who stand for egalitarian ideals, equal access and opportunities, and the importance of civil and human rights. This is the image we like to project to others. Ironically enough, the impression management strategies most well-intentioned people use to uphold this image are those used by White supremacists and avowed racists as well. Although the latter group consciously tries to deceive others by portraying their tactical selves in public, most ordinary citizens try to deceive not only others, but themselves as well.

In all probability, the majority of those attending the social function had much at stake in their portrayal of themselves as racially unbiased. When the topics of race and gender were introduced into the conversation, it immediately raised a red flag or warning for those engaged in the conversation: "Be careful about what you say and how you say it. You don't want to be misunderstood and be mistakenly perceived as a racist or sexist. It is best to avoid the topic and/or superficially discuss it. Don't say what you truly think or feel." This is a theme and psychological dynamic we will explore in another chapter.

The Strategies and Techniques of Acting

People possess an arsenal of self-presentation strategies they use to enhance their favorable image to an audience and to be liked, be seen positively, and be consistent with what society deems appropriate (Bolino & Turnley, 1999). Self-disclosure, for example, is used to selectively disclose information about the self that others will perceive favorably. *Selective self-presentation* may involve self-promotion in one form or another. For example, many at the fund-raiser talked about the important jobs they have held, actions taken in the past to promote voter registration, interesting vacations they had taken, and their standing in the community (Roberts, 2005). Name-dropping was very common as several guests would mention personally knowing important politicians or having socialized with Hillary Clinton. With respect to racial or gender credentials, people may stress that they are members of the Southern Poverty Law Center, have many Black friends, supported the Equal Rights Amendment, and support human rights. Other information or facts about themselves that may be at odds with the impression they hope to project are downplayed or not disclosed to the audience.

Managing appearances is another tactic where the goal is to control or manufacture an image of yourself so that others will perceive you in a certain way. This tactical strategy is intended to present a false, exaggerated, or misleading image in many ways. For example, physical appearance and control of nonverbal behaviors are consciously planned or exercised in interpersonal interactions. For the man, wearing a suit or not, the color of the tie (red = power), or dressing more casually (turtleneck and jacket), and for the woman, formal dress or evening gown, color coordination, and importantly jewelry are all intended to convey an image important to the actor. The suit may be intended to convey power and authority, the turtleneck and jacket one of an academic intellectual, and jewelry may be a statement of status and affluence. Managing appearances is also very important in the nonverbal behavior of the guests. Body posture, facial expression (smiles), head nods, appropriate eye contact, and physical closeness are all used to indicate attentiveness to others, to communicate agreement, and to convey a positive feeling and interest to the other person (real or not).

The most widely used impression management strategy, however, is that of *ingratiation*, first identified by E. E. Jones (1964) in his book of the same name. Since that time many in social psychology and organizational behavior have investigated its manifestation, dynamics, and impact. Not only is it used to increase the attractiveness and likability of the actor, but it can enhance interpersonal relationships and build harmony among individuals, groups, and organizations (Bolino & Turnley, 1999; Goffman, 1959; Rosenfeld, et al., 1995). In essence, ingratiation can be expressed in any number of ways. First, *opinion conformity* is often used to align your opinions, beliefs, and feelings with people you are trying to ingratiate yourself to. In this case you are trying to increase your attractiveness with and influence others through pronouncements of similarity ("I liked that movie too!" "Voting is a right in this country." "Yes, racism is abhorrent."). Expressions of agreement with such beliefs and opinions occur despite disliking the movie, believing that voting is a privilege and not a right, and not wanting your son or daughter to marry a person of color or outside of their racial group. *Other enhancement* is another ingratiating tool where compliments or saying positive things about the other person are used. Flattering the person's dress style, handling of a difficult situation, sense of humor, or intelligence are examples. Compliments vary from true admiration, to exaggerations, to outright falsehoods.

Impression management strategies tend to enhance a favorable image of the self, downplay possible negative attributions of the self by others, and mask or conceal the authentic self for the purpose of social harmony. The politeness protocol dictated by the social context, and by the desire to be viewed favorably by others, all work in unison and in an intersecting manner to ensure that potential conflict, expression of differences, and antagonisms are concealed, minimized, and diluted in the interpersonal transactions that occur (Sue, 2013). Race talk or discussions of race have the potential to be divisive topics that can destroy social synchrony in interpersonal interactions. It is a socially taboo topic that often pushes powerful emotional hot buttons in people; exposes major differences in worldviews; creates discord, disagreement, and conflict; and threatens social harmony. When topics on race, racism, power, and privilege arise in conversations, the ground rules governing how they are handled and discussed among individuals are triggered and influenced by the norms of social context, the impression management strategies used by participants, and the implicit and explicit conflict-avoidant transactions. In such situations, a conspiracy of silence operates to prevent the authentic self from emerging, and what is presented in the tactical self is often inauthentic in order to preserve social harmony. The storyteller observed that discussions on race seemed superficial as people danced around the topic or failed to weigh in on it, which is often the result of impression management strategies employed by participants.

Individuals who follow the politeness protocol script are rewarded by validation and acceptance by other cast members; those who refuse to follow the master script or who violate and transgress the social norms and standards of acceptable conduct are punished. In social situations they are either ignored or avoided. Applying this to the opening scenario where the topic of race arose illustrates principles operating from the politeness protocol that prevented honest dialogues on race from occurring. First, the central character (psychologist and educator) had much at stake in his self-identity, as someone who had spent his entire professional career researching racism and antiracism, and perhaps having personal experiences with prejudice and discrimination in his life. Although he is not immune from using impression management strategies, his ideas and observations about breaking gender and racial barriers probably came from his authentic self. The group he conversed with may or may not have agreed with his remarks, but the topic seemed to make some people very uncomfortable.

When a discussion between the storyteller and another guest developed, it exposed a potential clash of racial realities and threatened to expose differences in the perception of race between the two men. In Chapter 3, we characterized this transaction as White talk (master narrative) at odds with back talk (counter-narratives by people of color). When the other man stated that race and gender were no longer barriers to advancement, that we should be a color-blind nation, and that we should vote for the most qualified person, the educator found the statements to be an invalidation of his racial reality. All three of these statements have been identified as forms of racial microaggressions (Sue et al., 2007). When the educator attempted to cite support for his position that race is always a factor in electoral politics, observers in the group felt uncomfortable; some handled the situation by remaining silent and not weighing in on the discussion, and others politely excused themselves from the group. None of them chose to take sides, to seek further clarification, and/or to express their own opinions on this matter. In other words, it was clear from their nonverbal communications that the main actors in the developing dialogue had violated the politeness protocol. Even the educator's wife sensed the violation, actively intervened in the discussion (elbowing the man and pretending to ask for a Perrier), and in private admonished him for raising the topic and becoming so animated. She indicated that he was a source of embarrassment to her and that discussions of race were inappropriate in this situation. In other words, she was telling her husband to adhere to the politeness protocol; impressions of him, and by association her, needed to be managed more carefully. The husband dutifully complied, and as indicated in the scenario, never brought up the race topic again.

The dynamics and outcomes in this vignette are telling and shine a light on the incompatibility of honest racial dialogues with many situational social norms. On a broader level, the culture and norms of our society offer cues for impression management; and, on a societal and organizational level, policies and practices instruct, support, and demonstrate appropriate social behaviors on racial interactions and race talk. These norms and our need to present a pleasant and agreeable front (image) mean that race talk is to be avoided or to be discussed in only the most superficial manner. Avoiding conflict, being noncontroversial, and preserving group harmony are rewarded while those who violate the politeness protocol are punished through social isolation, rejection by the group, and/or having negative attributions made about them; they are troublemakers who lack social skills and are offensive, impulsive and disagreeable, mean and hurtful, too emotional, or oversensitive. The politeness protocol is a powerful and inflexible norm and transgressing it brings on major condemnation.

It would be irresponsible not to note that impression management is a natural and inherent strategy employed by everyone. The strategies are also used by people of color and women to achieve certain goals. For these groups, however, the strong power differential between them and majority group members means they must exercise caution and restraint when confronted with topics or situations with racial or gender implications. For example, employees of color are often placed in situations where they must adapt or mold their behaviors to conform to the norms of the organization in order to advance or receive favorable ratings while employed. Whether impression management tactics are functional or dysfunctional, adaptive or maladaptive depends on the short- and long-term consequences to the individual employing them and for the ultimate good of our society.

THE ACADEMIC PROTOCOL AND RACE TALK

Studies suggest that the majority of educators claim to value diversity in classroom settings, and believe it represents a potential learning environment where cross-racial interactions and racial dialogues can present opportunities to develop the awareness, knowledge, and skills to function in a pluralistic society (President's Initiative on Race, 1998, 1999). Despite this strong belief, most teachers report making few changes to facilitate race talk, and feel uncomfortable and unprepared to deal with potentially heated exchanges on the topic (Pasque et al., 2013; Sue, Torino, et al., 2009). Indeed, most teachers report they are motivated to help students dialogue on race and racial topics, but feel limited, fearful, and constrained from doing so. What accounts for this large discrepancy between the desire of teachers to facilitate discussions and their inability to take effective action or produce the conditions that would evoke positive outcomes? Part of the answer seems to lie in the values and assumptions inherent in academia and the teaching profession itself.

Just as the politeness protocol sets standards and norms for discussions on race in social situations, the academic environment, especially the classroom, can also be likened to a different theatrical stage in which scripts for race talk are implicitly followed by faculty, and by default, their students (hooks, 1994; Valentine et al., 2012). The conditions that would facilitate a meaningful difficult dialogue on race, for example, may be at odds with learning assumptions, policies, and practices of the academic environment (hooks, 1994; Palmer, 2007). What has been called the academic protocol, for example, emphasizes a learning environment characterized by objectivity, rationality, and intellectual thought and inquiry (APA Presidential Task Force, 2012; Young, 2003). Race talk, however, is highly subjective, is intense, relies on storytelling, and is emotive in nature. The academic protocol is deeply rooted in our educational system and arises from White Western notions of science as exemplified in the scientific method (Highlen, 1996; Walsh & Shapiro, 2006). In Western science, the experimental design is considered the epitome of methods used to ask and answer questions about the human condition or the universe. The search for cause and effect is linear and allows us to identify the independent variables, the dependent variables, and the effects of extraneous variables that we attempt to control. It is analytical and reductionist in character. Extraneous variables that need to be controlled or eliminated are often the emotions, opinions, and preconceived notions of researchers, teachers, and participants.

Truth seeking in Western science operates from several basic assumptions: (a) Empirical reality is valued over experiential reality; (b) the mode of knowing is accomplished through breaking down phenomena into distinct and separate units or objects; (c) data, facts, and knowledge (truth) exist when they can be observed and measured via one of the five senses; and (d) universal principles are the hallmark of science so that cultural influences and differences are minimized. The concepts of separation, isolation, and even individualism in human relationships are hallmarks of the Euro-American worldview and, thus, not surprisingly, are foundational to our educational system.

From the perspective of education, learning and the acquisition of knowledge takes a reductionist approach to describing data, facts, information, and phenomena. The attempt to maintain objectivity, autonomy, and independence in understanding the physical world and human behavior is strongly stressed. Such tenets have resulted in separation of the person from the group (valuing of individualism and uniqueness), science from spirituality, man/woman from the universe, and thoughts from feelings. Within this framework exists a mind–body dualism in which the mind is legitimized in education while the body (spirit, emotions, and feelings) is not considered important in intellectual inquiry (Tatum, 1992). The road to knowledge and enlightenment in education is manifested in three major characteristics of Western science and education: focus on (1) empiricism, (2) reason and rationality, and (3) reductionism. All three tend to work against meaningful and successful race talk in classrooms.

Empirical Reality Versus Experiential Reality

The scientific way of knowing is based upon empirical tests that establish verifiable facts that represent the building blocks of knowledge and ultimately truth (Heppner, Wampold, & Kivlighan, 2008). In one form or another, most educators are trained to value scientific thinking that is data driven, supported by empirical evidence, and gathered through objective systematic means. The material taught in classes and the information imparted by teachers are theoretically based upon objective facts or truths, rather than upon subjective opinions, beliefs, and potentially contaminating biases (C. J. Goodwin, 2003). Thus, opinions, beliefs, feelings, knowledge, ideas, and information have credibility and reliability only when put to an empirical test. As we have seen in previous chapters, race talk is about storytelling or bearing witness to one's lived reality or experience (Bryan et al., 2012; Willow, 2008). Oftentimes, race talk from the perspective of people of color is inherently anecdotal and includes stories of the pain and suffering of racism, and is subjective in nature, experiential, and unverifiable in the immediacy of the moment.

Most professors and many teachers conduct their classes, however, in a manner that values a sterile decorum in which topics of race, gender, and sexual orientation are discussed in a businesslike manner and in a highly intellectualized fashion (hooks, 1994; Tatum, 1992). This feature of the academic protocol evaluates and judges the legitimacy of classroom information and learning through empirical evidence rather than experiential evidence. Empirical evidence is the source of knowledge that is required in determining reality and truth (observation and experimentation). The *senses* (what is seen, heard, smelled, or touched) are the primary source of empirical evidence. Although talking or testimony about past experiences, memories, feelings, and observations also serve as sources of evidence and derive from some sensory experience, they are considered to be secondary or indirect ways of knowing.

Thus, when dialogues on race occur in the classroom, experiential reality is not considered as reliable and valid information because it is contaminated by opinions, idiosyncratic experiences, emotions, and personal values. As a result, knowledge acquired and accepted through storytelling is considered to be an inadequate source of information and generally false. Many educators perceive dialogues or conversations on race as an exchange of opinions and ideas that are not necessarily grounds for the advancement and accumulation of knowledge. They stress the need for empirical reality and attempt to downplay experiential reality (it is less credible, trustworthy, valid, and reliable). The terms *hard science* and *soft science* exemplify this clash or division between the status of disciplines associated with the physical sciences and the social sciences. Physical sciences adhere strongly to empirical reality, whereas the social sciences (psychology, sociology, and anthropology) are considered less scientific; as a result, social sciences often attempt to mimic the higher status of physical sciences by adopting quantification, objectification, and logic/rationality to studying the human condition. In many respects, such an approach ultimately distances "ways of knowing" or renders the means of asking and answering questions about the human condition to an abstract hypothetical level that dilutes, diminishes, and disconnects empirical reality from experiential or lived realities. The following story illustrates this disconnection.

Years ago a Nigerian educator told me a story about a White female teacher hired to teach elementary school subjects to White students in a community where a major multinational corporation had a plant in Nigeria. Many of the employees were U.S. Americans who lived near the plant and who brought their families over to the country. The classroom consisted of U.S. students and Nigerian students whose parents were also employed by the corporation. During one of the class periods the teacher posed a math problem to the class.

Teacher: There are four blackbirds sitting on a tree. You take a slingshot and kill one of them. How many are left?

Johnny, White U.S. student (raising hand excitedly): Teacher, teacher, I know the answer!

Teacher: Johnny, what is the answer?

Johnny: That is sooo easy . . . four take away one is three!

Nigerian student (interrupting): No, no, no . . . that's not right teacher! The answer is zero!

Teacher (puzzled): I'm afraid that is the wrong answer. Johnny is right! Four take away one is three.

In this case, both Johnny and the teacher are operating from empirical and hypothetical reality in how to ask and answer questions about the physical world and human condition. Teachers who teach hard sciences and math frequently operate under the assumption that math is math and that truth can be discerned through empiricism. From this framework, Johnny has come up with the correct answer. The Nigerian student, however, might be operating under experiential reality or lived experience. Were the teacher to inquire as to how the he arrived at his answer, the Nigerian student might have explained in this fashion: "Teacher if you shoot one bird, the others aren't stupid enough to stay around. They will *all* fly away."

Whose answer is correct, the White or Nigerian student's? Empirical reality and experiential reality are only problematic in teaching when we pose an either/or dichotomy. Bridging both is important. In this case, the teacher might have asked the question differently: "There are four blackbirds seated on a tree. You take a slingshot and kill one of them. How many flew away?"

Reason Versus Emotion

Dialogues on race may ultimately push hot emotional buttons in students and teachers alike and may cause heated exchanges among and between them. We have already explored some of the reasons these strong feelings are generated, but when they occur in the classroom they are most often perceived by educators as the three Ds: disruptive, dysfunctional, and disrespectful. Emotions such as anger and frustration, for example, are disruptive to Western European classroom decorum where calm discussions filled with logic and reasoning are philosophically aspects of appropriate student and faculty conduct (Valentine et al., 2012). Classrooms are political spaces, microcosms of race relations in the broader society, and teachers represent the agents that enforce the types of interactions dictated by the norms of the learning environment (Sue, 2010; Valentine et al., 2012).

Most educators consider the strong expression of emotions, especially anger, as disruptive and not conducive to learning. In interpersonal relationships, anger is often manifested as blaming others, attacking their points of view, and/or belittling them. Even if such expressions of anger occurred elsewhere, most of us are uncomfortable and ill prepared to deal with any type of intense anger. Feelings of defensiveness often arise, for example, when hot racial topics make their appearance between students of color (who feel their points invalidated and silenced) and White students (who feel unjustly blamed or accused of being racist). The prevailing implicit assumption in academic circles is that emotions are antagonistic to reason, that learning occurs when topics are discussed calmly. When a discussion on race becomes heated, students are admonished by teachers to not let their emotions get the best of them, to calm down, and to speak to one another with respect (Sue, 2010). Anger is seen as dysfunctional (even pathological) during race talk, so instructors feel compelled to control its intensity and expression. To accuse, blame, or attack someone through the expression of anger is also considered disrespectful. Because classroom spaces are created by those in power, teaching and student learning are conducted through the lens of teaching norms, beliefs, and values that dictate what topics are educational and how they should be discussed.

One of the major obstacles to race talk is the common assumption that different cultural groups operate according to identical speech and communication conventions. Black styles of communication are often high key, animated, heated, interpersonal, and confrontational. Many emotions, affects, and feelings are generated (Hall, 1976; Shade & New, 1993; Weber, 1985). In a debate, Blacks tend to act as advocates of a position, and ideas are to be tested in the crucible of argumentation (Banks & Banks, 1993; Kochman, 1981). White middle class styles, however, are characterized as being detached and objective, impersonal and nonchallenging. The person acts not as an *advocate* of the idea, but as a *spokesperson* (truth resides in the idea). A discussion of issues should be devoid of affect because emotion and reason work against one another. One should talk things out in a logical fashion without getting personally involved. African Americans characterize their own style of communication as indicating that the person is sincere and honest, while Euro-Americans consider their own style to be reasoned and objective (Irvine & York, 1995).

Unfortunately, blanket discouragement of heated expressions serves to discourage students from honestly expressing their true thoughts, attitudes, and feelings about race and racism as well the true thoughts, attitudes, and feelings from others as well. Studies reveal that difficult dialogues on race are filled with heated and oftentimes explosive emotions, and that attempts to suppress or limit their expression actually lead to detrimental learning consequences for White students and students of color (Sue, Lin, et al., 2009; Sue et al., 2010). With respect to White Americans, Sara Winter (1977) provides us with insights as to the types of emotions likely to be elicited in race talk, the bases of the reactions, and why well-intentioned Whites prefer not to talk about race or racism. Yet, as she explains, experiencing embedded or nested feelings associated with our beliefs and memories about different groups are preconditions to dealing with our anxieties associated with race and racism. Using Black Americans as an example, she states,

> Let me explain this healing process in more detail. We must unearth all the words and memories we generally try not to think about, but which are inside us all the time: "nigger," "Uncle Tom," "jungle bunny," "Oreo"; lynching, cattle prods, castrations, rapists, "black pussy," and black men with their huge penises, and hundreds more. (I shudder as I write.) We need to review three different kinds of material: (1) all our personal memories connected with blackness and black people including everything we can recall hearing or reading; (2) all the racist images and stereotypes we've ever heard, particularly the grossest and most hurtful ones; (3) any race related things we ourselves said, did or omitted doing which we feel bad about today.... Most whites begin with a good deal of amnesia. Eventually the memories crowd in, especially when several people pool recollections. Emotional release is a vital part of the process. Experiencing feelings seems to allow further recollections to come. I need persistent encouragement from my companions to continue. (p. 3)

Such a journey in the classroom cannot be accomplished in a manner devoid of feelings and without emotional release. Indeed, to close off the expression of these feelings leads to a sterile discussion that separates the head from the body and soul. In many classrooms, for example, debates or dialogues on race adhere to the academic protocol, which is dispassionate and objective, devoid of emotions and affect. The challenge for education as we shall see in the later chapters is not that one way of knowing and learning is better than the other, but for educators to integrate both to make education, self-knowledge, and understanding meaningful and life changing.

Objectivism Versus Subjectivism

One of the most basic tenets of scientific thinking is *objectivity*, which is intended to be the cornerstone of establishing universal laws and truths devoid of human factors that may contaminate the acquisition of facts and knowledge (C. J. Goodwin, 2003; Heppner et al., 2008). These human factors involve the personal opinions, values, and biases of researchers, scholars, and teachers that are viewed as impediments to seeking truth. The roles of investigators and by extension effective teachers are ones of maintaining objectivity, being detached, and controlling emotions that may unduly compromise or undermine logic/rationality. The extreme extension of this role is that the scientist, scholar, and educator can be characterized as business-like or machine-like in their search for knowledge and in their teaching. In reality, we recognize that no person can completely separate himself/herself from his/her beliefs, attitudes, and values and be completely objective.

When topics such as race, racism, Whiteness, and White privilege are discussed in classrooms or any other situation for that matter, they become deeply personal, emotional, and subjective (McIntosh, 2002; Willow, 2008; Young, 2003). According to Palmer (2007), objectivity in teaching is the major culprit that creates disconnection between teachers, their subjects, their students, and the ability to learn from lived experience:

> For objectivism, the subjective self is the enemy most to be feared—a Pandora's box of opinion, bias, and ignorance that will distort our knowledge once the lid flies open. We keep the lid shut by relying exclusively on reason and facts, logic and data that cannot be swayed by subjective desire.... The role of the mind and the senses in this scheme is not to connect us to the world but to hold the world at bay, lest our knowledge of it be tainted.
>
> In objectivism, subjectivity is feared not only because it contaminates things but because it creates relationships between those things and us—and relationships are contaminating as well. When a thing ceases to be an object and becomes a vital, interactive part of our lives—whether it is a work of art, an indigenous people, or an ecosystem—it might get a grip on us, biasing us toward it, thus threatening the purity of our knowledge once again.
>
> So objectivism, driven by fear, keeps us from forging relationships with the things of the world. Its modus operandi is simple; when we distance ourselves from something, it becomes an object; when it becomes an object, it no longer has life; when it is lifeless, it cannot touch or transform us, so our knowledge of the thing remains pure. (p. 52)

Some have argued that concepts of objectivity are fueled by Western values strongly manifested in the Protestant work ethic. Basic to the ethic are the concepts of separation and individualism: (a) The individual is the psychosocial unit of operation, (b) the individual has primary responsibility for his or her own actions, (c) independence and autonomy are highly valued and rewarded, and (d) one should be internally directed and controlled. Consistent with this orientation is our nation's heavy reliance on asking and answering questions about the human condition through sensory information as defined by the physical plane of reality (Western science). We are often told to be objective, that rationality is the ability to separate ourselves from the issues, and not to let our emotions get in the way. Our worship of science reveals the value placed on symbolic logic, analytical and linear approaches, and the ability to tease out parts from the whole. The results of this overriding philosophy of life are also reflected in our educational system, legal system (individual rights), standards of healthy development and functioning (autonomy, independence, and being your own person), definition of the family (nuclear family vs. extended family), and even religion (separation of church and state).

While individualism as a value has many positive components, is it possible that its extreme form may lead to an unhealthy separation between people? When you objectify others, see them as distinct from you, and perceive your relationships with people as less desirable than separation and objectification, is it possible that you may also be prone to dehumanize them? Because your world revolves around you, others are less important. Others become objectified, and in many cases dehumanized as well. You will have little regard for others, see them as separate from you, and experience little empathy for them. During World War II and the Vietnam War, for example, referring to the Japanese and Vietnamese in demeaning racial epithets such as Japs, Gooks, and Slants frequently dehumanized Asians. They were not seen as human beings, but rather subhuman aliens, evil, and animals that should be wiped off the face of the earth and destroyed. They were the true Yellow Peril frequently referred to in our historical relationship with Asians. Such an approach made it easier for our soldiers to kill them.

A similar analogy can be made to that of racial hatred in the United States. Persons of color are perceived as other beings: subhuman, criminals, untrustworthy, animalistic, uncivilized, aliens, dangerous, lazy, unintelligent, and the dregs of society. Thus, you have little empathy for them and believe that a civilized society would be better off without persons of color. Such a belief, whether spoken or not, makes it easy for outright racists to enact violence and cruelty upon persons of color without guilt or compassion. It also allows the majority of White Americans to sit idly by and bear witness to the cruelty and oppression inflicted upon a subhuman group of humans without protest.

After all, as long as you do not feel connected to the other beings and do not perceive them as part of you, injustice and oppression are not disturbing.

If your disconnection from others allows racism to thrive, then the solution might lie in becoming connected with one another by viewing humanity as all-encompassing and inherently unifying. In that respect, if the *us-and-them* thinking is replaced by the collective *we*, then what happens to one person happens to all. If injustice were carried out against a member of another race, we would all feel the pain and bear the responsibility in rectifying the situation. Successful facilitation of race talk offers the potential for empathic understanding and connections to those we view as other beings, and it enhances our spiritual connection with all of humanity.

CHAPTER FIVE

Color-Blind Means Color-Mute

Sometime back in California, my former colleague (Dr. Alvin Jones, an African American faculty member) and I were involved in starting a Third World Counselor's Training Program for our educational psychology department. We trained students who wanted to specialize in cross-cultural counseling (now referred to as multicultural counseling) and who desired to work in communities of color. One of the requirements for being admitted was to be interviewed by two faculty members in the department. The cross-cultural counseling program was one of many specialties offered by the department but students could interview with any faculty member. I recall a morning in which a prospective White student showed up at my office and requested one of the two admission interviews. He indicated his interest in minority mental health and wanted very much to study in the program. I greeted him warmly and the following conversation ensued:

DWS: So, glad you are interested in the program. Let's talk about your reasons for applying to the program, but before we do that, I wonder have you interviewed with any other faculty member?

Student: Yes, I have.

DWS: Oh good, so I won't have to repeat material about admissions you may already have. Who did you speak with?

Student: I'm sorry, I can't remember the name, but *he* was very friendly and helpful.

DWS: Oh, so it was one of my male colleagues.

Student: Yes.

DWS: Can you describe him?

Student (looking very uncomfortable): His office is down the hall ... and well, he's a real good dresser.

DWS: That's nice, but what did he look like?

Student: Well, I, I, I just don't know how to describe him. He's about your height ... very nicely decorated office with interesting international sculptures.

DWS: Anything else?

Student: Oh yes, his hair ... he has short, kinky hair.

DWS: Oh, you mean Dr. Jones.

Student: Yes, yes, that's his name (sounding relieved that Dr. Jones had been identified).

At that time it struck me as humorous that it took so long to identify my colleague. If the student had simply stated, "I don't remember his name, but he's the Black professor at the end of the hall," we could have ended the query immediately, as my colleague Alvin Jones was the only African American faculty member in a department of approximately 20 others. All were White except for the two of us.

Questions: Why was it so difficult for the student to use race as a descriptor for the African American faculty member? Did the student not notice the race of my colleague? Is it possible for anyone to be color-blind? What does noticing or not noticing the race of another person mean? Is it difficult for you to publicly acknowledge the race of individuals you interact with? What makes it difficult for you?

The 4-year-old White girl was sitting in a grocery cart being pushed by the mother down the aisle as she was selecting various cuts of beef at the meat counter. At one aisle, the mother paused to read the labels on a selection of beef roasts she was considering. At the other end of the aisle another customer (Vietnamese man) approached and scanned other cuts of meat. The young child was obviously very interested in the man and kept staring at him as he approached. When he paused next to the mother, the girl leaned over, nearly sticking her own face in that of the man to get a better glimpse of him. Loudly the child exclaimed, "Mom look at his eyes . . . look at eyes . . . they are funny." The lady was initially puzzled at the words of her daughter, but when she looked up and saw the Vietnamese customer, her face flushed beet red. It was obvious that she was embarrassed and horrified that her daughter was pointing to the man's slanted eyes. She quickly shushed the young child and pushed the cart away at a rapid pace. At the end of the aisle the mother whispered reproaches to her daughter and admonished the young child for her comments. "We don't say things like that. It's not nice. Be quiet." (Anonymous workshop participant's story)

Questions: Why do you think the mother was so horrified at what her daughter said about the Vietnamese man? In what ways does the example of the mother and child's reactions to the Vietnamese customer provide lessons as to our discomfort about noticing and talking about race? What do you think are the lessons being taught to the child? Can you recall incidents in your early childhood that may account for your feelings and discomfort related to race talk?

To be color-blind is to be color-mute! In other words, if you profess not to see or notice racial differences, you cannot talk about them. In both of these cases, the color-blind protocol, or color blindness, is operating in such a manner as to discourage the acknowledgment of noticing race and, thus, making conversations about race mute. As in the politeness and academic protocols, color blindness works against honest racial dialogues by intentionally or unintentionally ignoring race and/or physical differences associated with it.

In the first example, it was obvious that the student was uncomfortable using race as a descriptor of my colleague and danced around its acknowledgment by using every other conceivable depiction possible: the location of his office, his mode of dress, his height, his friendliness, the decorations in his office, his hair style, and so on; everything but the fact that he was Black. At the end of the interview with the prospective student, when our conversation returned to his hesitancy in acknowledging Dr. Jones's race, it was clear that the topic was very uncomfortable for the candidate. He lacked fluency in talking about his reactions (rhetorical incoherence), spoke haltingly, was obviously very anxious about the topic, and made reference to the fact that he had not noticed that my colleague was Black. Although finding this unbelievable,

I felt sufficiently sorry for the young man that I did not pursue the issue further. But it was clear to me that the young student was very concerned about being perceived as racist and thought that pretending not to see color would help him appear nonracist (Apfelbaum, Sommers, & Norton, 2008).

In the second scenario, we get an inside developmental view of how the muting of race talk begins early in life. From childhood, people are taught that noticing differences is impolite and to be discouraged, and that there is something wrong with doing so. The young White girl had no qualms pointing out that the Vietnamese man had eyes that looked different from her own and those of her parents, but the mother expressed horror at the child's honest public observation about this difference. The mother's reaction communicated clearly to the child that talking about racial differences was a taboo topic. But, there is a deeper and more insidious socialization process that is occurring here. When we ask the question Why is it so bad to publicly notice and talk about differences?, the answers provided by scholars give meaning to the color-blind phenomenon (APA Presidential Task Force, 2012; Neville et al., 2013).

"Colorblindness refers to a set of beliefs that individuals' group membership or physical appearance is not and should not be influential in how we perceive, evaluate, make decisions about, or formulate public policy toward them" (APA Presidential Task Force, 2012, p. 9). In other words, color blindness is a belief that race should not and does not matter in judging a person's character and should not influence decisions or actions toward individuals or groups, which overlooks the notion that racism continues to be a significant negative factor in the lives of people of color. It can be said to be comprised of three overlapping processes: (1) attempts to deny differences by adhering to the idea of sameness and equity (color-evasion), (2) attempts to disassociate problematic racial beliefs from implicitly held ones (stereotype-evasion), and (3) attempts to avoid acknowledging the continuing existence of structural or institutional racism in society (power-evasion). All three comprise a sophisticated intersecting series of ideological beliefs that possess powerful personal and sociopolitical meanings and consequences (Apfelbaum et al., 2008; Bonilla-Silva, 2006; Frankenburg, 1997; Neville et al., 2000; Neville et al., 2013). All three may operate consciously on an intentional level or outside the level of conscious awareness on an unintentional one. Regardless, by intentionally or unintentionally ignoring race and racial differences, race is relegated to being an insignificant factor in the lives of people of color. As long as one professes color blindness, race talk is avoided and muted. Let us explore the meaning and consequences of the three dimensions of color blindness and how they impact race talk.

COLOR-EVASION: "WE ARE ALL THE SAME UNDER THE SKIN"

In an insightful and important article on color-blind racial ideology, Neville et al. (2013) identify several forms of color blindness, one called color-evasion, which involves the denial of racial differences by emphasizing sameness. Color-evasion appears to have two primary purposes. First, it is an aspirational and philosophical goal intended to reduce prejudice, discrimination, and unfair treatment of people of color. Second, it represents a belief in sameness or a philosophy that we are all human beings, Americans, and the same under the skin. In a major study of 2,000 Millennials (those ages 14 to 24), for example, it was found that 73% believe color blindness should be an aspirational goal in society; 68% believe seeing race prevents society from becoming color-blind; and 70% believe they don't see racial minority groups any differently than they see White people (MTV, 2014). Let us first discuss and analyze the aspirational goal of being color-blind.

Color Blindness: An Aspiration Goal

The goal of attaining a race-neutral society can be accomplished through forgetting about race. As long as one does not see race, discrimination on the basis of differences is discouraged and/or eliminated. The erroneous assumptions contained in this philosophy can be stated in the following way: (a) It is possible for individuals to be color-blind or to not see race, (b) not acknowledging and talking about race will make one appear nonprejudiced, and (c) color blindness as a means to promote equality can be successful (Apfelbaum, Pauker, Sommers, & Ambady, 2011). Research reveals that it is nearly impossible not to notice race, especially the physical features of people of color. Of all the dimensions of social categorization, psychologists overwhelmingly conclude that racial recognition and categorization (using electrocortical and other measures) are among the quickest and most automatic cognitive processing responses made by individuals (Ito & Urland, 2003; Montepare & Opeyo, 2002). Ironically, many White Americans claim they are unable to racially categorize or do not do so (Norton, Sommers, Apfelbaum, Pura, & Ariely, 2006). Explaining the phenomenon of color blindness or the discrepancy between perception of racial differences and its conscious acknowledgment has been labeled *strategic color blindness* (Apfelbaum et al., 2008).

In their attempts to appear nonprejudiced, many well-intentioned Whites employ a strategy to make them appear free of bias by not acknowledging and talking about race even when race is a relevant factor (APA Presidential Task Force, 2012). Many studies suggest, however, that this strategy may backfire and actually make the person appear more prejudiced (Apfelbaum et al., 2008; Tynes & Markoe, 2010; Vorauer & Kumhyr, 2001; Vorauer & Turpie, 2004). In general, these studies indicate that when involved in an interracial dyad or when placed in an environment in which race is salient, many White participants become concerned that whatever they say or do may be construed as being prejudicial. Self-regulation strategies or impression management (being careful what to say or how to say it, or pretending not to notice race) may be employed, but they exact a psychic toll on the person, resulting in considerable depletion of psychological resources (Richeson & Shelton, 2007).

In one study, for example, it was found that participants who chose not to notice racial differences when interacting with Black participants displayed less friendly nonverbal behaviors and were judged by observers as more prejudiced (Apfelbaum et al., 2008). High anxiety about a racial theme makes many Whites dance around the topic of race, and their speech patterns are often characterized by rhetorical incoherence such as ambiguous references, stuttering, topic diversion, and mispronunciation of key words related to race (Utsey et al., 2005). In other words, people of color interpret these verbal and nonverbal behaviors as evasive, biased, and prejudiced; the speakers have something to hide and the hidden truth is racial prejudice.

It appears that Whites who wish to appear nonbiased in interracial interactions spend considerable cognitive effort monitoring their behavior so they will not appear racist; it was found that these participants subsequently performed poorly on a cognitive task because energies were diverted toward creating a favorable image of themselves (Richeson, Trawalter, & Shelton, 2005). Depending on the tactics employed, some studies do suggest that the regulatory efforts of Whites can create short-term positive perceptions of them (being unbiased, increased warmth, and social desirability), but that the ultimate cost of not acknowledging and talking about race perpetuates deep misunderstanding between the parties (Shelton et al., 2005).

Color blindness as a means to attain social justice and equity has also been shown to be highly unsuccessful in eliminating prejudice and discrimination (APA Presidential Task Force, 2012; J. M. Jones, 1997; Neville et al., 2013; Plaut et al., 2009). In a study designed to test the merits of an environment that professes the importance of either color blindness or multiculturalism, the investigators explored both effects upon employees in institutional work environments (Plaut et al., 2009). A multicultural ideology stresses the importance of group differences and celebrates their positive contributions, whereas a color-blind ideology stresses ignoring or minimizing group differences. Both approaches, on the surface, argue for equality, equal access and opportunity, and the importance of fairness and justice. The findings were extremely revealing. First, they found that minimizing group differences reinforced majority group dominance and minority group marginalization in the workplace. In a climate of color blindness, it appears that employees of color feel excluded and disengage from their work roles, resulting in lower productivity. Second, in contrast, it was found that a multicultural orientation promoted inclusive behaviors among Whites, enhanced engagement of both parties, and reduced marginalization (Purdie-Vaughns, Steele, Davis, Ditlmann, & Crosby, 2008). Many other studies have arrived at similarly related conclusions. When multiculturalism and color blindness are experimentally manipulated and measured, findings suggest that color blindness actually predicts greater bias, whereas multiculturalism predicts lower bias (Neville et al., 2000; Plaut et al., 2009; Richeson & Nussbaum, 2004).

Thus, the belief that a race-neutral society can produce procedural justice for all groups and that it will end prejudice and discrimination is not supported by research on color-blind racial ideology. Neville et al. (2013) conclude several things about color-evasion: (a) Ignoring race or color is actually harmful to the well-being of people of color in a highly racially stratified society, (b) those who endorse a color-blind ideology actually engage in a higher rate of racially insensitive behaviors, and (c) attaining a racially color-blind society is unattainable and only reinforces racism and societal inequality. Thus, the three basic assumptions of color blindness—that it is possible not to notice racial differences, that it will make one appear less prejudiced, and that it provides a path to equal access and opportunity—are not supported by the psychological literature.

Color Blindness: Belief in Sameness

A second component of color-evasion is based on the subconscious assumption of sameness or the idea that differences between human groups are so troublesome that it is best to emphasize our similarities. In general, the concept of sameness has been used as a strategy of color-evasion, although it can also be rooted as a subconscious ideology as well. Here are some very common statements that have the impact of attempting to deny, diminish, or dilute the noticing of differences, thereby working against race talk.

- "People are people." "We are all human beings." "We're all Americans." "We're all the same under the skin." "There is only one race, the human race."

- "We should emphasize our similarities, not our differences." "I don't see color at all." "We should be a color-blind society." "Everyone should be treated the same."

- "We should all learn to blend in." "If you immigrate to this country, you should assimilate and acculturate." "When in Rome, do as the Romans do." "We are a melting pot."

These statements have been found to be considered racial microaggressions by people of color because they deny their racialized experiences (Sue, 2010). They also contain several distorted underlying thoughts/premises of current color-blind racial ideology (J. M. Jones, 1997; Neville et al., 2013). First, there is an explicit assumption that people are people, and we are all human beings who share many similarities with one another. Second, differences are divisive, negative, and act as barriers to human relationships. Third, the ultimate goal of assimilation and acculturation is exemplified in the melting pot concept; everyone should desire and work to become the same. Like all familiar sayings that arise from history and age-old usage, there is much truth to them. The problem, however, lies in the dual but antagonistic meaning of these statements.

Yes, differences can prove divisive, but isn't it related more to how people perceive differences rather than the differences themselves? For example, is skin color the problem or is it society's perception of color that is at fault? Yes, stressing commonalities is important, but does it mean differences are bad, deviant, or wrong? Yes, we are all the same under the skin, and human beings, but why is being human defined from a White, Western perspective? Yes, we should treat everyone the same, especially if differential treatment is discriminatory in nature. But, can treating everyone the same result in unfairness? Yes, it is important to learn the language and culture of the society you reside in; but should it be at the cost of losing your cultural heritage and group identification? These are loaded questions when we probe into how color blindness, and by default Whiteness, has infiltrated the answers. Let me first address the issue of diluting differences and operating as if we are all the same under the skin. As Shakespeare's character Shylock stated, "When I cut myself, do I not bleed?"

A White Euro-American colleague once stated to me, "Derald, why are you always talking about cultural differences? When I look at you, I don't see you as an Asian American at all. You're no different than me. We're both Americans.

Why can't we simply relate to one another as human beings? After all, there is only one race in this world. It's called the human race" (White Euro-American colleague).

I have come to increasingly understand the hidden meaning of these statements. In most cases, there is an implicit equation that a human being is the same as being White. The speaker is usually saying something like this: "Differences are divisive, so let's avoid acknowledging them and seek out our commonalities. I'm uncomfortable with racial differences, so let's pretend they don't exist. To keep me comfortable, just pretend to be White. Meet me on my ground and we'll do fine."

According to this stance, being a human being or an American are the same as being White. Whiteness surrounds the use of these terms, and on a conscious and subconscious level, there is an aversion to seeing race, color, or differences (Sue, 2003). Color blindness uses Whiteness as the default key and represents a racially motivated defense (Zetzer, 2011; Zou & Dickter, 2013). The pretense by White Americans of not seeing color is motivated by the need to appear free of bias and prejudice or by fears that what they say or do may appear racist, or it is an attempt to cover up hidden biases (Sue, 2013). To be color-blind not only denies the central importance of racial differences in the psychological experience of minorities (racism and discrimination), but also allows the White person to deny how his or her Whiteness intrudes upon the person of color.

STEREOTYPE-EVASION: "I DON'T BELIEVE IN THOSE STEREOTYPES"

Let us return to the early grocery store example of the interaction between child, mother, and the Vietnamese man. It was clear that the young girl was expressing a naive curiosity of physical differences she observed between the shape of the man's eyes and her own. There was no good or bad judgment attached to the observation; no imputation of meaning. She was simply trying to make sense of the observed physical difference. The daughter's exclamation, however, caused deep embarrassment to the mother, who communicated that talking about these differences was inappropriate, bad, and prejudicial, that these differences should never be publicly stated or admitted. But, we may ask, why is the mother so upset with the daughter noticing physical differences and what lies behind her motivation to avoid race talk? The answer probably lies in her own association of racial differences with deviancy, inferiority, and negativity; unfortunately, these associations are being unwittingly passed on to her own child.

Psychologists believe that in early childhood (up until 3 or 4 years of age), children are relatively naive about the meaning of racial and cultural differences, although they do recognize social categories and reveal a preference for facial features of their own group (Cassidy, Quinn, & Humphreys, 2011; Shutts, Banaji, & Spelke, 2010). Although these early implicit signs of racial awareness are present (Dunham, Baron, & Banaji, 2008), the social meanings attached to these differences are either absent or minimal; children at this age find race difficult to articulate, and they appear to be unaware of social norms related to it (Aboud, 1988; Hirschfield, 2001). There is a tendency to be innocent, open, and spontaneous regarding racial differences. Such an open and naive orientation becomes less characteristic as the socialization process proceeds. The negative reactions of parents, relatives, friends, and peers toward other racial groups influence the perceptions of children. It is important to note that such messages send mixed signals to children, who are also taught that prejudice and discrimination are wrong, that we are all equal under the law, and that we should treat everyone the same.

Through a process of social conditioning, however, White children are increasingly taught to associate only positive qualities with their own race and negative ones with other racial groups. The process of our cultural conditioning occurs through significant others (Sue, 2003), our educational curriculum (Minow, Shweder, & Markus, 2008), the mass media (Cortes, 2008), and institutions in society (APA Presidential Task Force, 2012; J. M. Jones, 1997). Even at 5 to 6 years of age, cultural and racial identities are still quite amorphous, but a burgeoning negative association of race to people of color begins to emerge under the influence of societal forces. Of special importance are parental reactions to racial groups (shushing children for mentioning racial differences and implying something wrong about them) communicated either implicitly or explicitly (Boysen & Vogel, 2008; President's Initiative on Race, 1999). At around the age of 10 or 11, racial differences between groups crystallize into prejudice toward groups of color (Apfelbaum et al., 2011). Unfortunately, these associations are also a powerful socialization factor for children of color, who may internalize them.

In one study of children ages 10 to 17, for example, it was found that all children regardless of race were more likely to couple negative qualities with characters of color (delinquent, criminal, poor, lazy, and less intelligent) and White characters with positive qualities (more money, intelligent, and educated) in television and movies (Children Now, 1998). The continued societal association of people of color with pathology, deviancy, inferiority, and lesser beings are often manifested in the stereotypes we hold of different racial groups. The following racial stereotypes and images are embedded in our collective consciousness and some form of their manifestations may be held by people at varying levels of awareness (Sue, 2010):

- African Americans: hostile, angry, impulsive, dangerous, drug dealers, criminals, pimps, prostitutes, addicts, unintelligent, mentally retarded, low skills, lack abstract thinking, concrete, inhuman, animalistic, undesirable, smelly, unkempt, dirty, mentally ill, abnormal, insatiable sexual appetite.
- Asian Americans: spies, sneaky, backstabbers, disloyal, slanted eyes, stingy, subhuman, model minority, bright, hardworking, obedient, studious, quiet, good in math and science, wealthy, passive, lack leadership skills, poor interpersonally, men are unmasculine/sexually unattractive, women are domestic, exotic, and sexual pleasing.
- Latinas/os: illegal aliens, foreigners, drug dealers, farm workers, poor, welfare recipients, tax avoiders, domestic servants, unskilled, criminals, dangerous, untrustworthy, greasy, sloppy, irresponsible, lazy, never on time, carefree, uninhibited, poor English, uneducated, stupid, religious.
- Native American Indians: alcoholics, drunkards, nonverbal, uneducable, retarded, savages, animalistic, uncivilized, blood thirsty, primitive, subhuman, superstitious, never on time, poor, passive, noncompetitive.

Almost all studies on attitudes toward groups of color, however, indicate that explicit expressions of biased beliefs and attitudes have declined dramatically over the past 45 years (Dovidio et al., 2002; Gaertner & Dovidio, 2005). Many social scientists believe that the blatant expression of prejudice and bias have morphed into a contemporary or modern form of racism (DeVos & Banaji, 2005; Dovidio et al., 2002; Sue, Nadal, et al., 2008). Because social, political, and legal institutions condemn the expression of bias and bigotry, because we disapprove of unequal treatment and racism, and because our nation has become more aware of the falsehoods associated with stereotyping, society now considers it socially unacceptable to profess the inferiority of persons of color. Thus, most of us on a conscious level can recognize stereotypes when they are presented to us and we can denounce and disown them as being untrue. The methods used to measure explicit bias, however, are prone to social desirability and political correctness and do a poor job of tapping underlying implicit attitudes. Thus, it is possible to consciously know that a stereotype of African Americans (being less intelligent) is inaccurate, but harbor the belief subconsciously (Devine, 1989; Dovidio & Gaertner, 2000).

Dissociating the negative aspects of race related to people of color, however, is a monumental task that has shown mixed results. White Americans have been more successful in disengaging the relationship of deviancy to racial differences on a public or conscious level than in an unconscious or implicit one (Baron & Banaji, 2006; Boysen & Vogel, 2008). One especially noteworthy study of 6-year-olds, 10-year-olds, and adults drives home the point that there is a difference between explicit (conscious) and implicit (unconscious) expressions of bias toward groups of color (Baron & Banaji, 2006). In this particular study, researchers used two variations of the Implicit Attitudes Task (IAT), an adult version and a child version, to measure biased evaluations of Blacks. In general, implicit measures of bias operate under the assumption that reaction time differences between associating Black and White names with pleasant and unpleasant words provide a measure of the degree of bias possessed by a participant. It is similar to studies that measure reaction times of police officers' decisions to shoot or not shoot a Black or White suspect when placed in a potentially threatening situation (Correll et al., 2007).

The IAT has been used successfully in numerous studies to measure automatic associations related to unconscious bias of specific social categories such as people of color (Greenwald, McGhee, & Schwartz, 1998). Using this method, Baron and Banaji (2006) found that implicit and explicit biases diverged as the age of participants increased: (a) At age 6 years, both implicit and explicit attitudes were roughly similar; (b) at age 10 years, the beginnings of a dissociation began to occur—that is, explicit bias began to decline while implicit bias remained unchanged; and (c) at adulthood, explicit bias dropped dramatically, but again implicit bias remained unchanged. What may be even more surprising is a study conducted by Boysen and Vogel (2008) that attempted to measure the effects of formal multicultural training in combating bias and stereotypes attributed to African Americans, lesbians, and gay men. Although explicit bias declined significantly with formal training, implicit bias toward these groups remained unchanged.

The effects on race talk are highly correlated with these findings and may indicate people's attempts to cling to conscious (explicit) beliefs of equality while disavowing their unconscious (implicit) biases. One method of doing this is to avoid talking about race by espousing color blindness. By ignoring race and not talking about it, the incongruence and conflict between hidden biases and stereotypes with conscious beliefs of equity remains hidden (Sue, 2010). Support for this assertion can be found in a study of children ages 8 to 11 (Apfelbaum et al., 2011). The investigators found that (a) older children ages 10–11 were more likely to avoid using race as a descriptor than their younger counterparts, and (b) their responses mirrored that of their adult counterparts (Apfelbaum et al., 2008).

Several important conclusions can be drawn from these studies. First, we have made considerable progress in combating conscious forms of bias and stereotyping. Second, although successful in dealing with overt expressions of bias, implicit biases in well-intentioned people remain relatively untouched and strong. Third, although formal education and training seems effective in combating explicit bias, it appears to have less success in ameliorating implicit attitudes. Fourth, it may be that remediation is less effective than prevention and starting at a young age (childhood) to combat stereotypes may offer a more effective solution. Last, it is clear that color blindness may be seen as part of a strategy to internally combat recognition of implicitly held biases. We will return to this latter theme shortly in Chapter 7.

POWER-EVASION: "EVERYONE CAN MAKE IT IN SOCIETY, IF THEY WORK HARD ENOUGH"

The third function of color blindness is the attempt to diminish, ignore, or deny the existence of cultural, structural, and institutional racism in our society, which is labeled *power-evasion* by Neville and colleagues (2013). Avoiding race talk is to avoid the acknowledgment of power and privilege held by many Whites over their brothers and sisters of color. Further, it makes invisible the harmful impact cultural and institutional racism have upon people of color (psychological well-being and standard of living) and places the blame for their current plight upon those groups most oppressed (victim blame). It is most aptly expressed in the myth of meritocracy; anyone can succeed in society if they simply work hard enough, the world is wide open to everyone, and everyone has equal access to the fruits of their labor. Power-evasion is often-times linked to the invisibility of cultural and institutional racism. According to J. M. Jones (1997) cultural racism is the individual and institutional expression of the superiority of one group's cultural heritage over another, and institutional racism resides in the programs, policies, and practices of organizations.

Power-evasion has several consequences: (a) It denies the racialized experiences of people of color (that they are disadvantaged), (b) it denies the existence of privilege enjoyed by Whites (that they are advantaged), (c) it perpetuates the myth of meritocracy, (d) it masks or makes invisible structural inequities in our society, (e) it sustains the social hierarchy by providing a cover of innocence, and (f) it justifies inaction in tackling racial inequities brought about through power and privilege (APA Presidential Task Force, 2012; J. M. Jones, 1997; Neville et al., 2013; Ponterotto, Utsey, & Pedersen, 2006; Sue, 2003). Being color-blind, and thus color-mute, prevents us from hearing back talk where there is danger that we will unmask the realization of the power and privilege that resides in Whiteness.

Power-evasion, the denial of power imposition, has its cultural origins in the historical concepts associated with the melting pot, assimilation, and acculturation. As more and more White immigrants came to the North American continent, the guiding principle of blending the many cultures together became codified into such terms as *the melting pot* and *assimilation/acculturation*. The most desirable outcome of this process was a uniform and homogeneous consolidation of cultures, in essence for everyone to become the same. The ultimate hope was that these early immigrants would forge a new national identity in which there would be a shared language, culture, and history (Takaki, 1998). As the many groups began to coalesce, a general American culture began to emerge that served as a reference point for immigrants and their children: the middle-class cultural patterns of largely White Protestant Anglo-Saxon and White ethnics from European countries (Britain, Germany, Ireland, Italy, and so forth).

If there is anything that can be termed *White culture*, it is the synthesis of ideas, values, and beliefs coalesced from descendants of White European ethnic groups in the United States (Barongan et al., 1997). While acknowledging the dangers and limitations of overgeneralizing, the European American worldview can be described as possessing some of the following values and beliefs, which often form the foundations of our programs, policies, practices, and structures of institutions: rugged individualism, English language, mastery and control over nature, a unitary and static conception of time, religion based on Christianity, separation of science and religion, and competition (Katz, 1985; Ponterotto et al., 2006). If the merging of European cultures into an American one was the result of assimilation and acculturation, you may ask, how is the melting pot concept a myth?

First, the melting pot seems to have been meant for White Euro-Americans only. A basic important tenet of assimilation and acculturation is the existence of a receptive society. That is, once a person has learned the language and customs of the group and now accepts those desired values, he or she should become a full member of the society with all the rights and privileges that follow. But, despite how acculturated people of color become, they are never fully accepted by the dominant culture. Persons of color are constantly reminded of their inferior status and second-class citizenship, and are told in no uncertain terms that they are not welcomed or desired.

Although most White immigrant groups were confronted with prejudice and oppression when first arriving in America, their experiences in the United States have been qualitatively different than the experiences of people of color (Takaki, 1998). In a significant way, European immigrants over the past century and racial minorities face opposite cultural problems. The new Europeans were seen as not American enough, and they were pressured to give up their strange and threatening ways and to assimilate. While it might take several generations, the offspring that were successful in this process could usually expect to become accepted citizens. African Americans, Asian Americans, and Latino Americans were second-class-status Americans. They were seldom welcomed and were told to stay in their place and not allowed into the mainstream culture of the privileged even when fully acculturated.

Second, there is something insidiously pathological about the melting pot concept in its assumption that groups should assimilate. Wehrly states, "Cultural assimilation, as practiced in the United States, is the expectation by the people in power that all immigrants and people outside the dominant group will give up their ethnic and cultural values and will adopt the values and norms of the dominant society—the White, male Euro-Americans" (1995, p. 5). Many psychologists of color, however, have referred to this process as *cultural genocide*, an outcome of colonial thought (Guthrie, 1997; Thomas & Sillen, 1972). Persons of color, more than their White brothers or sisters, are aware of the frightening implications of this expectation. Rather than a voluntary process, it is one of forced compliance, an imposition of the standards of the dominant group upon the less powerful one. Thus, the melting pot (a seemingly harmless and neutral concept) is in actuality a justification for political imposition. The European colonization efforts toward the Americas, for example, operated from the assumption that the enculturation of indigenous peoples was justified because European culture was superior (Barongan et al.,

1997). Forcing the colonized to adopt European beliefs and customs was seen as civilizing them.

In the United States, this practice was clearly seen in the treatment of Native Americans where their lifestyles, customs, and practices were seen as backward and uncivilized, and attempts were made to make over the heathens (Duran, 2006; Gone, 2010). Such a belief is also reflected in Euro-American culture and has been manifested in attitudes toward other racial/ethnic minority groups in the United States as well. "Racial/ethnic minorities would not encounter problems if they just assimilate and acculturate." Unfortunately, the dilemma facing people of color is being sold a false bill of goods: "If you assimilate, you will bear the fruits of our society."

Third, many White Americans are fond of saying, "When in Rome, do as the Romans do. Shouldn't people who immigrate to this country or those who reside in it acculturate? After all, when I travel abroad, I have to accept the ways of another country. This is only common sense." Let us, for the moment, assume that assimilation is desirable and that becoming a part of your country of residence is important. The question is this: *Shouldn't we, therefore, all become Native Americans? Further, why aren't we?* Answering these two questions brings us into the realm of sociopolitical discussions of power. It is clear that assimilation is not a concept of equality, but one of power. Who has the power to determine the direction of assimilation? The early immigrants to the North American continents imposed their will upon the indigenous people of the land. They had no inclination or thoughts to assimilate or acculturate to the customs and norms of the American Indians. True assimilation and acculturation is based upon an equal status relationship, wherein different groups have equal influence upon one another.

MYTH OF THE MELTING POT

In summary, the melting pot concept is a falsehood. It is a White Euro-American concept meant for Whites only. The myth of the melting pot is predicated on several false assumptions: (a) a receptive society, (b) an equal status relationship between culturally different groups, and (c) its morally and politically neutral character. In reality, the melting pot is used to mask White supremacy and White privilege (topics, as we have seen, that impede race talk). Its goals are to perpetuate an imbalance of economic, social, and political power; control the gateways to power and privilege; and determine which groups will be allowed access to the benefits, privileges, and opportunities of the society. One might even conclude that the ideal of melting is to become as White as possible.

In contemporary times, power imbalance and imposition continues in the form of institutional racism. J. M. Jones (1997) has defined institutional racism as

> those established laws, customs, and practices which systematically reflect and produce racial inequities in American society. If racist consequences accrue to institutional laws, customs, or practices, the institution is racist whether or not the individuals maintaining those practices have racist intentions. Institutional racism can be either overt or covert (corresponding to de jure and de facto, respectively) and either intentional or unintentional. (p. 438)

Institutional racism that benefits or favors Whites is seen in all facets of our society: bank lending practices, access to health care, housing, jobs, education, media portrayals, law enforcement, and court decisions that mete out justice. Although individual acts of racial discrimination hurt people of color on an individual level, systemic racism embedded in our society hurts literally millions of marginalized persons in our society.

The existence of institutional racism shields the operation of White privilege (a topic covered in Chapter 9) through what is called standard operating procedures (SOPs), which represent the rules, habits, procedures, and structures of organizations that oppress persons of color while favoring Whites. The SOPs may be applied equally to all groups, but serve to maintain the status quo. Space does not allow an extended discussion of these policies and practices that shield and mask their discriminatory effects, but some are listed here (Sue, 2003).

- Systemic societal forces that produce segregation, allowing only certain groups to purchase homes in affluent neighborhoods, resulting in differential worth of real estate.
- Bank lending practices that consider credit worthiness on the basis of location, inevitably discriminating against minority communities.
- Inequitable school financing in which property taxes of wealthy communities produce greater educational resources than poorer communities.
- Segregated schools that dispense inferior education to one group, but advantaged education to another.
- Biased curricula, textbooks, and materials that reaffirm the identity of one group while denigrating others.

- Educational testing that is normed and standardized on a White, middle-class population; the results are culturally biased test instruments used to track minority students into non-college-bound classes.
- Teachers and counselors with expectations, attitudes, and racial perceptions that result in beliefs that students of color are less capable, often resulting in a self-fulfilling prophecy among minorities as though true.
- School tracking systems that may unfairly perpetuate inequities in education.
- Hiring policies and practices that utilize the old boy's network to recruit and hire prospective employees.

In conclusion, to be color-blind is to be color-mute. It hides the ugly secrets of racial inequities, power, and privilege, and White Americans' personal complicity in the perpetuation of racism. Race talk is frightening because it threatens to destroy the fabric of naïveté and innocence that has shielded many from acknowledging their continuing roles as unintentional oppressors in a cultural context that is inherently unfair to people of color. It allows color-blind individuals to escape responsibility for taking action to end injustice, unfairness, and racism in our society.

Why Is It Difficult for People of Color to Honestly Talk About Race?

CHAPTER SIX

"What Are the Consequences for Saying What I Mean?"

Dear Brothers and Sisters of Color:

I write . . . to you and to those White folks who have marched with us against racism and shown that their hearts are in the right place. Throughout our people's histories, we have had to contend with invalidation, oppression, injustice, terrorism, and genocide. Racism is a constant reality in our lives. It is a toxic force that has sought to

- strip us of our identities,
- take away our dignity,
- make us second-class citizens,
- destroy our peoples, cultures, and communities,
- steal our land and property,
- torture, rape, and murder us,
- imprison us on reservations, concentration camps, inferior schools, segregated neighborhoods, and jails,
- use us as guinea pigs in medical experiments, and
- blame our victimization upon the faults of our own people.

Attempts to express these thoughts have generally been met with disbelief and/or incredulity by many of our well-intentioned White brothers and sisters. We have been asked, "Aren't you distorting the truth? Where is your proof? Where is your evidence?"

When we attempt to provide it, we are interrogated about its legitimacy, told that we are biased or paranoid, and accused of being dishonest in how we present the facts. After all, they say, "Our nation is built upon life, liberty, and the pursuit of happiness. It was founded upon the principles of freedom, democracy, and equality." Yet, these guiding principles seem intended for Whites only! In the classic book, *Animal Farm* (Orwell, 1945), when the issue of inequality arose, the character in a position of power justified the treatment by stating, "Some are more equal than others." Rather than offer enlightenment and freedom, education and healing, and rather than allowing for equal access and opportunity, historical and current practices in our nation have restricted, stereotyped, damaged, and oppressed persons of color.

For too long people of color have not had the opportunity or power to express their points of view. For too long our voices have not been heard. For too long our worldviews have been diminished, negated, or considered invalid. For too long we have been told that our perceptions are incorrect, that most things are well with our society, and that our concerns and complaints are not supported. For too long we have had to justify our existence, and to fight for our dignity and humanity. No wonder that we are so tired, impatient, and angry. Yet, as people of color, we cannot let fatigue turn into hopelessness, nor anger into bitterness. Hopelessness is the forerunner to surrender, and bitterness leads to blind hatred. Either could spell our downfall!

It is important for us to realize that despite these indignities, we have persevered and become stronger. We have survived through our collective strength. We have survived through our heightened perceptual wisdom. We have survived through our ability to read the contextualized meanings of our oppressors. We have survived through our bicultural flexibility. We have survived through our families and communities. We have survived through our spirituality and our religion. We have survived through our racial/ethnic identity and pride. We have survived through our belief in the interconnectedness of the human condition.

Unlike many of our White brothers and sisters who are untested, we have demonstrated superhuman resiliency in the face of adversity. Our perseverance in battling the forces of racism comes (a) from understanding the strengths and assets developed by our ancestors as they fought oppression and (b) from our cultural values, mores and traditions.

As persons of color, we have been subjected to inhuman stressors in our lives: (a) poverty, high unemployment rates, and lower standards of living; (b) conflicting value systems imposed by a White Euro-American society; (c) a history of broad governmental actions that have led to the enslavement of Black Americans, the internment of Japanese Americans, and the colonization of Native Americans; and (d) constant microinvalidations and microaggressions that strike at the core of our group identities.

In light of the historical and continuing experiences of oppression, even I marvel at our ability to continue our lives in such a normative fashion. It seems that White America exhibits minimal appreciation for the incredible strength and resiliency that we have shown in surviving and sometimes flourishing in the face of racism. Our experiences of oppression have required us to sharpen and hone our survival skills to such a degree that they now represent assets. We have learned this through the courageous and undefeatable actions of our ancestors who showed us the way. It is ironic that overcoming adversity has led us to develop an ability to understand the minds of our oppressors with astounding clarity.

So, when we begin to become tired and discouraged, when hopelessness seems just around the corner, and when we wonder what good our actions are doing, we need to remind ourselves of the strengths and assets we possess; many of them taught to us by our ancestors. We need to take pride in the fact that our heightened perceptual wisdom, ability to rely on nonverbal and contextual meanings, and bicultural flexibility has proven keys to our survival. (Sue, 2003, pp. 257–259)

Questions: How much knowledge do you have about the historical treatment of groups of color in the United States? What do you know about the colonization of Native Americans, enslavement of Black Americans, incarceration of Japanese Americans, and malicious treatment of Latinos? Were they ever covered in detail in social studies or history courses? If so, were they generally downplayed and minimized? As a person reading the letter, do you believe what is being expressed or are they simply gross exaggerations? If true, how do you think these historical events affect the worldviews of people of color? On a personal level, what do these facts mean to you and the life you are living? What are the strengths and assets possessed by people of color that I mention? In what ways have they helped people of color survive in a monocultural society and even thrive?

This open letter to brothers and sisters of color outlines the immense historical and current challenges people of color have encountered in their day-to-day lives. I wrote it at a point in my life when I was beginning to doubt whether the voices of those most oppressed in our society were being heard by well-intentioned White brothers and sisters. The struggle to tell our stories and have them acknowledged and validated continues to this very day. The content of this letter touches upon reasons why race talk may prove difficult for people of color. This chapter covers the historical experiences of people of color in White America, the struggle for dignity and survival in a hostile and invalidating culture, the power of racism in affecting their lived realities, and the survival mechanisms they have developed and employed. These experiences have taught people of color to be wary about what Whites profess about themselves, to be constantly vigilant about the motives and actions of others, and to approach the world with a healthy skepticism when racial issues arise. As such, it has a drastic impact on the willingness of people of color to honestly talk about race and racism to their well-intentioned White brothers and sisters.

In this chapter are clues as to why people of color find it difficult to talk about race with their White counterparts. Although they are more willing to discuss topics of race and to bear witness to their lived realities, people of color feel silenced, invalidated, and punished by Whites when they attempt to do so (Bell, 2003; Sue, Lin, et al., 2009; Sue, Torino, et al., 2009). Further, to constantly have to explain their life circumstances, to justify their perceptions and reactions, to not have their groups' histories known, and to be wary of the consequences for truth telling in the face of an unreceptive audience is exhausting and energy depleting. To them, the actual avoidance of race talk imposed upon them by White Americans denies their experiential reality, forces them to be disingenuous, and assails their integrity (Hanna et al., 2000; Harlow, 2003).

Thus, many people of color must deal with the sting of racism, ostracism, and stigma (S. A. Goodwin, Williams, & Carter-Sowell, 2010; K. Williams, 2011) and live in silence (Sue, Nadal, et al., 2008) or mold their behaviors in such a way as to meet the expectations of White Americans (Boyd-Franklin, 2010). In race talk they must either remain silent or say only what White folks want to hear. Being shackled by these forces means a denial of their humanity and represents an invisible world of pain and suffering that must be endured to the obliviousness of White America. To understand the dilemma faced by people of color in race talk we must first become aware of (a) the situational context of oppression that they live under, (b) the ensuing psychological costs associated with racism, and (c) the negative personal and group consequences for breaking their silence.

ETHNOCENTRIC MONOCULTURALISM

Scholars and researchers have noted that the high frequency and cumulative burden of a lifetime of oppression in the form of racism are realities in the lives of people of color (Banks, 2004; Clark, Anderson, Clark, & Williams, 1999; Pierce, 1995; M. P. Rowe, 1990; Solórzano, Ceja, & Yosso, 2000; Steele, Spencer, & Anderson, 2002; Sue, Capodilupo, et al., 2008). Although old-fashioned racism (overt forms of racial hatred such as hate crimes) has declined, it appears to have morphed into a more subtle, covert, and insidious form of racial bias known as *aversive racism* and *racial microaggressions* (APA Presidential Task Force, 2012; Dovidio et al., 2002; Sue et al., 2007). Racial microaggressions are the everyday slights, indignities, insults, put downs, and invalidations directed toward persons of color by well-intentioned Whites who are unaware that they have engaged in prejudicial and discriminatory behaviors (Sue et al., 2007). The power of racial microaggressions is in their invisibility because they represent a subconscious worldview of inclusion–exclusion, superiority–inferiority, normality–abnormality, expressed through the norms, values, and standards derived from a White Euro-American perspective that are imposed upon marginalized groups in our society (Sue & Sue, 2013). The racial reality expressed in the open letter is usually outside the level of conscious awareness of most White Americans. Indeed, White peoples' perceptions and beliefs about race and its current status in our nation are often diametrically opposed to those held by brothers and sisters of color. In theory both groups may disagree with one another on the manifestation, dynamics, and impact of racism and these different perspectives are not necessarily harmful or disadvantages to one group or another. This statement would be generally true if both groups shared an equal or nearly equal status relationship to one another. When they do not, however, the group with the power to impose their standards upon the lesser powered group can result in oppression. Racism is one such form of oppression (Hanna et al., 2000; J. M. Jones, 1997).

Ethnocentric monoculturalism is an umbrella of individual, institutional, and cultural forces that demeans, disadvantages, and denies people of color equal access and opportunities (Ponterotto et al., 2006; Sue, 2004).

It is composed of five intersecting components that have major detrimental consequences to socially devalued groups in our society: (1) belief in the superiority of one group, (2) belief in the inferiority of other groups, (3) manifested and supported by institutions, (4) deeply embedded in an invisible veil of White racial ideology, and (5) possessing the power to impose a racial reality upon less powerful groups.

Component 1—Belief in Superiority

Within the United States, there is a strong belief in the superiority of White Euro-American cultural heritage (history, arts/crafts, language, traditions, religion, values, etc.) as expressed in the mores, values, and standards of the group. Descriptors of the dominant group may contain phrases such as *more civilized* and *more advanced* to refer to the positive qualities of the group, and can be manifested in aphorisms such as *being gracious, being ladylike,* and *being classy,* which are filled with normative values that dictate the type of behaviors deemed appropriate and acceptable. In race talk, for example, being calm and rational in discussing issues and not letting one's emotions get the best of him or her are often norms imposed upon participants. Behaviors that deviate from these norms are considered undesirable, irrational, or inappropriate, and generally negative characteristics are attributed to those who break the norms. The underlying White Euro-American belief here is that emotion is antagonistic to reason. As mentioned earlier, these standards may actually stifle rather than facilitate an honest discussion of race.

In ethnocentric monoculturalism, White Americans may possess conscious and subconscious feelings of superiority and a belief that their ways of doing things are the right ways and normative. Such values and perceptions inundate nearly all aspects of White Euro-American existence and behavior. They encompass physical characteristics (value on light complexion, blond hair, and blue eyes) to cultural characteristics such as belief in Christianity (monotheism), individualism, capitalism, protestant work ethic (meritocracy), control of emotions, standard English, and the written versus oral tradition (Anderson & Middleton, 2011; Capodilupo & Kim, 2013; Garrett & Portman, 2011; Katz, 1985). People possessing these traits and values are perceived more favorably and generally have greater access to the rewards and privileges of the society. McIntosh (2002) refers to many of these as *White privilege,* a knapsack of invisible unearned assets that can be cashed in each day to their advantage, but that are not available to people of color. Some examples include curricular materials that portray White Americans positively, seeing members of their race widely represented in the mass media, entering retail stores without being suspected of being a shoplifter, freedom to choose the neighborhood Whites choose to live in, and so on. White privilege is a topic that will be discussed further in Chapters 8 and 9. Unfortunately, people of color who do not possess these traits or characteristics of the dominant group may be perceived in a negative light that disadvantages them.

Component 2—Belief in Inferiority of Others

Because other racial/ethnic groups may differ significantly from the majority group, their cultural values, customs, traditions, language or linguistic traits, and cultural/religious observances may be perceived as inferior (J. M. Jones, 1997; Sue, 2004). Historically, for example, Native Americans and their culture have been described as primitive, uncivilized, and/or even pathological. Thus, under the umbrella of ethnocentric monoculturalism, the lifestyles of people of color can be considered inferior to White Western norms and values. In contrast to the majority group, physical characteristics such as dark skin, black hair, and brown eyes, and cultural differences such as religious beliefs (Islam, Confucianism, polytheism, etc.), linguistic characteristics (speaking with an accent, nonstandard English, use of nonverbal communication, bilingualism, etc.), collectivism, and shared wealth may be considered less desirable (Capodilupo & Kim, 2013; Garrett & Portman, 2011; Katz, 1985).

With respect to race talk, differences in communication styles become very important to understand as we will see in Chapter 7. Conversation conventions in Euro-American society, for example, assume that the behaviors and rules for speaking or interacting with others are universal and those who deviate from them are considered uneducated or breaking the mold of good conduct. For example, a popular dictum in U.S. dialogues is that controversial issues should be discussed objectively and with emotional restraint. African American styles, however, are high keyed, animated, confrontational, and heated with considerable affect (Kochman, 1981; Stanback & Pearce, 1985). Among African Americans such a style does not connote irrationality but positive passion. Such styles are believed to indicate sincerity, authenticity, and genuineness; from the perspective of Whites, however, the style suggests lack of objectivity, irrationality, and/or potential violence (Hall, 1976; Shade & New, 1993).

In many cases Whites may perceive this style coming from a Black person as threatening, intimidating, and potentially violent (Kochman, 1981). In a racial dialogue, communication style differences may not only portray the behaviors of socially marginalized groups as inferior and undesirable, but may trigger stereotypes from Whites of the angry, hostile, and violent Black man or woman. Likewise the reticent, subtle, and quiet communication style of Asian Americans may be seen by Whites as being passive, inhibited, unfeeling, and guarded. Among traditional Asian culture, however, indirectness and subtlety in expressing oneself are seen as signs of maturity, wisdom, and appropriateness.

Component 3—Manifestation in Institutions

Ethnocentric monoculturalism is almost always manifested in the programs, policies, practices, and structures of institutions in our society. Chain-of-command systems; management systems; hiring, retention, and promotion systems; performance appraisal systems; education and training systems; and employer–employee relationship systems dictate and control the lives of employers, employees, teachers, students, and customers in nearly all aspects of life. All of us are touched by the organizations that employ us and/or in which we are required to seek their goods and services. It goes without saying that such organizations are generally monocultural in nature (White Euro-American) that demand compliance (in the form of culture-bound rules and regulations) on the part of individuals who come in contact with them. Although most of us readily acknowledge the existence of individual racism, the biases of institutional racism are difficult to recognize because they are hidden within the fabric of the policies and practices of the organization (J. M. Jones, 1997). These organizational policies and practices may appear neutral and nondiscriminatory in nature because they are applied to everyone equally, but their effects are to disadvantage certain groups while advantaging others. This is why many women refer to sexism as creating a glass ceiling, an invisible barrier of organizational bias that allows men to be promoted to higher positions of management while keeping women from breaking through.

As mentioned earlier, J. M. Jones's (1997) definition of institutional racism labels it as a set of priorities and accepted normative patterns designed to subjugate, oppress, and force dependence of individuals and groups on broad societal values. It does this by sanctioning unequal goals, unequal status, and unequal access to goods and services. It prescribes lesser roles for people of color and sanctions them through selective enforcement of laws—blocking economic opportunities and outcomes—and the imposition of compliance through assimilation and acculturation. Institutional racism is any institutional policy, practice, or structure in governments, businesses, unions, schools, places of worship, courts, and law enforcement agencies that unfairly subordinate persons of color while allowing Whites to profit from such actions. Examples include housing patterns, segregated schools, discriminatory employment and promotion policies, racial profiling, inequities in health care, segregated churches, and educational curricula that ignore/distort the history of minorities.

When the policies, procedures, laws, and structures of society impede equal access and opportunity or even create unfair disparities in our society against persons of color, we have clear evidence of institutional racism. School tracking systems that unfairly perpetuate inequities; educational testing that is normed and standardized on a White population resulting in culturally biased test instruments; hiring policies and practices that utilize an old boy's network; biased curricula, textbooks, and materials that affirm the identity of one group while denigrating others; and inferior education based on the wealth of the school district all exemplify institutional racism. These rules and regulations, and their discriminatory outcomes, remain hidden and invisible to most ordinary citizens; people of color, however, are very aware of the detrimental toll they have on their standard of living.

Component 4—The Invisibility of White Racial Ideology in Worldviews

Ethnocentric monoculturalism operates through an invisible veil outside the level of conscious awareness and is reflected in worldviews of which racial ideology is embedded. The values and standards of superiority, inferiority, and norms associated with institutional policies and practices constitute a worldview of universality; everyone should ascribe to this reality and truth regardless of race, ethnicity, gender, sexual orientation, and so forth. The inability to see how the assumptions and biased practices exist in one's own beliefs and behaviors allows Whites to operate in a vacuum of naïveté and innocence that distances them from responsibility or the knowledge that their unawareness fosters complicity in the inequities of our society. This lack of awareness is infuriating to people of color, especially when they are unable to correct this misperception or even express their observations in a tentative manner. Most White Americans, for example, associate racism as residing only in White supremacists, the Ku Klux Klan, skinheads, and neo-Nazis. They do not see themselves as racist because that term belongs to the former group. The fact that they, as fair-minded and well-intentioned individuals, may harbor biases is a frightening prospect to entertain. That, as we have repeatedly emphasized, is why race talk is so threatening to their image as good, moral, and decent human beings.

Elsewhere, it was made clear that the socialization process imbues in citizens the biases and prejudices of the society: a belief that certain groups are lesser beings, that they are to be avoided, and that they are deserving of the lower status they occupy (Sue, 2003, 2004). These beliefs and attitudes are conveyed to us by family, friends, and neighbors, through our educational system, the mass media, and organizations. People soak up this cultural conditioning not through free choice, but through a painful process of social conditioning. No person acquired prejudices and misinformation through free choice; people were not born into the world wanting to be racist, sexist, or heterosexist. As long as biases remain hidden, however, responsibility for change at the individual, institutional, and societal levels can be avoided. The invisibility of White racial superiority and minority inferiority is a well-kept secret as long as people are not allowed to talk about it.

Component 5—Power to Impose

It goes without saying that all groups are ethnocentric, in that they perceive themselves, their cultures, and their communities in a positive light while viewing others less favorably. Further, all groups hold stereotypes, biases, and prejudices and can on an individual level discriminate against one another: People of color can discriminate against Whites and even against one another. But not all groups hold the *power* to impose their values and lifestyles on others, and thus hypothetically cannot oppress on a broader level. Many multicultural scholars contend that racism is about institutional power, a form of power that people of color just do not possess (APA Presidential Task Force, 2012; J. M. Jones, 1997; Sue & Sue, 2013). Thus, when filmmaker Spike Lee (African American) states, "Only Whites can be racist!," he is echoing the sentiments of many who have studied the manifestation, dynamics, and impact of racism. When White Americans unintentionally act in a prejudicial and discriminatory fashion toward people of color, they are backed by the full faith and credit of White Euro-American norms and values. When people of color unintentionally or even deliberately discriminate against Whites, they go against societal norms that work against them. In other words, people of color do not possess a share of the economic, social, and political power of White Americans, and have little ability to discriminate on a large-scale basis (Ponterotto et al., 2006). Thus, the harm of oppression is generally one-sided, from majority to minority groups.

POWER AND OPPRESSION

Indeed, ethnocentric monoculturalism has its roots in the Bill of Rights, Declaration of Independence, and the U.S. Constitution (Barongan et al., 1997). Over 200 years ago, Britain's King George III was forced to accept a Declaration of Independence from former White subjects residing as immigrants in what was to become the United States of America. The lofty language penned by its chief architect, Thomas Jefferson, was inspiring and served to shape and reshape the geopolitical and sociocultural landscape of the world many times over: "We hold these truths to be self-evident, that all men are created equal."

Although the moving language and tone spoke to freedom and self-determination, the hypocrisy and inconsistencies of the early founders remained hidden from them. That is, they did not seem to practice what they preached and remained oblivious to the contradictions. First, all 56 of the signatories were White males of European descent, hardly a representative sample of the gender composition of their population. Second, the language itself declared that "all *men* are created equal," leaving out half of the early immigrant women and those who followed. Third, many founders were slave owners, who could not recognize their own hypocrisy in considering Blacks to be less than human. Fourth, the history of this land did not start with the Declaration of Independence or the formation of the United States of America. It existed long before the early European immigrants arrived, but the history textbooks continue to portray the past from an ethnocentric perspective; history (Western civilization) started approximately 200 years ago. Last, related to this point, the early immigrants came to this country to escape persecution, but failed to recognize how they persecuted and oppressed the indigenous peoples (Native Americans) of this country. In fact, they took the land by force from Native Americans and claimed it to be divine destiny.

It is clear that the early founders had good intentions and meant well; they were not evil men whose conscious motivation was to oppress and dominate others. They were victims of their own social conditioning, trapped in their worldviews that made the majority of their biased attitudes, beliefs, and discriminatory behaviors invisible to them. Many people of color continue to believe that Whites today operate from ethnocentric monoculturalism, and that their biases and prejudices remain hidden from them still. Yet, as we now know, the history of the United States was formed from the fabric of racial oppression, domination, and discrimination (J. M. Jones, 1997). The Euro-American worldview continues to form the basis of our educational, social, economic, cultural, and political systems.

In many respects ethnocentric monoculturalism is about forced compliance and oppression directed toward people of color. They are asked to conform, change, assimilate, and acculturate to the norms and ways of the majority group or they will suffer the consequences. Ironically, as discussed in Chapter 5, even if people of color were to adopt White Euro-American ways, their visible racial/ethnic minority characteristics still prevent them from enjoying the full privileges and rewards of the society. Ethnocentric monoculturalism continues to value White Eurocentric ways of thinking, feeling, behaving, and being that do not fit the racial reality of people of color (Hanna et al., 2000; Sue & Sue, 2013). It is clear that the imposition of these standards on people of color represents cultural oppression: the unjust, cruel, and harsh exercise of power over various groups in our society. In his classic book, *Pedagogy of the Oppressed*, Freire (1970) describes how oppressors in colonized countries attempt to develop a culture of silence that prevents those oppressed from voicing their concerns. They do this through controlling and defining oppressed peoples in ways that undermine their identities and roles, and by silencing them through education and other institutions (shaping their racial realities to conform to that of the dominant culture). In this way, people of color, for example, are forced to comply and their objections are silenced and unheard (Hanna et al., 2000). Those who disobey, who break from the silence, and who do not conform are severely punished. To keep the voices of those most oppressed from being heard (back talk), the majority culture uses two major forms of forced compliance identified by Hanna and colleagues (2000).

First, racism can be expressed through oppression by force in which control and compliance of people of color can be attained through coercion, threat, or duress. A succinct description of this form of oppression follows:

> It is the act of imposing on another or others an object, label, role experience, or set of living conditions that is unwanted, needlessly painful, and detracts from physical or psychological well-being. An imposed object, in this context, can be anything from a bullet, a bludgeon, shackles, or fists, to a penis, unhealthy food, or abusive messages designed to cause or sustain pain, low self-efficacy, reduced self-determination, and so forth. Other examples of oppression by force can be

demeaning hard labor, degrading job roles, ridicule, and negative media images and messages that foster and maintain distorted beliefs. (Hanna et al., 2000, p. 431)

The definition of oppression by force is very applicable to the historical overt and abusive treatment of people of color: slavery, lynchings of Black people, physical and cultural genocide of Indigenous peoples, discriminatory legislation forbidding the ownership of land by Asian Americans, incarceration of Japanese Americans during World War II, low wages for hard labor by Latino immigrants, and so forth (Choney, Berryhill-Paapke, & Robbins, 1995; Gone, 2010; Grier & Cobbs, 1968; Hwang & Goto, 2009; Sue & Sue, 2013; Thomas & Sillen, 1972). In more subtle and less obvious ways, however, oppression by force continues for people of color, such as degrading job roles, ridicule, and negative media images.

A second form of oppression is that of deprivation—the flip side of imposition by force described as

the act that deprives another or others of an object, role, experience, or set of living conditions that are desirable and conducive to physical or psychological well-being. It also includes the deprivation of loved ones, respect, or dignity. Neglect is another form of oppression in which a person is deprived of love, care, support, or vital services as well as basic material needs such as food, shelter, and clothing. (Hanna et al., 2000, p. 431)

Many examples of deprivation can be recounted historically, such as the banning of religious and spiritual practices of Native Americans because they were considered subversive, and in contemporary times, people of color can be deprived of desirable jobs and their respect, dignity, and humanity (Barongan et al., 1997). Racial microaggressions, for example, not only attack and assail the identity of people of color, but they sentence them to second-class citizenship and deprive them of living conditions necessary for their physical and psychological well-being. Thus, oppression by force or deprivation creates undesirable and harmful conditions for people of color.

Effects on Trust–Mistrust

How people of color currently talk about race among themselves and to Whites differ significantly due to these historical events (Boyd-Franklin, 2010; Gone, 2009; Hwang & Gotto, 2009; Martinez & Gutierrez, 2010). Although the history and details of the forced enslavement of African Americans, widespread segregation of Latino Americans, passage of exclusionary laws against the Chinese, genocide of Native Americans, and internment of Japanese Americans are not in the critical consciousness of most Whites on a day-to-day basis, they have a large-scale impact on the mind-set of people of color. It should not be surprising then that many people of color view White Americans and their institutions with considerable mistrust (Sue & Sue, 2013). Indeed, such mistrust has been labeled by some psychologists as the *paranorm* that are oftentimes misinterpreted by Whites as pathological—paranoia or oversensitivity (Grier & Cobbs, 1968, 1971).

African Americans, for example, often make statements that The Man is out to get them; many Whites interpret such statements as paranoid and lacking a rational basis for such a belief (Guthrie, 1997; Parham, Ajamu, & White, 2011). Yet, history and anecdotal tales are replete with examples of how, in the face of historical oppression and discrimination, African Americans employ strategies (behaviors toward Whites) that have proven successful for survival in a racist society. *Playing it cool* is one such strategy that Blacks employ to conceal their true thoughts or feelings (rage and anger) and appear serene, calm, or nonreactive in the face of racism. Using this tactic is a survival mechanism aimed at reducing one's vulnerability to harm and exploitation in a hostile environment. True expression of thoughts and feelings endangers one's status in life and at the extreme can result in physical retaliation and death (being tortured, physically shackled, or killed by lynching). Thus the paranorm and its continued contemporary use have proven to be a functional survival mechanism. Interestingly, Grier and Cobbs (1968) consider the paranorm used by Blacks to represent an adaptive, functional, and healthy mechanism, rather than a dysfunctional one.

To understand this statement, it is important to be aware of how these behavioral patterns toward Whites were developed and how they affect the desire of people of color to self-disclose their true thoughts and feelings (Sue & Sue, 2013). These patterns were important for survival in a highly racist society and included indirect rather than direct expressions of hostility, aggression, and fear (Boyd-Franklin, 2003; J. M. Jones, 1997). During times of slavery, Blacks were forced to raise children who would fit into a segregated system and who could physically survive the indignities likely to be heaped upon them. Boyd-Franklin (2003, 2010) describes teaching Black children, especially males, (a) to express aggression indirectly in the face of insults and indignities, (b) to create as few waves as possible by engaging in ritualized accommodating/subordinating behaviors, and (c) to read the thoughts of others while hiding their own. These strategies involve a mild dissociation whereby Blacks separate their true selves from their roles as Negroes. The dual identity involves revealing the true self to only fellow Blacks, but the dissociated self to the prejudiced expectations of Whites. Along with playing it cool, another role often used is the *Uncle Tom* ploy whereby the Black person masquerades as docile, nonassertive, and happy-go-lucky. Passivity in slavery times was a necessary component of survival in order to keep the most menial jobs, to minimize retaliation, and to maximize survival of the self and loved ones.

There is a very common saying among people of color that goes like this: "If you really want to know what White folks are thinking and feeling, don't listen to what they say, but how they say it." In other words, the belief expressed is that Whites are often deceptive, and their words must be checked out through their tone of voice or other nonverbal behaviors that are least under conscious control. Among American Indians, the claim that "White men speak with forked tongues and mystify their words with White lies" is a similar accusation; Whites are not truthful in stating what they think or believe. These statements and beliefs continue to contemporary times in which Whites are believed to hold biases, prejudices, and stereotypes that they consciously or unconsciously attempt to conceal. The orientation of people of color and their perception of many Whites can be described in the following passage:

> When one Black person talks privately with another, he or she might say "Look, we don't have to jive each other or be like White folks; let's be honest with one another." These statements reflect the familiar Black saying that "talk is cheap," that actions speak louder than words, and that Whites beguile each other with words.... In contrast, the White mind symbolizes to many Black people deceit, verbal chicanery, and sterile intellectivity. For example, after a long discourse with a White person, a Black individual might say: "I've heard what you've said, but what do you really mean?" (Smith, 1981, p. 154)

Coping With Oppression—Heightened Perceptual Wisdom

In the face of oppression and adversity, people of color have developed a heightened sense of observation and awareness that allows them to notice and recognize aspects of threat and danger posed by the environment and specifically White Americans (Hanna et al., 2000; Miller, 1986). It is often stated that people of color and other oppressed and marginalized groups possess an exceptional clarity of vision and truth that is discomforting to those who are most empowered. Sternberg (1990) coined the term *perspicacity* to refer to the power of accurate perception; it allows the person to see beyond the obvious, to read between the lines, to not be easily fooled, and to intuitively understand the motives, intent, and meaning of others. Women, for example, develop their perceptual abilities as one of the few means of coping when denied power and status (Miller, 1986); the battered wife becomes hypersensitive to the moods and behaviors of her husband in order to survive and minimize further abuse. Employees are aware of the power differential between themselves and others who hold power over them so they become attuned to the routine of their bosses, their habits, customs, moods, and behaviors.

Ironically, Whites do not realize that possessing unchecked power and control over others often results in the dimming of their own perceptiveness and leads to a distorted reality. This is because their high status and power means they (a) seldom have to worry or even think about people of color, (b) use only one another to validate their sense of a false racial reality, and (c) inaccurately define people of color from a stereotypical template. It deprives them of seeing the world and others as they really are (Hanna et al., 2000). People of color often say, "We understand White folks better than they understand themselves." A White male boss who hires employees of color, for example, may take pride in his belief that he is a kind, compassionate person who is free of bias. He is unaware, however, that employees who work under his authority consider him to be deceiving himself, and his behavior toward them is considered degrading and biased. Becoming aware of the customs and contradictions of the dominant group is a coping mechanism that maximizes survival.

People of color have been forced to operate within a predominantly White culture, and are taught the history, mores, and language of Western society from the moment of birth (Banks, 2004). They have been exposed to a Euro-American educational curriculum, work for White-controlled places of employment, and are subjected to a White justice system. In other words, they have been immersed in the prejudices of their oppressors and their biased institutions. Thus, their survival depends on how accurately they are able to discern the truth as it relates to the thoughts and actions of White Americans. For their survival, they have had to become hypervigilant in discerning the motives, attitudes, and the often unintentional biased contradictions of their White brothers and sisters. Their intuitive insights about White Americans and their biases often cause great discomfort and consternation to those in the dominant group. It is precisely this fear of being unmasked in the eyes of persons of color in public that creates much of the difficulty that Whites have in speaking about racism and oppression. Yet, it is exactly this heightened perception and wisdom that represents a valuable asset and an aspect of optimal human functioning among persons of color.

People of color must rely heavily on their intuitive and experiential reality to discern the truth about people they encounter. As indicated earlier their ability to accurately read nonverbal communication and discern the truth is also a strength developed in the knowledge that nonverbal behaviors are least under conscious control and more likely to reveal where others are coming from. Their ability to read nonverbal cues accurately and efficiently has long been important for the survival of persons of color. Clues to conscious deceptions and unconscious biases can be seen more readily through facial expressions, bodily movements, hesitations in speech, and so forth. People of color, for example, frequently give examples of the need to be vigilant when traveling in unknown parts of the United States. Not only must they be alert to possible dangers to their physical survival, but their psychological survival is also at risk. They must be able to discern the double messages being sent to them by both intentional and unintentional racists.

In general, perspicacity and heightened sense of awareness of persons of color have been developed through the ages and from the continual day-to-day experience of persons of color in their interactions in White America. The perceptual wisdom they developed has allowed them to perceive the mind of White folks and oppressors with stark clarity and to cut through the smokescreen of deception. Past and present discriminatory situations serve as a tangible factor in the mistrust of many Whites, and people of color are likely to approach any discussions of race and racism with wariness and vigilance for potential bias and threat from Whites. Ironically, Whites are often perceived as potential oppressors with biases (whether conscious or not) unless otherwise proven. The issue is not whether one is unbiased, but how aware, honest, and open their White counterparts are to their prejudices and stereotypes, and whether these biases will interfere with the White person's ability to relate to persons of color. People of color often approach race talk with these questions: What makes you any different than my White teacher, White neighbor, or White employer who said one thing but meant another? How aware are you of your racial biases and will they interfere with our ability to form a working relationship? How a White person handles these challenges will either enhance or negate the success of race talk with their brothers and sisters of color.

CHAPTER SEVEN

"To Speak or How to Speak, That Is the Question"

Several years ago, a Fortune 500 company requested my services to work with Asian American employees in their workforce. Apparently, they had taken a survey on employee satisfaction and found that a large number had expressed dissatisfaction with their roles in the company; felt that they were not promoted when otherwise qualified; and expressed a desire to leave the company in the near future. As Asian Americans represented nearly 20% of their technical workforce and were highly valued, the company was very concerned about the financial costs to hire and retrain future workers. I was called in as a consultant to help with leadership training and to conduct workshops on assertiveness and communication styles for their Asian American employees. The company's definition of the problem (lack of Asian American employees in upper management) was (a) that it resided in the individual deficiencies of Asian American employees; (b) that they were unassertive, passive, noncompetitive, and lacked leadership skills; and (c) that training to achieve company-defined leadership criteria offered the best solution.

As a consultant with knowledge about Asian American culture and behavior, I was struck by how closely the problem definition paralleled societal stereotypes of this group: Asian Americans are passive, inhibited, and unassertive; make poor leaders and managers; are poor in people relationships, but make good scientists and technical workers.... In my meetings with the executive team, nearly all felt that Asian employees lacked the necessary qualities for leadership. When I asked how it was that businesses in Hong Kong, Taiwan, Japan, and other Asian companies were so successful, several in the executive team posed the possibility that Asians in Asia were more assertive than their counterparts in the U.S. I indicated to them that this was not the case, but that Asians consider leadership competence to be a person who is able to work behind the scenes, building group consensus, and motivating the team to increase productivity. When I suggested that they ask employees to identify the top individuals who were most instrumental in the success of their teams, several Asian American employee names would consistently be mentioned. Interestingly, these individuals were never put forth as candidates for promotion to the managerial ranks. (Sue, 2008, p. 161)

Questions: What experiences have you had in interacting with Asians and Asian Americans? If you were to characterize their communication styles, how would you describe them? Do they tend to be more quiet, low keyed, and reticent than their White counterparts? Relative to others, are they more likely to be humble and nonassertive when debating or arguing over a point? How might this affect race talk? Are these traits mere stereotypes or relatively accurate?

Years ago when attending a faculty meeting, I witnessed an interaction between a Black male faculty member, Daryl, and several of his White colleagues. The Search Committee had spent considerable time deliberating the hiring of a new faculty member of which one candidate was a Latina among a short list of three White males. As the discussion continued, it became increasingly heated. The dialogue went something like this:

Daryl (Black faculty member speaking passionately): With the changing demographics, we would be remiss in our educational responsibilities if we graduate students without the awareness, knowledge, and skills needed to function in a pluralistic society. Sylvia Sanchez is at the top of my list of candidates. Her specialty is in multicultural education, and we would for the first time be hiring not only the first Spanish-speaking educator, but the first woman in our department.

Jack (White faculty member): I'm less interested in hiring the first of anything, other than who is the most qualified!

Daryl (sounding annoyed): What are you saying? That because she is Latina that she is not qualified? What type of racial bias is that?

Jack: Don't take what I'm saying out of context. I just believe the most qualified person should get the offer, and it should not be based on race or gender. It's just not fair to hire someone because they are Latina.

Daryl (raising his voice): Don't give me that bullshit. Are you committed to cultural diversity or not?

Jack: That's not the issue and you know it. I resent your accusation! My personal feelings aren't at issue here, but the needs of the program are. I'm not going to sit here and be insulted.

Bill (White faculty member, interrupting the exchange): Look now, let's tone it down. Before we consider your recommendation, it's also important for us to consider the many needs of our program. I think that's what Jack is saying. Sanchez's experience in multicultural education is fine, but we need someone with strong quantitative skills, someone who could easily transition into teaching our research and statistics courses. We need someone who will fit into the program and that we feel comfortable working with.

Daryl (leans across toward Bill and punctuates his remarks by pounding the table): I can't believe what I am hearing from you all. I'm getting pissed off! This is just a bunch of intellectual bullshit! Preserve the old boy's network—is that what you are saying? Is this faculty committed to cultural diversity or not? I don't want to hear a bunch of excuses! Where are you all coming from?

(Bill looks uncomfortable and pushes his chair away from Daryl.)

Daryl (observes Bill's distancing actions, smiles wryly, and comments): Don't worry. I'm not going to hit you.

Chair (White male): Daryl, pleeease . . . calm down. Don't let your emotions get the best of you. Let's talk about this in a calm and rational manner. It doesn't matter about what we personally think. We should consider the needs of the program.

Daryl (turns to the Chair): What! Are you saying I'm not rational?

Jack (interrupting quickly): Mr. Chairman, I vote that we table this discussion.

Questions: What do you see happening in this interaction between Daryl and the rest of the White faculty? Is Daryl irrational and out of control? In what ways may communication styles be creating misunderstandings between the participants? What images or stereotypes may Bill possess about Black men? Can you identify the norms and values guiding what is considered appropriate and inappropriate behavior in this discussion? Why was the discussion tabled and did it resolve the situation?

COMMUNICATION STYLES

These two vignettes represent our introduction into the area of *communication styles* and how they affect racial dialogues. On one end of the continuum are styles represented by many Asian Americans where subtlety, indirectness, and restraint of strong feelings are considered appropriate behavior when discussing or debating a point of view (B. S. K. Kim, 2011; Sue & Sue, 2013); on the other end are styles represented by some African Americans where directness, passion, and confrontation tend to be normative (DePaulo, 1992; Irvine & York, 1995; Kochman, 1981). Both communication styles appear to result in different perceptions of the communicator. Using the opening examples, let us look at how communication style differences interpreted through the lens of a Western European framework may create misunderstandings (Wolfgang, 1985).

Asian American Styles

In the first vignette about Asian American employees, it appears that their communication or leadership styles were at odds with that valued by the company (Sue, 2008). A close examination of the company's performance appraisal system (criteria) used for hiring and promoting employees to middle and upper management positions contained words and phrases such as *assertive and aggressive, take charge, competitive, dynamic and forceful,* and *highly visible.* These descriptors seem rooted in Western values of individualism, control, dominance, and competition where winning and success are judged to be leadership qualities residing in the individual. Asian cultural values, however, stress the importance of collectivism, harmony, indirectness, subtlety, and cooperation in interacting with others. Leadership, according to Asian standards, is attributed to the person who works behind the scenes, gathering group consensus, involving all in the decision-making process, and motivating team productivity. Avoiding the limelight and sharing credit for team performance (humility) are valued attributes of workers who are informally acknowledged by their peers as leaders.

The communication style of Asian American employees is being viewed as an obstacle to leadership positions within the company. They are perceived as lacking the abilities and skills to take charge of others, to be forceful, and to be able to make tough decisions. They are viewed as passive, unassertive, unfeeling, and too uncomfortable to deal with overt conflicts that may arise in interpersonal situations—social stereotypes that are widespread in our society about Asians (B. S. K. Kim, 2011). If the criteria used for promotion were an accurate reflection of managerial effectiveness, then a strong argument could be made about the importance of Western European standards of leadership. But, as we have seen, when team members were asked to identify individuals most responsible for group productivity, it was often Asian names that rose to the surface. Thus, we can conclude that the performance appraisal system was culture bound, and potentially biased toward Asian American employees. In this particular case, Asian American employees are unfairly shut out of managerial and executive positions because of the beliefs held by the executive team regarding what constitutes leadership.

Such misinterpretations of Asian American behaviors are often made in the classrooms as well. Teachers and fellow White students often describe them as relatively quiet, shy, seldom contributing to discussions, and having difficulty relating to other classmates. They are oftentimes described as being disinclined to express their true thoughts and feelings, overly cautious, guarded in their behaviors, and relatively passive in the face of the give-and-take characteristic of interpersonal conflict (Leong, Wagner, & Tata, 1995). As we will shortly see, race, culture, and gender influence how people behave and communicate. The problem is not in the differences of how people communicate, but in the failed understanding of their meanings, and the detrimental actions taken by those in positions of authority who hold stereotypes.

African American Styles

The second vignette demonstrates how the communication style of African Americans appears to pose the greatest misunderstanding among White Americans and other groups because of not only cultural, but sociopolitical reasons as well. In terms of verbal, emotional, and behavioral expressiveness, African American styles of communication occupy the other end of the spectrum from those of Asian Americans (Kochman, 1981; Sue & Sue, 2013).

We have already seen how the racial reality of Whites and African Americans may differ significantly from one another, but these differences may be compounded by racial styles of interaction. The dialogue between Daryl and his White colleagues points to a number of possible misunderstandings being exacerbated by communication styles.

First, in a debate or dialogue, African American styles tend to be passionate and animated, and ideas are tested in the crucible of argumentation and confrontation (Kochman, 1981; Shade & New, 1993). The presence of affect is considered sincere, unifying, and healthy, and the advocacy of the speaker suggests an honest connection to the idea or topic. Daryl's challenging behavior and manner of presentation may represent his honesty and authentic connection to the ideas and beliefs he advocates. On the other hand, White styles of communication are in marked contrast to the conversation conventions of most Black Americans; Whites believe that discussions should be devoid of affect; that one serves as a *spokesperson* (truth resides in the idea) not as an *advocate*; and that the debate should be objective, detached, and reasoned (Irvine & York, 1995). From the White perspective, Daryl lacks objectivity and is allowing emotions to cloud his judgment. From Daryl's perspective, however, his White colleagues are inauthentic, and he is disinclined to believe that they do not possess an opinion or a connection to their beliefs. His constant attempts to have his colleagues express their opinions are thwarted by what Daryl views as subterfuge to hide their biases. Their constant avoidance of stating where they personally stand or what they believe suggests his White colleagues' insincerity in the dialogue.

Second, Black styles of communication distinguish between an argument used to debate a difference of opinion, and one that ventilates anger and hostility (DePaulo, 1992; Irvine & York, 1995; Kochman, 1981). In the former, the debate with strong affect is tempered by a positive attitude toward the material, while in the latter there is more passion than sincerity and a negative and abusive attitude toward the opponent. Daryl is positively oriented toward cultural diversity and is advocating it forcefully (not angrily). African Americans can easily distinguish between the two, but White Americans have great difficulty (Kochman, 1981). The White colleagues seem to believe that Daryl is out of control and too emotional. Bill's distancing behavior, for example, seems to imply that he believes Daryl may become violent; Jack's motion to table the discussion also reflects this belief. It is interesting to note Daryl's reaction to the nonverbal behavior of Bill; he sarcastically reassures him by saying, "Don't worry. I'm not going to hit you." Apparently, he is well aware that the stereotype of the angry and potentially violent Black male affects his interactions with many Whites. This is an important point we will return to shortly.

NONVERBAL COMMUNICATION

It is clear that expressing one's thoughts, beliefs, attitudes, and feelings is influenced by race, culture, ethnicity, gender, and other sociodemographic factors. When discussing a topic, expressing a point of view, or debating an issue, differences in communication styles often confuse rather than clarify issues; in many cases they may actually create greater conflict even when both parties hold the same beliefs. Communication styles acknowledge the importance of those factors that go beyond the content of what is said. Some communication specialists believe that only 30% to 40% of what is communicated conversationally is verbal (Condon & Yousef, 1975; Hall, 1959; Ramsey & Birk, 1983; Singelis, 1994). What people say and do is usually qualified by other things that they say and do (Wolfgang, 1985). A gesture, tone, inflection, posture, or degree of eye contact may enhance or negate the content of a message.

Communication styles have a tremendous impact on our face-to-face encounters with others. Whether our conversation proceeds with fits or starts, whether we interrupt one another continually or proceed smoothly, the topics we prefer to discuss or avoid, the depth of our involvement, the forms of interaction (ritual, repartee, argumentative, persuasive, etc.), and the channel we use to communicate (verbal–nonverbal versus nonverbal–verbal) are all aspects of communication style. Some refer to these factors as the *social rhythms* that underlie all our speech and actions. Differences in communication style are most strongly manifested in nonverbal behaviors that transcend the written or spoken word. Three of these involve proxemics, kinesics, and paralanguage.

Proxemics

The study of *proxemics* refers to perception and use of personal and interpersonal space (Mindess, 1999). Clear norms exist concerning the use of physical distance in social interactions. Edward Hall (1959, 1969) identified four interpersonal distance zones characteristic of U.S. culture: intimate, from contact to 18 inches; personal, from 1.5 to 4 feet; social, from 4 to 12 feet; and public (lectures and speeches), greater than 12 feet. In our society, individuals seem to grow more uncomfortable when others stand too close rather than too far away. These feelings and reactions associated with a violation of personal space may range from anxiety, intimidation, anger, and conflict (Pearson, 1985). On the other hand, we tend to allow closer proximity to people whom we like or feel interpersonal attraction toward. Some evidence exists that personal space can be reframed in terms of dominance and status. Those with greater status, prestige, and power may occupy more space (larger homes, cars, or offices). Men tend to be more apt to intrude on the personal space of women because of their greater sense of power and dominance.

Furthermore, cultures dictate different distances in personal space. For Latin Americans, Africans, African Americans, Indonesians, Arabs, South Americans, and French, conversing with a person dictates a much closer stance than is normally comfortable for Euro-Americans (J. V. Jensen, 1985; Nydell, 1996). When Daryl moves physically closer to Bill during their dialogue, it is possible that the Bill perceives it as an intrusion or an act of hostility. Likewise, Bill's desire for greater physical distance from Daryl may suggest to Daryl a lack of engagement and honesty.

Kinesics

While proxemics refers to personal space, *kinesics* is the term used to refer to bodily movements. It includes such things as facial expression, posture, characteristics of movement, gestures, and eye contact. Much of our assessments of personality traits are based on expressions on people's faces (Pearson, 1985). We assume that facial cues express emotions and demonstrate the degree of responsiveness or involvement of the individual. For example, smiling is a type of expression in our society that is believed to indicate liking or positive affect. People attribute greater positive characteristics to others who smile; they are intelligent, have a good personality, and are pleasant (Singelis, 1994). However, when Japanese smile and laugh, it does not necessarily mean happiness but may convey other meanings (embarrassment, discomfort, shyness, etc.).

Among some Japanese and Chinese, restraint of strong feelings (anger, irritation, sadness, and love or happiness) is considered to be a sign of maturity and wisdom. Children learn that outward emotional expressions (facial expressions, body movements, and verbal content) are discouraged except for extreme situations. The lack of facial expressions may be the basis of stereotypes, such as the statement that Asians are inscrutable, sneaky, deceptive, and backstabbing.

Eye contact is, perhaps, the nonverbal behavior most likely to be consciously or subconsciously noted by people. It is not unusual for people to infer incorrect meaning to either an avoidance of eye contact (shy, unassertive, sneaky, or depressed) or to prolonged eye contact—staring (attentiveness to hostility). This lack of understanding has been played out in many different scenarios when Black–White interactions have occurred as we saw in the last chapter. In many cases it is not necessary for African Americans, for example, to look at each other in the eye to communicate attentiveness (Smith, 1981). Many White teachers may be prone to view African American students as being inattentive, sullen, resistant, or uncooperative. Going through the motions of looking at the person and nodding the head is not necessary for many African Americans to indicate that they are listening (Hall, 1974, 1976).

Paralanguage

The term *paralanguage* is used to refer to other vocal cues that individuals use to communicate. For example, loudness of voice, pauses, silences, hesitations, rate, inflections, and the like all fall into this category. Paralanguage is very likely to be manifested forcefully in conversation conventions such as how we greet and address others and take turns in speaking. It can communicate a variety of different features about a person, such as age, gender, and emotional responses, as well as the race and sex of the speaker (Banks & Banks, 1993; Lass, Mertz, & Kimmel, 1978; Nydell, 1996).

There are complex rules regarding when to speak or yield to another person. For example, WhiteAmericans frequently feel uncomfortable with a pause or silent stretch in the conversation, feeling obligated to fill it in with more talk. Silence is not always a sign for the listener to take up the conversation. In Asian culture, silence is traditionally a sign of respect for elders. Furthermore, silence by many Chinese and Japanese is not a floor-yielding signal inviting others to pick up the conversation. Rather, it may indicate a desire to continue speaking after making a particular point. Often silence is a sign of politeness and respect rather than a lack of desire to continue speaking.

The directness of a conversation or the degree of frankness also varies considerably among various cultural groups. Observing the English in their parliamentary debates will drive this point home. The long heritage of open, direct, and frank confrontation leads to heckling of public speakers and quite blunt and sharp exchanges. Britons believe and feel that these are acceptable styles and may take no offense at being the object of such exchanges. However, U.S. citizens feel that such exchanges are impolite, abrasive, and irrational. Relative to Asians, Euro-Americans are seen as being too blunt and frank. Great care is taken by many Asians not to hurt the feelings of or embarrass the other person. As a result, use of euphemisms and ambiguity is the norm. On the other hand, African Americans may be so direct and frank about racial matters that it intimidates and creates discomfort for White Americans.

NONVERBAL COMMUNICATION IN RACE TALK: SOCIOPOLITICAL CONSIDERATIONS

As mentioned in Chapter 6, there is a common saying among African Americans: "If you really want to know what White folks are thinking and feeling, don't listen to what they say, but how they say it." In most cases, such a statement refers to the biases, stereotypes, and racist attitudes that Whites are believed to possess but that are consciously or unconsciously concealed. For people of color, survival, as discussed in Chapter 6, is based on their ability to discern the motives of White Americans, and as mentioned earlier, nonverbal communication is the road to accurately ascertaining them.

Nonverbals as Reflections of Bias

The power of nonverbal communication is that it tends to be least under conscious control. Studies support the conclusion that nonverbal cues operate primarily on an unawareness level, that they tend to be more spontaneous and more difficult to censor or falsify, and that they are more trusted than words (DePaulo, 1992; Singelis, 1994). People of color and other marginalized groups operate from this belief. In our society, for example, we have learned to use words (spoken or written) to mask or conceal our true thoughts and feelings. This is often the case in race talk as evidenced in the interaction between Daryl and his White colleagues. Note how many of our politicians and lawyers are able to address race issues in the media without revealing much of what they truly think or believe.

Nonverbal behavior provides clues to conscious deceptions or unconscious bias (Utsey et al., 2005). There is evidence that the accuracy of nonverbal communication varies with the part of the body used: Facial expression is more controllable than the hands, followed by the legs and the rest of the body (Hansen, Stevic, & Warner, 1982). If people are unaware of their own biases, their nonverbals are most likely to reveal their true feelings. It is notable that studies suggest that women and minorities are better readers of nonverbal cues than are White males (Hall, 1976; Jenkins, 1982; Pearson, 1985; Weber, 1985). Much of this may be due to their need for physical and psychological safety related to *survival*. For an African American person to survive in a predominantly White society, he or she has to rely on nonverbal cues more often than verbal ones.

An African American male colleague gives the example of how he must constantly be vigilant when traveling in an unknown part of the country. Just to stop at a roadside restaurant may be dangerous to his physical well-being. As a result, when entering a diner, he is quick to observe not only the reactions of the staff (waiter/waitress, cashier, cook, etc.) to his entrance, but the reactions of the patrons as well. Do they stare at him? What type of facial expressions do they have? Do they fall silent? Does he get served immediately, or is there an inordinate delay? These nonverbal cues reveal much about the threat or safety of the environment around him. He may choose to be himself or play the role of a humble Black person who leaves quickly if the situation poses danger. Interestingly, this very same colleague talks about tuning in to nonverbal cues as a means of *psychological survival*. He believes it is important for people of color to accurately read where people are coming from in order to prevent invalidation of the self. In a racial dialogue, these survival mechanisms often come into play in helping them understand others and the context.

Too often, people of color are placed in situations where they are asked to deny their true feelings in order to perpetuate *White deception*. Statements that people of color are oversensitive (paranoid?) may represent a form of denial. When a colleague of color makes a statement such as "I get a strange feeling from John; I feel some racial bias coming out," White colleagues, friends, and others are sometimes too quick to dismiss it with statements like, "You're being oversensitive." Perhaps a better approach would be to say, "What makes you feel that way?" rather than to negate or invalidate what might be an accurate appraisal of nonverbal communication.

Nonverbals as Triggers to Biases and Fears

Often people assume that eliminating bias is a straightforward process that involves the acquisition of knowledge about the various racial/ethnic groups. If we know that Asian Americans and African Americans have different patterns of eye contact and if we know that these patterns signify different things, then we should be able to eliminate biases and stereotypes that we possess. Were it so easy, we might have eradicated racism years ago. While increasing our knowledge base about the lifestyles and experiences of marginalized groups is important, it is not a sufficient condition in itself. Our racist attitudes, beliefs, and feelings are deeply ingrained in our total being. Through years of conditioning they have acquired a strong irrational base, replete with emotional symbolism about each particular racial/ethnic group. Simply opening a text and reading about African Americans and Latinos/Hispanics will not deal with our deep-seated fears and biases.

One of the major barriers to effective communication in a race dialogue is the common assumption that different cultural groups operate according to identical speech and communication conventions. In the United States, it is often assumed that distinctive racial, cultural, and linguistic features are deviant, inferior, or embarrassing (Kochman, 1981; Singelis, 1994; Stanback & Pearce, 1985). These value judgments then become tinged with beliefs that we hold about Black people: racial inferiority, being prone to violence and crime, quick to anger, and a threat to White folks (Irvine & York, 1995; Weber, 1985). The communication style of Black people (manifested in nonverbals) can often trigger off these fears.

The situation between Daryl and his White colleagues seems to represent just such an example. While African Americans may misinterpret White communication styles, it is more likely that Whites will misinterpret Black styles. The direction of the misunderstanding is generally linked to the activating of unconscious triggers or buttons about racist stereotypes and fears they harbor. As we have repeatedly emphasized, one of the dominant stereotypes of African Americans in our society is that of the hostile, angry, prone-to-violence Black male. The more animated and affective communication style, closer conversing distance, prolonged eye contact when speaking, greater bodily movements, and tendency to test ideas in a confrontational/argumentative format all contribute to Whites' belief that their lives are in danger, à la Bill and Jack's reactions to Daryl's communication style.

BEING CONSTRAINED AND SILENCED: IMPACT ON PEOPLE OF COLOR

How does this context of forced compliance, attempting to function in a White Euro-American normed environment, affect the ability and desire of people of color to discuss issues of race? In a series of studies designed to address this question, it was found that participants of color constantly referred to issues of forced compliance, humiliation, and loss of integrity not only when deciding how and when to speak about racial topics, but in many other situations where race did not appear directly involved (Sue, Capodilupo, et al., 2008; Sue, Lin,

Torino, Capodilupo, & Rivera, 2009; Sue, Nadal, et al., 2008; Sue et al., 2011). Two aspects of race talk were identified in our studies for people of color. The first was the participants' awareness of the potential social impact that their race had on White colleagues, neighbors, friends, and strangers. The awareness was associated with their attempts to manage racial stereotypes and racial social stigma that others might unwittingly impose upon them (Harlow, 2003; Sue, Nadal, et al., 2008). The second aspect was situations in which racial microaggressions were directed at these people of color or that they witnessed directed at others. In both cases, these situations often triggered an intense internal struggle about being true to the self and expressing their thoughts honestly or modifying them to avoid negative consequences.

Managing Racial Stigma and Stereotypes

Simply having to interact and communicate with White Americans in different situations—being aware of one's own racial differences and how they may be perceived—was enough to evoke considerable conflict. The research participants in our studies, for example, described multiple incidents involving the pressure to conform to White standards of communication, modifying how they said things and behaved, and the need to fit in and almost act White (Sue, Nadal, et al., 2008). In order to be acceptable and professional, one 25-year-old Black female asserted the following: "In a professional setting, you really have to sort of masquerade your responses. You can't say what's really on your mind, or you have to filter through so many different lenses till it comes out sounding acceptable to whoever's listening" (p. 334). The tactic of modifying one's behavior and/or how one speaks to a White audience seems linked to counteracting perceived stereotypes, fostering a positive image, avoiding reactions that would result in negative outcomes (loss of a promotion, ostracism, being labeled as a troublemaker, etc.), and maintaining one's current elevated status (Harlow, 2003; C. Jones & Shorter-Goodsen, 2003; Ridley, 2005).

An example of the last point is the plight of professors of color who theoretically occupy a high-status position in academia. White professors in institutions of higher education are generally perceived as competent, capable, and possessing special expertise in their field of study, and when teaching classes, students generally accept them as more knowledgeable. Although this statement may hold for White professors, it is not necessarily true for faculty of color (Harlow, 2003; Stanley, 2006; Turner, Gonzalez and Wood, 2008). Several studies suggest that Black professors, for example, feel compelled to provide proof that they deserve to hold the position of professor to White students and colleagues. In our society, White male professors have statuses that are consistent and even anticipated by their White students and colleagues, while Black professors occupy a racial status that is inconsistent with faculty status. Doubts about their academic and leadership credentials are constantly entertained by faculty of color about how they are perceived and may lead to communication and behavioral strategies when they enter a classroom, as stated by two Black faculty members:

First professor:
And I think when I walk in there, other things go through their minds. Probably whether or not I'm good, whether or not I'm tough, whether or not this is going to be a blow-off class for them, whether I'm an affirmative action professor, whether I'm going to be one of those attitudes kind of professor, whether I'm going to be a racist professor, whether I'm going to be the kind of professor who makes white people feel bad about what has happened to black people in America. (Harlow, 2003, p. 353)

Second professor:
I give my credential the first day of class. And I do feel to some extent I have to, and I know nobody else (in this department) does.... So tomorrow I'll stand in front of class and tell them all that I've done and blah, blah, blah.... I've found if I don't do that, I don't get the respect that I would deserve. I'd get more people challenging what I say about (the discipline). (Harlow, 2003, p. 356)

The fear that others will see a Black professor as cold, mean, and intimidating; as unqualified; or as an affirmative action hire forces many to alter the way they behave, respond, and communicate even prior to an interracial encounter. This means they must alter their natural way of communicating or risk being seen as caricatures or stereotypes. We have already mentioned that communication style differences can often trigger stereotypes, biases, and fears from the majority group (Kochman, 1981; Sue & Sue, 2013). This is especially true for African Americans, who must deal with the dominant stereotype of being seen as unintelligent, hostile, angry, and prone to violence.

Dealing With Racial Microaggressions

We have repeatedly emphasized how the daily lives of people of color are filled with incidents of racial microaggressions delivered by well-intentioned Whites and/or through ethnocentric monoculturalism. The microaggressive content encountered by people of color includes *assumption of criminality, lesser intelligence, alien in own land, color blindness, myth of meritocracy, second-class citizenship,* and *pathologizing communication styles* (Sue et al., 2007). When a communication style difference triggers off other microaggressive content (stereotypes—the shy, passive Asian American or the angry Black man/woman), it can be especially demeaning, humiliating, and invalidating to a person of color. When microaggressions occur, they precipitate powerful reactions on a cognitive, behavioral, and emotional level within people of color that have major effects on race talk (Harlow, 2003; Sue, 2010; Sue, Lin, et al., 2009).

Cognitive

On a cognitive level, people of color often report an internal dialogue on whether to speak or not to speak at the moment of a potentially racist occurrence. Many questions are likely to be on the mind of the person: "Did what I think happen, really happen? Was this a deliberate slight or an unintentional one? Is it worth raising an issue or should I just let it go? If I point out the microaggression, how do I prove it? What are the consequences or most likely outcome? Will I be seen as a troublemaker?" Experience has taught many people of color that their observations will be invalidated, that they may be perceived as having a bone to grind with White people, that they are troublemakers, or that they are simply oversensitive (Sue et al., 2011; Sue, Lin, et al., 2009). People of color also recognize the power differential that often resides in favor of the perpetrator so that raising the issue may result in the teacher, employer, neighbor, or others taking actions that impact negatively on the person (not getting a promotion, receiving a lower grade, or having others avoid you).

Behavioral

On a behavioral level, many people of color feel caught in a trap and must change their behavior to conform to the situation or expectations of the majority group. In a classroom situation, for example, one Black student stated, "For me, I know that if I'm in class with people and I don't want to come across as the angry Black woman... I'm not going to stand up and scream" (Sue, Lin, et al., 2009, p. 187). Many Black students report that to convey their message and have it received the right way, they cannot be emotional while speaking. Squelching their natural style of communication to conform to White talk was often described as humiliating. They described the psychological costs as being inauthentic, having sold out, not being true to the self, and a deep sense of losing one's own integrity. Behaviorally, people of color seemed unanimous in ascertaining the degree of threat (danger) or support they were likely to receive in the situation if they brought up the issue. In a classroom situation, for example, students of color report that their decision to engage race talk often depended on the nonverbals they observed among White students and faculty. Behaviors such as eyeball rolling, shifting or slouching in chairs, fidgeting, changing the topic, becoming quiet, and avoiding eye contact were cues of resistance, that the situation was unsafe for students of color, and that the White students and faculty were disinclined to engage in race talk (Harlow, 2003; Sue, Lin, et al., 2009; Sue, Nadal, et al., 2008).

Emotional

In the face of microaggressions, whether in the workplace, classroom, or other public forums, the emotional toll for people of color can be great (Sue, 2010). Three large categories of emotional reactions were identified. First, many people of color report being *incensed* when they felt their integrity was being assailed. Microaggression themes that dealt with criminality, lower intelligence, and being a perpetual foreigner or treated as a second-class citizen (lesser human being) brought on feelings of anger, frustration, annoyance, and sometimes rage. In most cases being treated as inferior or a subhuman being was insulting and offensive. Second, *anxiety* and outright fear of the personal consequences for raising issues of bias and unfairness were always on the minds of the targets. In many cases, people of color described enduring humiliation in silence for fear of retaliation from those with authority and power. Third, many describe an *emotional exhaustion* of having to constantly deal with a never-ending onslaught of microaggressions and being placed in a no-win, damned-if-you-do-and-damned-if-you-don't situation. If a person chooses to confront the microaggression, energy must be expended in defending oneself, oftentimes with negative consequences. If a person chooses not to confront the situation, he or she must endure the affront in silence, often berating oneself for not having the courage to act on his or her convictions.

CONCLUSIONS

In general, our explication in Chapter 6 about ethnocentric monoculturalism and the history of oppression directed at persons of color, along with our discussion of communication styles and the manifestation of racial micro-aggressions in this chapter, provide valuable insights into why race talk may prove difficult for African Americans, Asian Americans, Latino/Hispanic Americans, and Native Americans. Racial dialogues are microcosms of race relations in the United States; reenact the biases, prejudices, and stereotypes of the wider society; invalidate and punish dissenting voices; and force compliance on groups of color. For people of color, race talk symbolizes their lived experience in which they are forced to navigate two worlds on a daily basis: their own world and the White world. The dual navigation creates feelings of uneasiness and disingenuousness and fosters a feeling of being inauthentic and superficial. As stated by Pierce (1995, p. 277), these dual and contradictory dilemmas "create stressful confusions about how to resist oppressions versus when, where, and how to accommodate it."

Why Is It Difficult for White People to Honestly Talk About Race?

CHAPTER EIGHT

"I'm Not Racist!"

In the last two chapters we specifically addressed the reasons why race talk proves difficult for people of color. In the next two chapters, we focus on reasons why many Whites find the topic disconcerting as well as difficult. The discomfort in racial dialogues leads to *cognitive avoidance, emotional avoidance,* and *behavioral avoidance.* These forms of avoidance are illustrated in one form or another by the following authors.

> To date, my biggest discovery is that I didn't really believe that people were being discriminated against because of their race. I could hear them say it, but in my head, I kept running a parallel reason from the White perspective. A Chinese lady says that her party had to wait longer while Whites kept getting seated in front of them. I say, other people had made reservations. A Black man says that the receptionist was rude, and made him wait longer because he's Black. I say she had a bad day, and the person he was there to see was busy. A Puerto Rican couple says that the second they drove into Modesto...a cop started tailing them, and continued to do so until they reached their hotel, which they opted to drive right on by because they didn't feel safe. I say, there's nothing to be afraid of in Modesto. It's a nice little town. And surely the cop wasn't following you because you're Puerto Rican. I bet your hotel was on his way to the station. I know that for every story in which something bad happens to someone because of their race, I can counter it with a White interpretation. And while I was listening with a sympathetic ear,

I silently continued to offer up alternative explanations, benign explanations that kept my world in equilibrium. (Rabow, Venieris, & Dhillon, 2014, p. 189)

I have a fear of speaking as a member of the dominant group.... My feelings of fear stem from not wanting to be labeled as being a racist. I think that fear also stems from the inner fear that I do not want to know what happens to people of color every day. I may not directly be a racist, but not reacting or speaking up to try to change things is a result of my guilt.... This is a frightening prospect because I do not want to see the possibility that I have been a racist. Awareness is scary. (Rabow et al., 2014, p. 192)

All the white people I know deplore racism. We feel helpless about racial injustice in society, and we don't know what to do about the racism we sense in our own groups and lives. Persons of other races avoid our groups when they accurately sense the racism we don't see.... Few white people socialize or work politically with people of other races, even when our goals are the same. We don't want to be racist—so much of the time we go around trying not to be, by pretending we're not. Yet white supremacy is basic in American social and economic history, and this racist heritage has been internalized by American white people of all classes. We have all absorbed white racism; pretense and mystification only compound the problem.... We avoid black people because their presence brings painful questions to mind. Is it okay to talk about watermelon or mention "black coffee"? Should we use black slang and tell racial jokes? How about talking about our experiences in Harlem, or mentioning our black lovers? Should we conceal the fact that our mother still employs a black cleaning lady?... We're embarrassedly aware of trying to do our best, but to "act natural" at the same time. No wonder we're more comfortable in all-white situations where these dilemmas don't arise. (Winter, 1977, p. 24)

Questions: Why is it so difficult for many White people to honestly talk about race? In looking at the statements of the three authors, can you discern themes that may shed light on this question? Why do you think the first author has difficulty believing the stories told by people of color? What is the most salient fear that the second author avoids facing? Where do the feelings of guilt come from? What function do you believe these emotions have upon race talk? When talking about race and racism, have you ever experienced the helplessness, conflicts, and discomfort expressed by the third author? Does the feeling of helplessness lead to inaction? If race talk evokes the many reactions described here, is there little wonder that most Whites would prefer to avoid race talk?

The three narratives provide clues as to what race talk is likely to evoke in well-intentioned White Americans: denial and strong emotions such as fear, guilt, confusion, and helplessness. These powerful psychological emotions prevent Whites from engaging in honest race talk by denying the lived realities of people of color; inducing avoidance strategies such as minimizing or diminishing the importance of the topic; and hedging, mitigating, or excusing one's own beliefs and actions (Rabow et al., 2014; Todd & Abrams, 2011; van Dijk, 1992, 1993). Let's explore in further depth the meaning and implications of the three narratives provided here.

COGNITIVE AVOIDANCE—RACISM DENIAL

First, the account by the first author reveals a pattern of entertaining alternative explanations to the stories told by persons of color about their experiences of prejudice and discrimination. Although the author describes listening sympathetically, it was clear that he or she silently did not believe that these were instances of racism; other more benign explanations could account for the events described. This is not atypical for many White Americans when they listen to stories of discrimination from people of color (Bolgatz, 2005; Young, 2003). They are seen as exaggerating or misperceiving situations. But, by remaining silent, the author may have unintentionally communicated inauthentic agreement. In this situation, the White person may have lost a valuable opportunity to have a meaningful dialogue with persons of color, and to more deeply understand the worldview of the person. Only in an honest exchange of ideas can true communication occur.

Silence has been identified as one strategy used by many Whites to mask or conceal their true thoughts and feelings about racial issues (Sue, 2010; Sue, Torino, Capodilupo, Rivera, & Lin, 2009; van Dijk, 1992). Ironically, depending on the context of silence and how it is mitigated by nonverbal behavior, the communication is often misinterpreted in a negative light. At worst, the recipient may infer racial bias and, at best, it may be seen as indifference (Kochman, 1981; Ramsey & Birk, 1983; Tatum, 1992). As mentioned previously, attempting to appear nonprejudiced through silence, avoidance, and lack of disclosure may actually make someone appear more biased because great energy is expended to conceal thoughts and feelings, thereby making the person appear less friendly or involved (Apfelbaum, Sommers, & Norton, 2008; Sue, 2010).

Denial through disbelief, unwillingness to consider alternative scenarios, distortion, fabrication, and rationalization are all mechanisms frequently used by Whites during race talk to prevent them from thinking about or discussing topics of race and racism in an honest manner (Feagin, 2001; Sue, Rivera, Capodilupo, Lin, & Torino, 2010; van Dijk, 1992). Denials that work against honest race talk come in many forms. There is denial that they are prejudiced, denial that racism still exists, denial that they are responsible for the oppression of others, denial of their advantaged and privileged status, denial that they hold power over people of color, and even denial that they are White (Feagin & Vera, 1992; McIntosh, 2002; Sue, 2010; Tatum, 1992; Todd & Abrams, 2011).

All these denials are played out in both conscious and unconscious ways that are often confusing and anxiety provoking for White Americans when they talk race. Little wonder that when White Americans break their silence on the topic, their verbalizations have been observed to be unclear, anxiety ridden, constricted, ambiguous, filled with qualifiers, tentative, and oftentimes, *incoherent* (Bonilla-Silva, 2006; Utsey, Gernat, & Hammar, 2005). The result is that the well-intentioned White participant is rightly or wrongly perceived as being hung up about race, being biased and prejudiced, having something to hide, and not being truthful.

People of color are very aware of and sensitive to the language of denials that often occur outside the level of conscious awareness of White Americans (Hanna, Talley, & Guindon, 2000; van Dijk, 1992). In race talk, White denials occur in everyday conversations, textbooks, news media, and all forms of public and organizational settings. Denials take many shapes and when used by Whites in a conversation on race and racism, they trigger warning signals to people of color about the motives of the speaker. Several categories of denials can be identified.

Denials of Personal Bias, Prejudice, and Discrimination

"I have nothing against Blacks, but *my customers are uncomfortable with them.*"
"*I know this may sound racist*, but I'm going to say it anyway."
"I have nothing against interracial marriages, *but I worry about the children.*"
"I'm not biased because *I have a Chinese sister-in-law.*"
"I'm not racist; *I have several Latino friends.*"
"I believe *the most qualified person should get the job.*"
"I'm not prejudiced, but *I can see how other Whites can be racist.*"

In a society where the norms, values, and laws prohibit racial discrimination and prejudice, to be perceived as a racist is abhorrent and to be publicly condemned (Apfelbaum et al., 2008; van Dijk, 1992). The preceding representative statements allow Whites, however, to express, convey, justify, and legitimate personal racial/ethnic bias through disclaimers and denials that mask personal prejudice. In many respects they translate the biased opinions to ones of fact (rather than prejudice), and/or offer a rationalization that justifies their substance/concerns. A person may state, for example, that they are not against interracial marriages, but legitimately express their hidden bias through concern about biracial offspring and the many challenges such children will encounter in life. Or, when a White employer tells a candidate of color that he or she believes the most qualified person should be hired, the employer disclaims any possible personal bias if the job is offered to a White person. Another ploy taken by many Whites is to acknowledge and discuss racism as residing only in other people, but that they are free of it. This is often reinforced through self-deception: beliefs that true racism is only reserved for extreme acts of racial hatred (hate crimes) and resides only in White supremacists, and that they are personally immune from inheriting racist beliefs and attitudes.

All of these strategies allow the person to hide his or her prejudice through distortion or provide a seemingly alternative rational or legitimate reason. Further, they are nearly impregnable to unmask in that they are difficult to argue against. Who would argue, for example, against hiring the most qualified individual? Likewise, statements that one has friends or even relatives of color are intended to disclaim personal prejudice by providing proof through association. Or, stating that something may sound racist warns others not to misconstrue their statement, because what is about to be said is honest and not racist. Thus, to the listener, if it comes across as bias, it represents a misinterpretation (the problem resides in the misperception of the person listening—he or she is to be blamed).

Denials of Societal Bias, Prejudice, and Discrimination

"We live in a *postracial era*."
"Whites aren't prejudiced; look how we elected the *first Black president*."
"Racism is a *thing of the past*."
"My parents and grandparents *didn't own slaves*."
"We *aren't responsible for the sins of our forefathers*."
"*Anyone can succeed* in this society if they work hard enough."
"We are *not a racist society*."

All of these statements represent a denial that group- and institutional-based racism exists in society, or at least that it no longer serves as a significant force in the lives of people of color. It relegates racism to a thing of the past; inaccurately diminishes the effects of historical injustices on contemporary inequities; suggests a level playing field in which anyone, regardless of race, creed, or color, can succeed; assumes a fair and just society; and blames people of color for their own victimization (blaming the victim). In many ways, these forms of denial are likely to evoke stronger negative reactions from people of color during race talk because individual disclaimers affect mainly interpersonal relationships, but societal disclaimers strike at the heart of the omnipresent and continuing lived reality of racism encountered in the day-to-day lives of people of color.

Although individual discrimination is hurtful and takes a toll on the psychological well-being of persons of color, societal bias also impacts the standard of living by creating disparities in education, employment, and health care (J. M. Jones, 1997; Sue, 2010). Although people of color see the election of Barack Obama as a major milestone in the history of the United States, their lived realities continue to indicate that racism, bias, and discrimination are alive as well. It frustrates them that their White brothers and sisters are unable to see the world through realistic lenses.

Denials Through Deflection

"I don't like to always have to say things that are *politically correct*."
"People of color keep playing *the race card*."
"White people this . . . White people that . . . why are White people *blamed for everything?*"
"You are being *paranoid and oversensitive*."
"You shouldn't take it that way because it was *not my intention!*"
"Why does *everything always have to be about race?*"
"This is really *not a race issue*, but a class issue."
"People of color *are equally racist*."
"*Affirmative action discriminates* against Whites."
"Whites are now the *victims of reverse discrimination*."

In race talk, denials through deflection are defensive preemptive strikes against potential implicit or explicit accusations of racial biases (van Dijk, 1992). In many cases, they tend to portray people of color as the ones who are unfair in race dialogues and that their assertions or allegations are suspect and without substance. These verbal exchanges are intended to imply a deficiency in either the communicator or in the idea through changing the topic, invalidating the legitimacy of an assertion, minimizing the importance of the issue, pathologizing a response, and equating one form of oppression with another.

First, claims of reverse racism especially on topics of affirmative action allow majority group members (Whites) to turn the tables on their accusers by implying they are now the ones being discriminated against. Although this flies in the face of all economic, educational, and employment data (APA Presidential Task Force, 2012; J. M. Jones, 1997), the focus of the debate now becomes one of portraying White Americans as the victims. Second, another ploy often used is to dilute and diminish the importance of the issue is relegating racism to one of many forms of social injustices: classicism, sexism, heterosexism, ableism, or ageism. Whites advocating this approach assert that fairness is to provide equal time to discussing and considering these many isms, and that they may be the primary issue, not racism. Third, shifting the focus from action to intention is another maneuver often used in race talk by Whites. Here the person who may have engaged in behaviors or made a statement perceived as biased claims, "I did not intend it that way." The relationship of intent to action is often used in criminal law to determine the degree of responsibility of the perpetrator (murder and manslaughter varies depending upon the intent). In race talk, shifting the topic to intent is tactically very effective because proving biased intent is virtually impossible.

Other forms of deflection involve claiming that people of color are equally racist, and are biased against Whites and one another. Although true in some cases, the strategy allows Whites to absolve their feelings of guilt ("People of color are racist too!"), provides an excuse for inaction ("Why should we change? These people can't even get along with one another."), refocuses the issue of racism as equally distributed among all groups ("Big deal, all groups are racist."), and allows blurring the distinction between individual bias and the power of White systemic oppression ("Your experiences of discrimination are no different than mine.").

Portraying people of color as the problem is often manifested in claiming that the race card is being played and/or that Whites are forced to be politically correct in their pronouncements. The implication here is that issues of race and racism when mentioned by people of color are not legitimate (playing the race card for an ulterior purpose) and that political correctness prevents honesty or truth from being expressed by Whites. In essence, allegations of playing the race card and the pressures of political correctness are games of verbal jujitsu used by dominant group members to portray and redefine White talk as the silenced, oppressed, and dissenting voice, while back talk is portrayed as the untouchable incorrect stance that needs to be challenged. These allegations are conservative ploys used to silence back talk and allow White talk to dominate and to reinforce the master narrative of Whiteness. People of color who attempt to break away from these constraints earn labels as being troublemakers, people who have an ax to grind with White folks, or who are being excessively paranoid and oversensitive.

EMOTIONAL AVOIDANCE—FEAR, GUILT, AND OTHER FEELINGS

Why are denials so prevalently used by White Americans in race talk? The opening narrative provided by the second author reveals fears, anxieties, and feelings of guilt related to increasing awareness of his or her own biases. The author readily admits to a reluctance to talk about race and racial issues for fear of being labeled a racist, fear of realizing his or her own racism, the guilt experienced by virtue of silence and inaction, and not wanting to acknowledge the daily pain suffered by people of color. In many respects, this last point raises an important awareness that is being strongly defended against by the White author. If indeed, he or she has unwittingly engaged in racist behaviors and has unknowingly allowed systems of injustice to flourish, the pain and suffering inflicted upon people of color is partly due to his or her own complicity in a racist system. This proves to be a frightening and uncomfortable realization for many White Americans. Blinders of naïveté, innocence, and obliviousness become removed when awareness of racism and its dynamics increases.

In Chapter 2, we identified four major fear categories experienced by White Americans when race talk occurs: (1) fear of appearing racist, (2) fear of realizing their racism, (3) fear of confronting White privilege, and (4) fear of taking personal responsibility to end racism. The latter two fears will be explored more thoroughly in the next chapter; in this section we concentrate primarily on the emotional experience of White Americans as they become increasingly aware of their racist attitudes, feelings, and behaviors (Sue, 2013). Although fear and anxiety are the major emotional reactions by Whites as they enter a discourse on race, many other nested or embedded feelings make their presence felt as well (Sue et al., 2010; Sue, Torino, et al., 2009; Tatum, 1992; Todd & Abrams, 2011). Unless these are acknowledged and deconstructed, they will continue to hold an invisible power over Whites, making it difficult to gain insight into their psychological conflicts and preventing them from freely discussing issues of race, racism, and Whiteness (Tatum, 1992, 2002). In a number of studies, White participants have identified several powerful emotions experienced during race talk that interfered with their ability to engage in a meaningful discourse on race (Sue et al., 2010; Sue, Torino, et al., 2009; Todd & Abrams, 2011).

Anxiety and Fear

Anxiety is the primary subjective emotion encountered by Whites during race talk. In fact, one of our studies (Sue et al., 2010) identified a global aspect of fear and apprehension that exists in many Whites even prior to a discussion of race. It is best understood as a generalized predisposition of existing feelings or thoughts (dread) associated with topics on race. The power of social conditioning and the attendant taboos provide a biased lens through which Whites approach, view, and interpret the meaning of race talk. Thus, when race talk presents itself, they are already inclined to approach it in a guarded manner and to view it as a potentially unpleasant experience. Regardless, all our participants described their fears of engaging a conversation on the topic because they could be misunderstood or perceived as being racist. Others went further, however, in describing having to confront the realization that they were, indeed, racist, or at least acknowledge that they had stereotypes, biases, and prejudices toward people of color. The insight and awareness is so painful and fearful because it directly challenges White people's self-image of themselves as good, moral, and decent human beings who do not discriminate. Facing this potential awareness created high levels of anxiety and resulted in maneuvers to avoid confronting their meanings.

As mentioned previously, silence or not participating in the discussion, denials of personal and societal racism, or physically leaving the situation were notable ploys used in race talk. Many of the fears (being perceived as racist and/or realizing they were racist) were acknowledged by our White participants (Sue et al., 2010; Sue, Torino, et al., 2009). They described physiological reactions of anxiety like a pounding heart, dry mouth, tense muscles, and perspiration. One participant stated, "I tried hard to say something thoughtful and it's hard for me to say, and my heart was pounding when I said it." Others described feeling intimidated in the discussions, stammering when trying to say something, being overly concerned about offending others, having a strong sense of confusion as to what was going on, censoring thoughts or statements that could be misunderstood, feeling reluctance in expressing their thoughts, being overwhelmed by the mix of emotions they felt, and hearing constriction in their own voices.

These thoughts, feelings, and concerns blocked participants from fully participating in a race dialogue because they became so concerned about themselves (turning inward), that they could not freely be open and listen to the messages being communicated by people of color. Indeed, their whole goal seemed to be a defensive stance to ward off the messages and meanings being communicated to them that challenged their worldviews, themselves as racial beings, and their potential roles as oppressors.

Defensiveness and Anger

Although defensiveness and anger are two different emotions, studies seem to indicate a high relationship between the two (Apfelbaum et al., 2008; Sue, Torino, et al., 2009; Zou & Dickter, 2013). One represents a protective stance and the other an attempt to strike back at the perpetrator (in many cases statements by people of color). In race talk, many White participants described feeling defensive (unfairly accused of being biased or racist, blamed for past racial injustices, and responsible for the current state of race relations): "I'm tired of hearing 'White people this . . . White people that' . . . Why are we always blamed for everything?"

When people of color talk racism, Whites seem to interpret statements as a personal accusation, and rather than reach out to understand the content, respond in a defensive and protective posture. In many cases, even statements of racial facts/statistics such as definitions of racism, disparities in income and education, segregation of neighborhoods, hate crime figures, and so forth arouse defensiveness in many Whites. Their defense response to a racial dialogue is seen as protection against (a) criticism ("You just don't get it!"), (b) revealing personal shortcomings ("You are racist!"), or (c) perceived threat to their self-image and egos ("I'm not a racist—I'm a good person."). Because of this stance, Whites who feel attacked may engage in behaviors or argumentative ploys that present denials and counterpoints because they view the racial dialogue as a win–lose proposition. Warding off the legitimacy of the points raised by people of color becomes the primary goal rather than listening and attempting to understand the material or point of view.

When Whites feel wrongly accused, they may respond with anger and engage in a counterattack when a racial topic arises. It appears that anger in race talk stems from two sources: (1) feeling unfairly accused (defensiveness) and/or (2) being told their substance, stance, or position taken is wrong. When back talk occurs, many Whites may feel offended and perceive the allegations as a provocation or an attack that requires retaliation. Anger may be aroused when Whites feel offended ("How dare you imply that about me."), wronged ("I am deeply hurt you see me that way."), or denied their good standing ("Don't associate me with racists!"). Unlike defensiveness that defends one's own stance, anger turns its attention to attacking the threatening behavior of others. Given the choice of the fight-or-flight response, Whites make a choice to take verbal action in stopping the threatening accusations. The strategy used is to discredit the substance of an argument and/or to derogate the communicator, often through a personal attack (angry Black man/woman). In many respects, anger and defensiveness may become so aroused that the person loses control of their self-monitoring capacities and the ability to accurately assess the external environment. These latter two characteristics are extremely important for a successful dialogue on race.

Guilt, Regret, and Remorse

During race talk, many Whites admit to feeling guilty, although most tend to say that they "are made to feel guilty" by people of color, especially when unjustly accused (Sue, 2003). This statement actually suggests a distancing strategy in localizing guilt as external to the person rather than one rightfully residing and felt internally. Guilt as an emotion occurs when a person believes they have violated an internal moral code, and that they have compromised their own standards of conduct. The question becomes, why should Whites feel guilty when topics of race, racism, or Whiteness are discussed? If indeed they are not racist, not responsible for the racial sins of the past, and not responsible for current injustices, then neither would they feel guilt, nor could they be *made to feel guilty*. As seen in the statements by the second author at the beginning, the answer seems to be that at some level of consciousness, Whites realize that they have lived lies of self-deception and that they do hold responsibility for the current oppression of people of color in the United States, whether through action or inaction (Helms, 1992; Spanierman, Poteat, Beer & Armstrong, 2006; Tatum, 1992).

Some have coined the term *White guilt* to refer to the individual and collective feelings of culpability experienced by some Whites for the racist treatment of people of color, both historically and currently (Goodman, 2001; Spanierman, Todd, & Anderson, 2009; Tatum, 1992). In race talk, many Whites find guilt extremely uncomfortable because it means that they have violated a moral standard that they are disinclined to acknowledge. What is that moral standard? Being a good, moral, and decent human being who does not discriminate; being a nonracist; living a life that speaks to equality and justice; and being a humane person who treats everyone with respect and dignity are the positive standards that are being breached. Compromising these moral standards and beliefs and acting in ways that violate them bring on bad feelings of guilt and remorse.

Researchers have identified White guilt as one of the major psychosocial costs of racism for White individuals because it impacts empathic reactions to targets of racism (Spanierman et al., 2006; Spanierman et al., 2009; Todd & Abrams, 2011). In other words, guilt seems to have several functions in race talk. First, the manifestation of guilt among Whites signals an internal conflict involving transgression of moral standards and culpability. It may be experienced as a generalized low level of unease or discomfort, not fully acknowledged as guilt. Second, its presence in Whites signals that self-awareness of one's complicity in racism is beginning to bubble to the surface. Denial, mystification, and self-deception are weakening, and guilt, remorse, and regret are likely to follow if race talk is continued. The problem here is that guilt can serve a dual function; it propels people to take responsibility for their actions, or it negatively diverts and works against self-awareness. Third, unless handled effectively, guilt may work against successful racial dialogues. Spanierman and colleagues (Spanierman et al., 2006; Spanierman et al., 2009) find support for these two forms of guilt. They label this second type *fearful guilt* in which Whites exhibit not only high guilt, but high fear of interracial interactions as well. Empathic ability is seriously compromised and people exhibiting fearful guilt report the fewest number of interracial friendships. The main goal for fearful guilt is to defend and ward off awareness and to preserve the positive self-image of the self as a White person.

BEHAVIORAL AVOIDANCE—HELPLESSNESS AND HOPELESSNESS

Although helplessness and hopelessness can rightly be classified as emotions, they also border on providing direct excuses for inaction. The third opening author provides some insights into her feeling of helplessness and what she can do to deal with her creeping awareness of the racism that resides in her and others. When engaged in race talk, participants often describe two emotions that vary from helplessness (feeling powerless) to hopelessness (despair). These feelings are expressed by the author when she realizes the vastness and magnitude of individual, institutional, and societal racism; how they make themselves felt in all facets of human life; and how deeply racism is ingrained in the individual psyches of people and in the entire nation.

In most respects, the author's denial has broken down and her self-awareness places her in a very uncomfortable position. Individuals who have come to recognize and own their biased beliefs and prejudices, their roles in perpetuating racism, the pain their obliviousness has inflicted on people of color, and their privileged and advantaged position in society may feel overwhelmed by the magnitude of the problem. This may cause paralysis or inaction. Taking steps to make the invisible visible and to eradicate bias and discrimination requires concrete action. As long as the person feels helpless and hopeless, inaction will result.

Although guilt continues over realizing their culpability over past deeds, it is compounded by the knowledge that continued inaction on their part allows for the perpetuation of racism in the self and others. Thus taking action is a means to alleviate feelings of guilt. The emotions of helplessness and hopelessness make themselves felt in two different arenas: one is internal (personal change) and the other is external (system change). In race talk, for example, Whites at this juncture of development ask two primary questions.

First, is the question of *How does one change?* What needs to be changed? How does one become a *nonracist person?* How do I break the shackles of social conditioning that have taught me that some groups are more worthy than others and that other groups are less worthy? Many Whites often make these comments: "I don't know where to begin." "If I am not aware of my racism, how do I become aware of it?" "Tell me what I must do to rid myself of these prejudices." "Should I attend more workshops?" "I feel so confused, helpless, impotent, and paralyzed."

The second question is *What must I do to eradicate racism in the broader society?* While self-change requires becoming a *nonracist* person, societal change requires becoming an *antiracist* one. This latter role means becoming an advocate and actively intervening when injustice makes its presence felt at the individual level (objecting to a racist joke, confronting friends, neighbors, colleagues about their prejudices, etc.), and at the institutional level (supporting civil rights issues, making sure a multicultural curriculum is being taught in schools, openly supporting social justice groups, etc.).

Helplessness that is felt by Whites in race talk, unless adequately deconstructed as to what it means, can easily provide an excuse or rationalization for inaction. *What good would it do? I'm only one person, how can I make any difference? The problem is so big, whatever I do will only be a drop in the bucket.* Feeling helpless and hopeless are legitimate feelings unless used as an excuse to escape responsibility for taking any form of action. Helplessness is modifiable when the person is provided options and strategies that can be done to increase their awareness and personal growth, and when they are provided with the tools to dismantle racism in our society. We will address these change action strategies in the last few chapters.

Hopelessness, however, is one of despair and of giving up, a self-belief that no action will matter and no solution will work. Helplessness and hopelessness associated with the need for change and action can be paralytic. The excuse for inaction and thus avoiding race talk does not necessarily reside in simply knowing what to do, but in very basic fears eloquently expressed by Tatum (2002):

> Fear is a powerful emotion, one that immobilizes, traps words in our throats, and stills our tongues. Like a deer on the highway, frozen in the panic induced by the lights of an oncoming car, when we are afraid it seems that we cannot think, we cannot speak, we cannot move.... What do we fear? Isolation from friends and family, ostracism for speaking of things that generate discomfort, rejection by those who may be offended by what we have to say, the loss of privilege or status for speaking in support of those who have been marginalized by society, physical harm caused by the irrational wrath of those who disagree with your stance? (pp. 115–116)

In other words, helplessness and hopelessness are emotions that can provide cover for not taking action. They allow many Whites to not change for fear that their actions will result in the negative consequences previously expressed.

EMOTIONAL ROADBLOCKS TO RACE TALK

There are many other powerful emotions often experienced by Whites during race talk. They include sadness, disappointment, humiliation, blame, invalidation, and so on. These feelings, along with those already discussed can make their appearance in dialogues on race at any point. The unpleasantness of these emotions and their potentially disturbing meanings make avoidance of racial dialogues a common strategy used by White Americans. As we have seen, the politeness and academic protocols discourage the negative expression of intense feelings, and oftentimes consider it to border on irrationality. There is great fear that those involved in a heated exchange may lose control and begin attacking one another. In one of our studies, we found that White professors, for example, tried to dampen down the emotions in race talk and table the discussion for fear of losing control of the classroom situation (Sue, Torino, et al., 2009). Choosing not to deal with the conflict, however, led to the presence of an unresolved emotionally charged situation in the classroom that continued to affect the relationships between students despite not talking about it.

As long as emotions are left untouched, unacknowledged, and unexplored, they will serve as emotional roadblocks to successful race talk. Our research suggests that successful race talk must allow for the free expression of nested and impacted feelings, acknowledge their legitimacy and importance in dialogues, and be deconstructed so their meanings are made clear (Sue, 2013; Sue et al., 2010; Sue, Torino, et al., 2009). Rather than seeing emotions as a hindrance and barrier to race talk and rather than shutting them down, allowing them to bubble to the surface actually frees the mind and body to achieve understanding and insight. The cathartic relationship between memories, fears, stereotypic images, and the emotional release of feelings is captured in this passage by Sara Winter (1977, p. 27), who describes her own racial awakening:

> Let me explain this healing process in more detail. We must unearth all the words and memories we generally try not to think about, but which are inside us all the time: "nigger," "Uncle Tom," "jungle bunny," "Oreo"; lynching, cattle prods, castrations, rapists, "black pussy," and black men with their huge penises, and hundreds more. (I shudder as I write.) We need to review three different kinds of material: (1) All our personal memories connected with blackness and black people including everything we can recall hearing or reading; (2) all the racist images and stereotypes we've ever heard, particularly the grossest and most hurtful ones; (3) any race-related things we ourselves said, did or omitted doing which we feel bad about today.... Most whites begin with a good deal of amnesia. Eventually the memories crowd in, especially when several people pool recollections. Emotional release is a vital part of the process. Experiencing feelings seems to allow further recollections to come. I need persistent encouragement from my companions to continue.

Interestingly, when race talk is discussed, participants and scholars seldom describe positive emotions that come from such an undertaking. This begs the question "Is race talk always unpleasant?" The answer may lie in what stage of the racial dialogue participants have achieved. I must confess that only in a few instances of an extended racial dialogue (over several months in a classroom environment) have I witnessed expressions of elation, joy, and pride in a few of the White students. In these cases, it appears that they have achieved a fuller understanding of themselves as racial/cultural beings, developed meaningful interracial friendships, acknowledged their privileged status in life, increased their empathic abilities, realized that personal and systemic change is a lifelong commitment, and become allies in the struggle for equal rights (Kiselica, 1999; Spanierman et al., 2009). These personal changes are a lifelong journey, and expecting them to occur in a workshop, classroom, or singular event, even over an extended period of time, is an unrealistic expectation. Perhaps each success-ful individual racial dialogue should be perceived as planting seeds that will blossom fully in the near future.

CHAPTER NINE

"I'm Not White; I'm Italian!"

In a field study reported by Sue (2003), the following responses were obtained to the question "What does it mean to be White?"

42-year-old White businessman

Q: What does it mean to be White?

A: Frankly, I don't know what you're talking about!

Q: Aren't you White?

A: Yes, but I come from Italian heritage. I'm Italian, not White.

Q: Well then, what does it mean to be Italian?

A: Pasta, good food, love of wine (obviously agitated). This is getting ridiculous!

26-year-old White female college student

Q: What does it mean to be White?

A: Is this a trick question? . . . I've never thought about it. . . . Well, I know that lots of Black people see us as being prejudiced and all that stuff. I wish people would just forget about race differences and see one another as human beings. People are people and we should all be proud to be Americans.

34-year-old White female stockbroker

Q: What does it mean to be White?

A: I don't know (laughing), I've never thought about it.

Q: Are you White?

A: Yes, I suppose so (seems very amused).

Q: Why haven't you thought about it?

A: Because it's not important to me.

Q: Why not?

A: It doesn't enter into my mind because it doesn't affect my life. Besides, we are all individuals. Color isn't important.

(Sue, 2003, pp. 115–117)

Reflection Questions: Is this a fair or unfair question? Can you discern any common responses among the three given? In what ways do they differ? How do Whites view themselves as a racial/cultural group? What seems to prevent these three individuals from viewing themselves as White? If asked what it means to be White, would people of color also find difficulty answering the question? Why or why not? If you were to ask an African American or Asian American what it means to be Black or Asian American, how do you think they would respond?

These reflection questions are important to explore and consider because they potentially provide a deeper understanding of why racial dialogues are difficult to bridge. In Chapter 2 we identified four major fears that prevent many White Americans from openly addressing issues of race: (1) fear of appearing racist, (2) fear of realizing their racism, (3) fear of confronting White privilege, and (4) fear of taking personal responsibility to end racism. In the last chapter we addressed the first two fears, and in this one we focus upon the latter two.

WHAT DOES IT MEAN TO BE WHITE?

Research on Whiteness, White privilege, and White racial identity development point to one of the greatest barriers to race talk for many White Americans: *the invisibility of their Whiteness* (Bell, 2003; Helms, 1992; Spanierman, Poteat, Beer, & Armstrong, 2006; Tatum, 1992; Todd & Abrams, 2011). Just as ethnocentric monoculturalism and implicit bias achieve their oppressive power through invisibility, so too does Whiteness (Boysen, 2010; Sue, 2004). During a racial conversation, many Whites appear oblivious to the meaning of their Whiteness, how it intrudes and disadvantages people of color, and how it affects the way Whites perceive the world (Bell, 2002; Sue, 2013).

Indeed, denials of being White or confusion surrounding its meaning hamper awareness that could result in successful race talk (Todd & Abrams, 2011). The title of this chapter, "I'm not White; I'm Italian!" illustrates the denial and invisibility of Whiteness. Unfortunately, the omnipresence of Whiteness when unacknowledged oppresses people of color because it assails their psychological well-being and creates disparities in their standard of living (APA Presidential Task Force, 2012; J. M. Jones, 1997; Sue, 2010). The responses from these three White individuals provide us with the seeds of understanding the psychological dynamics of Whiteness (or the avoidance of talking about it).

First, it is clear that many White people do not see themselves as White, but as an ethnic group: Italian, Irish, German, Jew, and so on (Helms, 1990, 1992). Yet, although not true for most Jews, when pursued as to what being Italian means to the White businessman, he can only provide a superficial meaning of his ethnic identity. One might also surmise a degree of irritation and/or defensiveness experienced by the man at being asked such a "nonsensical" question. His emotional reaction itself is an important source of data in understanding the invisibility of Whiteness. For him, identifying with an ethnic group is less threatening and allows him to avoid identification with his Whiteness (Helms, 1992). The question becomes, therefore, what is threatening and what makes him defensive?

Second, unlike people of color, Whites seldom think about their racial/cultural identity (Rabow, Venieris, & Dhillon, 2014; Todd & Abrams, 2011). As mentioned earlier, people of color are very color conscious and aware of their racial/cultural differences and identities from the moment they awake in the morning until they go to bed at night. Indeed, the young female college student expresses surprise at being asked such a question, seems baffled by it, and finally responds with "never thought about it." Likewise, the female stockbroker also admits not thinking about her Whiteness, but both of them give slightly different reasons for not doing so. The luxury of never having to consider one's own Whiteness has been labeled by many as a form of White privilege, a concept we will shortly explore (McIntosh, 2002; Sue, 2010).

Third, when the latter two are asked as to why they don't think about their Whiteness, the college student casually mentions that Blacks associate

Whiteness with prejudice, whereas the stockbroker says it is unimportant to her because "it doesn't affect my life." The former response seems to suggest a certain degree of awareness of prejudicial associations with Whiteness, and her avoidance of thinking about being White may be a sign of defensiveness. The response that color is unimportant, and that Whiteness does not affect the stockbroker's life point to the myth of color blindness; one's racial identity has no bearing on the life circumstance of Whites and people of color (Helms, 1992). In this case the invisibility of Whiteness and color blindness are two sides of the same coin.

Last, it is important to note that both the college student and the stockbroker give responses that seem to dilute or minimize differences. The student expresses a belief that "people are people," that we "should see one another as human beings," and that we should just be proud "to be American." The stockbroker states that "color is unimportant," and that "we are all individuals." As mentioned in Chapter 8, both individuals try to avoid or deny group differences (racial) by only acknowledging the universal level (human beings) or the individual level (everyone is unique) of identity. By viewing people only as individuals or as human beings, Whites are often able to avoid the group level of identity, and thus avoid acknowledging race or color and the ensuing implications (Sue & Sue, 2013).

Based on these reactions and similar ones by other Whites, it is clear that the consciousness of being White is not easily entertained because of its invisibility and negative associations with prejudice that evoke defensiveness. What, we can ask, is the association with Whiteness that is so frightening and uncomfortable for many White Americans to acknowledge? We have a clue from the following response a Black male salesman made when asked the identical question.

39-year-old Black male Salesman

Q: What does it mean to be White?

A: Is this a school exercise or something? Never expected someone to ask me that question in the middle of the city. Do you want the politically correct answer or what I really think?

Q: Can you tell me what you really think?

A: You won't quit, will you (laughing)? If you're White, you're right. If you're Black, step back.

Q: What does that mean?

A: White folks are always thinking they know all the answers. A Black man's word is worth less than a White man's. When White customers come into our dealership and see me standing next to the cars, I become invisible to them. Actually, they may see me as a well-dressed janitor (laughs), or actively avoid me. They will search out a White salesman. Or, when I explain something to a customer, they always check out the information with my White colleagues. They don't trust me. When I mention this to our manager, who is White, he tells me I'm oversensitive and being paranoid. That's what being White means. It means having the authority or power to tell me what's really happening even though I know it's not. Being White means you can fool yourself into thinking that you're not prejudiced, when you are. That's what it means to be White. (Sue, 2003, pp. 118–119)

The response given by the Black salesman is markedly different from the other three responders by its specificity, clarity, and perspective. In essence, he believes being White means (a) having the power to define reality, (b) possessing unconscious biases that people of color are less competent and capable, (c) deceiving the self that one is not prejudiced, and (d) being oblivious to how Whiteness disadvantages people of color and advantages White people. This worldview is in marked contrast to the White respondents who would rather not think about their Whiteness, are uncomfortable or react negatively to being labeled *White*, deny its importance in affecting their lives, and seem to believe that they are unjustifiably accused of being bigoted by virtue of being White. Strangely enough, Whiteness is most visible when it is denied, evokes puzzlement/negative reactions, and is equated with normalcy. Few people of color react negatively when asked what it means to be Black, Asian American, Latino, or a member of their race. Most could readily inform the questioner about what it means to be a person of color.

Thus, in race talk, statements by Whites such as "Why is being White such a big deal?"; "There isn't anything like a White race"; "Your oppression is no different than mine"; "Being a woman, I've experienced oppression as well"; "We are all just human beings"; "When I've traveled abroad, I've been discriminated against as well"; "Can't we just relate to one another as individuals?"; and "We all have an equal opportunity to succeed" serve to inflame the senses of people of color because they fail to recognize the constant, continual, and cumulative experiences of racism on people of color, and the naive role the speaker plays in perpetuating the charade. In race talk, such statements go hand in hand with color blindness and the invisibility of Whiteness. They are both sides of the same coin and represent microaggressions that assail the racial identities of people of color and invalidate their experiential realities.

THE INVISIBILITY OF WHITENESS: WHAT DOES IT MEAN?

The failure to recognize the advantaged position of Whites and the disadvantaged position of people of color is acknowledged in the response by a Chinese American student, and by Robert Jensen, a White professor of journalism. In these two examples, we begin to see a converging of racial realities and the realization by a White man that being White means something radically different than being a person of color.

21-year-old Chinese American male college student (Ethnic Studies major)

Q: What does it mean to be White?

A: My cultural heritage class was just discussing that question this week.

Q: What was your conclusion?

A: Well, it has to do with White privilege. I read an article by a professor at Wellesley. It made a lot of sense to me. Being White in this society automatically guarantees you better treatment and unearned benefits and privileges than minorities. Having white skin means you have the freedom to choose the neighborhood you live in. You won't be discriminated against. When you enter a store, security guards won't assume you will steal something. You can flag down a cab without the thought they won't pick you up because you're a minority. You can study in school and be assured your group will be portrayed positively. You don't have to deal with race or think about it.

Q: Are White folks aware of their White privilege?

A: Hell no! They're oblivious to it. (Sue, 2003, p. 119)

Robert Jensen (White male professor of Journalism)

Q: What does it mean to be White?

A: I know I did not get where I am by merit alone. I benefited from, among other things, white privilege. That doesn't mean that I don't deserve my job, or that if I weren't white I would never have gotten the job. It means simply that all through my life, I have soaked up benefits for being white.

I grew up in fertile farm country taken by force from non-white indigenous people. I was educated in a well-funded, virtually all-white public
school system in which I learned that white people like me made this
country great. There I also was taught a variety of skills, including how to
take standardized tests written by and for white people. . . . There certainly
is individual variation in experience. Some white people have had it easier than me, probably because they came from wealthy families that gave
them even more privilege. Some white people have had it tougher than
me because they came from poorer families. White women face discrimination I will never know. But, in the end, white people all have drawn on
white privilege somewhere in their lives. (R. Jensen, 2002, p. 104)

In both of these responses we enter into one of the main fears experienced by
many White Americans. Engaging in race talk may potentially result in similar
realizations as that of R. Jensen (2002). It appears that the invisibility, denial,
and/or mystification of Whiteness for White Euro-Americans are related to
two underlying factors.

First, most people seldom think about the air that surrounds them, and how
it provides an essential life-giving ingredient, oxygen. We take it for granted
because it is plentiful in our everyday lives; only when we are deprived of
it, does it suddenly become frighteningly apparent. Whiteness is transparent
precisely because of its everyday occurrence, its institutionalized normative
features in U.S. culture, and because Whites are taught to think of their lives as
morally neutral, average, and ideal. To persons of color, however, Whiteness is
not invisible because it does not fit the normative qualities that make it invisible (Dyer, 2002). A fish in water, for example, requires oxygen for survival.
However, the medium to deliver it must be water, not air. The atmosphere that
symbolically represents White culture is quite noticeable to people of color,
and while nurturing to White Euro-Americans, it may prove less than healthy
for people of color.

Second, if Whiteness, as unearned privilege and advantage, is predicated on
White supremacy and the oppression of people of color and if Whites benefit
from it, then a frightening conclusion must be drawn: Whites have a stake in
racism and to be White is to benefit from racism (Wise, 2002). Little wonder
then that race talk is threatening and that many Whites avoid it in order not
to reach this conclusion. Racism hides in the background of Whiteness and is
protected through a conspiracy of silence that aids in making it invisible (Sue,
2005). As long as racism is an unacknowledged secret, it allows White people

to accept the unearned advantages of their skin color while allowing them to deny responsibility for how it disadvantages other groups (African Americans, Asian Americans, Latino/Hispanic Americans, and Native Americans; Harris, 1993; Tatum, 2002).

THE FEAR OF OWNING WHITE PRIVILEGE

Sue (2003) defined White privilege as

> the unearned advantages and benefits that accrue to White folks by virtue of a system normed on the experiences, values, and perceptions of their group. White privilege (a) automatically confers dominance to one group, while subordinating groups of color in a descending relational hierarchy, (b) owes its existence to White supremacy, (c) is premised on the mistaken notion of individual meritocracy and deservingness (hard work, family values, etc.) rather than favoritism, (d) is deeply embedded in the structural, systemic, and cultural workings of U.S. society, and (e) operates within an invisible veil of unspoken and protected secrecy. (p. 137)

White privilege continues to be a taboo topic for White people in our society. It is an unacknowledged secret that is overtly and covertly denied and protected through the use of self-deception and ground rules that prevent discussion and exploration. It protects Whites from realizing that they benefit from racism; as long as it is not talked about and is hidden from consciousness, they can maintain the illusion that they are not responsible for the state of race relations because they do not knowingly engage in racist behaviors. The invisible nature of White privilege serves to keep them comfortable, confident, and relatively oblivious to how it has the opposite effect on persons of color—harms, intimidates, oppresses, alienates, and makes for discomfort. Making the invisible visible through race talk is the first step toward dismantling the unfair and harmful nature of White privilege (Sue & Sue, 2013). The deconstruction of White privilege requires an analysis of its five basic components.

1. Automatically Confers Dominance Versus "I Made It on My Own"

Because we live in a society normed and standardized on White Euro-American values, most of the structures, policies, and practices of institutions are situated in such a manner as to pave the road for Whites while creating obstacles for other groups. The United States continues to favor White, Eurocentric ways of thinking, acting, and being that do not match the reality of people of color. In this respect, two sides of the coin are present: (1) on one side, White Privilege automatically confers dominance, control, and power to White Americans, and (2) on the other side, it automatically disempowers and oppresses people of color. On the one side, it automatically advantages one group; on the other side, it automatically disadvantages the other (McIntosh, 2002).

Most Whites would entertain the notion that being a person of color in this society subjects them to second-class citizenship. Yet it is intriguing that most White Americans would actively deny that they are advantaged automatically by this state of affairs. The Black salesman, for example, who says that White customers avoid him, view him as a well-dressed janitor, and always corroborate the information he dispenses with White salespeople is clearly disadvantaged (may make fewer sales). White salespeople, however, fail to see that the African American presence in the showroom actually ensures that they will make more sales (advantaged). The fact that White customers will seek them out and treat them as more knowledgeable and trustworthy validates them as superior sales representatives. The deception resides in the belief by Whites that the superior outcome (sales) reflects their individual efforts ("I made it on my own").

2. Exists on White Supremacy Versus "I'm Not Responsible for the Oppression of Others"

White privilege could not exist without White supremacy. White supremacy is a doctrine of racial superiority that justifies discrimination, segregation, and domination of persons of color based on an ideology and belief system that considers all other non-White groups inferior (J. M. Jones, 1997). Our discussion of ethnocentric monoculturalism provides the components of how White supremacy operates. Unlike individual acts of racism, White supremacy is more all-encompassing and insidious because it resides in the very institutional and cultural foundations of our society.

White supremacy and oppression go hand in hand. To maintain conformance and silence of persons of color, White supremacy as a doctrine and belief is instilled through education and enforced by biased institutional policies or practices that punish those who dare raise their voices in objection to their second-class status (Freire, 1970; Hanna, Talley, & Guindon, 2000). People are taught that Columbus discovered America, that the pioneers settled the West, that differences are deviant, the myth of the melting pot, positive portrayals of White people, negative portrayals of minority groups, that the internment of

Japanese Americans was based on national security (not racism), and that the Lewis and Clark expedition gave the United States a claim to the Oregon Territory. A particularly noteworthy and powerful example of White supremacy was the Manifest Destiny argument in the 1840s: All land owned by Native Americans was decreed by God to belong to White people.

The irrational sense of entitlement is a dominant feature of White privilege (McIntosh, 2002). And, more insidious, are the benefits that accrue to White folks from these historical events. Pretense and mystification about these facts only serve to perpetuate White supremacy, and the claim that Whites should not be blamed for the past injustices of their ancestors misses a vital point. They still benefit from the past injustices of their forebears! Thus, even if completely free of conscious racial prejudices and desire to forego or disclaim White privilege, Whites still receive benefits automatically and unintentionally.

3. Predicated on Favoritism Rather Than Meritocracy Versus "The Most Qualified Ought to Get the Job"

Earlier we gave the example of former president George W. Bush in which syndicated columnist Molly Ivins is often credited for saying that "George Bush was born on third base and believes he hit a triple." This statement represents the ultimate illusion of meritocracy—that those who occupy a favored position achieved their status through individual effort and merit alone. If you accept the concept of White privilege, then you must entertain the more realistic notion that many Whites did not succeed because of superior ability, but due to favoritism. George Bush did not become president of the United States solely because of hard work or superior intellect, but was born into a privileged family, given favored status by a White society (all his life attending the best White schools, living in the best White neighborhoods, obtaining the best White jobs, having to only deal with a White police force, etc.), and had opportunities not equally available to persons of color. Using the baseball analogy, while President Bush started on third base, most persons of color cannot even make it to the batter's box.

In the United States, our society arose from the cherished concept of rugged individualism; it is part of the Protestant ethic that believes there is a strong relationship between ability, effort, and success. People who succeed in our society work harder, have more skills, or are more competent. People who fail to achieve much in our society are seen as lazy, less capable, or less intelligent.

Democratic ideals such as *equal access to opportunities, everyone can make it in society if they work hard enough, liberty and justice for all, God helps those who help themselves*, and *fulfillment of personal destiny* are culturally conditioned into one's thinking. Behind these phrases lies one major assumption: Everyone operates on a level playing field. In the presence of White privilege, however, the playing field is tilted in such a way as to be an uphill trek for persons of color and a downhill one for Whites.

4. Embedded Systemically in Society Versus "The Cream Always Rises to the Top"

The idea that you are the master of your own fate unfairly blames minority citizens for their inability to achieve more in this society. It fails to take into consideration the systemic forces of racism, prejudice, and discrimination, and the operation of White privilege. People of color who suffer in poverty and unemployment and who live in the ghettos or barrios are blamed as suffering from deficiencies in their lifestyles or of possessing personal inadequacies. There is a triple purpose to the existence of White privilege: (1) to advantage White Americans, (2) to disadvantage persons of color, and (3) to attribute causes to individual deficiencies, thereby relieving White society of responsibility for perpetuating inequality.

It is becoming increasingly clear that the reasons for the plight of persons of color may not be solely internal but based upon systemic forces in society (J. M. Jones, 1997). We have already seen that the belief in meritocracy—that those who succeed have greater competence, superior skills, good work ethic, and high intellect—may be a myth: "The cream always rises to the top." White privilege is not confined to just the individual perceptions or actions of Euro-Americans. Indeed, a strong case can be made that institutional and cultural manifestations of White privilege are the invisible culprits, because they are systemically embedded in our society and have large-scale effects that dwarf individual actions of prejudice or discrimination.

Discriminatory benefits that favor Whites are seen in all facets of our society: bank lending practices, access to health care, housing, jobs, education, media portrayals, law enforcement, and court decisions that mete out justice. We are not talking about a few individuals hurt by White privilege, but literally millions of marginalized persons in our society. The existence of institutional racism shields the operation of White privilege through what is called standard operating procedures, which represent the rules, habits, procedures, and structures of organizations that oppress persons of color while favoring Whites (Sue, 2003).

5. The Unspoken and Protected Secret or "We Should Be a Color-Blind Nation"

The invisible whiteness of being maintains its viability precisely because it is a protected and seldom spoken secret. Avoidance of race talk is one means of protection. Not seeing color helps to mask these disparities and unfair advantages. In 1972, Ralph Ellison's book *The Invisible Man* described the invisible man syndrome where racial issues and color are diluted, ignored, or considered irrelevant. When originally formulated, the concept of a color-blind society was seen as the answer to discrimination and prejudice: Dr. Martin Luther King, for example, advocated judging people not by the color of their skin, but by their internal character.

Many White Americans, however, have distorted and or conveniently used color blindness as a means of color denial or, more accurately, power denial (Neville, Awad, Brooks, Flores, & Bluemel, 2013). An understanding of White privilege ultimately unmasks a dirty secret kept hidden by White Americans: Much of what they have attained is unearned, and even if they are not overtly racist, Whites cannot choose to relinquish benefits from it.

Getting White privilege out of the closet is difficult and resisted for these reasons. White privilege and its flipside, color blindness, mimic the norms of fairness, justice, and equity by whiting out differences and perpetuating the belief in sameness. The denial of power imbalance, unearned privilege, and racist domination is couched in the rhetoric of equal treatment and equal opportunity (Sue, 2003, 2005). As mentioned earlier, the programs, policies, and practices of institutions may be monocultural. They are applied equally to all groups so organizations and policy makers believe they are being imminently fair and not discriminating. Educational policy regarding IQ testing, use of college admission test scores, and hiring and promotion criteria in employment decisions are applied equally across all groups. Equal treatment in this case is discriminatory treatment because it has damaging differential impact on persons of color. Unfortunately, the belief in equal treatment masks the fact that the universal standards are White.

In closing, it becomes clear why many Whites prefer not to acknowledge Whiteness and White privilege. Race talk threatens to reveal deep-seated meanings and fears related to being White in this society. For, if the previous analysis is accurate, to be White means the following (Sue, 2003):

- To be socialized into a world of White supremacy.
- To inherit and benefit from a world of White privilege.
- To knowingly and unknowingly have a stake in the perpetuation of White racism.
- To deny the reality of people of color and to define reality from a White perspective.
- To be oblivious to one's own biases and prejudices.
- To possess the luxury of not exploring oneself as a racial/cultural being.
- To be able to equate a human being with being White.
- To be an oppressor, whether knowingly or unknowingly.
- To have been responsible for causing the pain and suffering of people of color.
- To be right.

FEAR OF TAKING PERSONAL RESPONSIBILITY TO END RACISM: MOVING FROM BEING NONRACIST TO BECOMING ANTIRACIST

Someone once made the following statement: "The ultimate White privilege is the luxury of acknowledging your privilege, but doing nothing about it." When Mark Cuban, owner of the Dallas Mavericks, stated in 2014 in reaction to the Donald Sterling incident that he was honest in saying he was prejudiced, was he actually manifesting White privilege? This statement is very meaningful because it represents the last major fear and hurdle to becoming *nonracist* and *antiracist*. These two are related concepts, but they refer to different aspects of personal development. Becoming *nonracist* means soul searching, individual change, and working on the self; becoming *antiracist* means taking personal action to end external racism that exists systemically and in the action of others. The invisibility of White privilege and Whiteness allows denial of the pain and suffering experienced by people of color, but more importantly, it absolves White Americans of personal responsibility for perpetuating injustice and allows them to remain passive and inactive.

To allow systems of injustice to exist and to deny complicity in the oppression of others means a denial of reality. To allow the continued degradation, harm, and cruelty to persons of color means diminishing one's humanity and lessening compassion toward the plight of the oppressed (Spanierman et al., 2006; Spanierman, Todd, & Anderson, 2009). To continue being oblivious to one's own complicity in such acts means objectifying and dehumanizing people of color. Awareness of one's role in the perpetuation of racism, and the pain inflicted on people of color would seemingly call for action on the part of White brothers and sisters. And herein lies one of the major obstacles in the path to social justice: Despite increasing awareness of the detrimental impact of racism and one's role in its perpetuation, social action does not seem to follow automatically or easily (Kawakami, Dunn, Karmali, & Dovidio, 2009).

In the numerous workshops and classes I have conducted on antiracism training, I have been impressed with how many White participants and students seem to make incredible progress in understanding themselves as racial/cultural beings, obtaining heightened awareness of the detrimental impact of racism and vowing that if they witnessed racist acts or unjust treatment of people of color, they would be compelled to intervene or take personal action. According to them, they could not live with themselves if they did not take responsibility to eradicate injustice. When these statements are made at the end of semester-long classes or lengthy workshops, they are heartfelt and sincere, filled with feelings of compassion, empathy, and respect for one another. White participants speak openly of their biases, indicate that if they heard racist or sexist jokes they would feel obligated to respond, that if a Black coworker was treated unfairly at work they would become an ally, and that, as parents, they would take action to make sure the curriculum of their schools would cover racial groups fairly. At that point in time, I have little doubt that participants and students mean what they say and say what they mean, that their hearts are in the right place, and that they are sincere; but, does it actually pan out in their future daily lives and social actions? Do they become nonracist and antiracist?

In a revealing study designed to shed light on the apparent paradox between awareness and action, investigators studied how people would feel and behave after witnessing an act of racism (Kawakami et al., 2009). Like many participants who undergo multicultural or racism awareness training, most Whites indicate that if they were to witness a racially biased incident or hear a racial slur, they would be very distressed and take immediate action. The investigators studied two groups of participants: forecasters (those who imagined the racial incident) and experiencers (those who actually witnessed the racial encounter). Those who imagined the racist incident tended to indicate they would be very upset to see the negative discriminatory condition, and would take some sort of action (rejecting the offender). Contrary to what people said they would feel (very distressed) and do (intervene), their predictions did not come true. The experiencers, who were involved in the racist situations, were not particularly disturbed, nor did the incidents affect their selection or acceptance of the offender.

In other words, the experimenters concluded that people tend to mispredict their affective and behavioral responses to racism. They actually seem to respond with indifference. The investigators suggested that despite public condemnation of racism and increasing awareness of its negative impact on people of color, well-intentioned Whites are disinclined to enforce egalitarian norms because of the cognitive and emotional toll required to do so. Bringing attention to the incident, confronting the perpetrator, rocking the boat, and having to go public requires considerable time, energy, and effort. Second, social deterrents to racism may be much weaker than public rhetoric implies. In this case, action (or rather inaction) speaks louder than words. Condemning racism is socially accepted, but not widely translated into corresponding action. Third, taking action may result in negative consequences for the individual, such as risking possible censure from family, friends, and coworkers who may be operating under the politeness, academic, and color-blind protocols. In this situation, significant others, including casual acquaintances, may actually discourage the individual from taking action or even verbally acknowledging it. So, contrary to what people say, they may actually fail to censure others who transgress egalitarian norms. The chasm between awareness and action is quite large.

Again, it appears that strong personal, institutional, and cultural forces work against antiracist actions on the part of White Americans who become liberated and aware of the dynamics of racism and Whiteness. On a personal level, family and friends may simply not possess the same critical racial consciousness of a loved one or acquaintance, may be unable to relate to him or her, may lack the ability to share his or her insights and new awareness, and may believe the person is making a mountain out of a molehill. The potential White ally experiences invalidation and marginalization from significant others, which can be quite painful: desiring others' nurturance, love, and affection and noting that it is being withheld or made contingent upon returning to the prior state of identity. During holidays when students spend time off campus with family, some report hearing a racist joke from a favorite aunt or uncle and objecting to it. They report that family members may tease them ("You've changed since going to that Ivy League school. What are they teaching you anyway? What liberal crap is the college filling your head with?"), or they may threaten to disown them from the family because of the disrespect shown.

Becoming antiracist, therefore, may mean significant changes in how Whites live their lives and may alter their relationships with family, friends, and coworkers as well as affect the environments in which they live (neighborhoods, communities, schools, and worksites). In many cases, estrangement may occur, and White allies may find that their new identities and commitments mean, at best, changing the relationships they have with others and, at worst, giving them up. This is a frightening prospect because the very people who have been important in their lives, people who have sustained and nurtured their old identities and people who have played an important role in their development, no longer can provide those nutrients to support their new nonracist awareness and antiracist actions. This change often presents a major challenge because the person may experience loneliness and the type of marginalization that people of color have constantly experienced. For many White Americans, the challenge and isolation may be too much, and they will return to their old ways allowing denial and self-deception to reestablish themselves.

The ultimate challenge of continuing to act on nonracist and antiracist identities cannot be accomplished alone. As we have discovered through all group movements, the potential White ally must find others who will walk with him or her, encourage him or her to continue the journey, and form new friendships and partnerships, especially among people of color. Studies suggest that antiracist people have greater racial diversity among friends, support affirmative action, possess greater cultural sensitivity and empathy, and are more prone to take social action to rectify injustices (Spanierman et al., 2009). The ultimate hope for change lies in having Whites (a) actively make Whiteness visible, (b) explore themselves as racial/cultural beings, (c) take responsibility for defining Whiteness in a nondefensive and nonracist manner, and (d) take antiracist actions aimed at the individual, institutional, and cultural levels (Hardiman, 1982; Helms, 1984, 1995). To do this, however,

White Americans will have to be willing to look at themselves honestly, to confront the truth about themselves and the world, and to liberate themselves from the invisible cultural conditioning of a racialized society. We will return to this topic shortly in Chapters 11 and 12 when we address White racial identity development and what parents, educators, and facilitators can do to enhance race talk.

Race Talk and Special Group Considerations

Interracial/Interethnic Race Talk: Difficult Dialogues Between Groups of Color

Race talk between people of color and within the groups possess similar and, at the same time, different racial/cultural specific issues. One would expect that people of color would have an easier time engaging in racial dialogues, but on certain topics it can be equally uncomfortable and difficult. I recently received the following personal communication from an Asian American female doctoral candidate at my institution:

> Hi Dr. Sue,
> I hope you're doing well. I know you're out for the Spring Semester, but I have a few questions I was hoping you might speak to about the "contested legitimacy" of Asians/Asian Americans adopting the use of the term "person of color." Meaning both White individuals AND other individuals of color contesting the belongingness of Asians to the umbrella community of "people of color."
>
> I've had a few recent experiences in group dialogues about race where I found myself feeling outside the conversation, and trying to make sense of what was happening in the moment.

In both instances, the groups were primarily organized for people of color, or attended dominantly by people of color. But as the conversation went on, I soon realized that my experiences were not the ones that were being talked about...that the implicit definition being used for "person of color" in the room meant African American/Black...and maybe Latino/a. NOT Asian/Asian American. Of course no one said that out loud. We're much too progressive and evolved for that. But it made me think about how even within the non-White/POC umbrella, Asians experience invalidation/invisibility/rejection. (Is this doubly rejecting?)

I'm not surprised when White people invalidate the experiences of racism felt by Asians. It's particularly stinging and confusing when it's from people of color. I've had people of color say I can't identify as a person of color, that I don't count as a racial minority...and then spout off model minority justifications of how my experience of racism is NOT the same as other groups, which is true. There are privileges I reap from the inaccurate model minority myth, whether or not I want them. Even at this institution I've noticed I get the benefit of the doubt from professors more than other students of color regarding my academic work/feedback. Nobody is surprised if I do well.

I guess my question is...how do Asian Americans engage in the conversation about race within the community of color? Have you ever felt like your "right" to identify as a person of color was contested by other people of color, or that dealing with the marginalized experience of invisibility as an Asian American was somehow less legitimate than the marginalized experience of explicit oppression? (aka "my experience of racism is worse than yours and therefore more legitimate"?) How have you responded?

If you've read this far, I thank you for taking the time. I hope this makes sense. I'm curious what your thoughts are, and would love to meet with you during your office hours when you return to campus. (Peggy L., February 2014)

Questions: (The following questions are addressed especially to people of color and secondarily to Whites.) Do you believe Asian Americans belong to the category People of Color? Are Asian Americans an oppressed minority group? When you think of Asian Americans, what are the first thoughts and images that come to mind? Are they a successful group or an oppressed group? Do African Americans, Asian Americans, Latino/Hispanic Americans, and Native Americans openly speak about their relationships with one another? Can different racial/ethnic groups be racist toward one another? Why is there so little focus and so much apprehension on race talk among and between people of color?

INTERRACIAL/INTERETHNIC RELATIONSHIP ISSUES

The e-mail message from the Asian American student and the ensuing questions lead us into a very sensitive and seldom addressed topic about interracial/interethnic relationships: conflicts and dialogues between groups of color (Orbe, Everett, & Putman, 2013; Sue & Sue, 2013). Most analysis of race talk focuses on Whites and people of color, and except for research done on intercultural communications (between nationalities), little focus has been given to dialogues between people of color in the United States (Oetzel & Ting-Toomey, 2013). Why has this been so? Are people of color less prejudiced than Whites? What types of misunderstandings and conflicts exist between people of color? Are people of color equally uncomfortable about race talk when it involves dialogues between them? Analysis of the e-mail correspondence provides hints and clues as to some of the major issues that have served to create tension between groups of color and the need to address them in race talk. I use primarily an Asian American and African American framework to illustrate the dynamics of race talk between these groups.

First, the Asian American female feels left out of the racial conversation because the experiences being described by group members seem to relate to mainly Black Americans. This observation involves a wider sociopolitical issue where most people, including Whites, perceive racial relationships as binary: *Black–White only* (Pew Research Center, 2012). So, when matters of prejudice or discrimination are brought up for discussion, other groups of color, such as Asian Americans, Latina/o Americans, and Native Americans, often feel left out of the dialogue and rendered invisible (B. S. K. Kim, 2011; Takaki, 1998). Thus, they often feel frustrated and that their issues are invalidated not only by Whites, but also by their African American brothers and sisters.

Second, the writer expresses the "contested legitimacy" of Asian Americans being considered "people of color" and by implication not being an oppressed minority group. Recently, an Asian American colleague told a story of how invalidated and angered she became when a Black colleague, during a diversity discussion, made reference to being the only person of color on the curriculum committee and that it was important to seek another. What was more disturbing was that White colleagues did not seem to notice my Asian American colleague's plight and racial identity. In other words, she seemed invisible at best, and at worst was considered to be White! In a hard-hitting article, "At Least You're Not Black: Asian Americans in U.S. Race Relations," E. H. Kim (1998) observes that Asian Americans in U.S. race relations are designated by society to be the in-between group (between Whites and other groups of color), and that this form of racial hierarchy is dangerous because it potentially creates interracial/interethnic conflicts and hard feelings. Why do so many people unintentionally (or intentionally) consider Asian Americans not to be people of color?

An answer to this question goes to the heart of the third point being made by the student. When other groups of color, including Whites, think about Asian Americans, one of the most prevalent images is that of a highly successful group that has made it in U.S. society (Pew Research Center, 2012). Indeed, the recent high-profile marriage of Mark Zuckerberg, founder of Facebook, to Priscilla Chan is not unusual in that 37% of recent Asian American brides are wed to a non-Asian groom (Pew Research Center, 2012). People point to how Asian Americans are more accepted by Whites than any groups of color, that they earn the highest incomes, are the best educated, and are the most satisfied with their lives (Pew Research Center, 2012). This has led many to claim that Asian Americans are a model minority, and past popular magazines have heralded the group with such titles as "Asian Americans: A Success Story" and "Asian Americans: Outwhiting Whites" (Sue & Sue, 2013). Such facts seem to suggest that Asian Americans are somehow immune to racism, are not victimized by it, and require no special concern. The model minority label, however, is a myth that will be addressed later. Its continued use in our society creates friction between Asian Americans and other groups of color.

Fourth, race talk between groups of color, especially when addressing personal and group experiences of racism, may be prone to the "who's more oppressed" trap (Sue, 2003). This is a game where one group claims that their treatment in society is worse than that of other groups. The student's correspondence seems to be alluding to the fact that her experiences of oppression are less legitimate than those being portrayed by Black students. The failure to bridge differences and understand one another is damaging and only serves to separate rather than unify. There is little doubt that each group, whether Native American, African American, Latina/o American, or Asian American, can claim that it has suffered immensely from racism. If we are able to truly understand our own group's oppression, it should make it easier to recognize the oppression of another. But to use one group's oppression to negate another group's is to diminish, dismiss, or negate the claims of another. It leads to separation rather than mutual understanding, a feature of race talk between groups of color that is divisive and counterproductive.

Last, it is clear that the student refers to her "privilege" as an Asian American because of the perceived stereotypes associated with her group and the apparent greater acceptance by White society of them. She relates experiences where professors and others hold positive stereotypes about the group, expect her to do well, and are not surprised by her performance. At some level, she realizes that this may be similar to White privilege and is disturbed by it. Again, the positive image of Asian Americans versus the negative ones of other groups may cause hard feelings and divisiveness (E. H. Kim, 1998). Indeed, when I was a young student in high school, I can recall my teacher scolding an African American student for not behaving in class. She would point me out in class and ask the Black student, "Why can't you people be more like Derald, who studies hard, doesn't disrupt the class, and just gets good grades?" Comments like this and many other similar ones would often make me feel very uncomfortable and alienate African American students from me.

RACE TALK: FEARS OF DIVIDE AND CONQUER

Why is race talk difficult between and among people of color? Why are some people of color hesitant to address interracial/interethnic differences? These are questions often asked privately by groups of color, but seldom publicly discussed for fear of negative consequences and the destruction of political unity (Orbe et al., 2013; Sue & Sue, 2013). It is clear that we are all products of our cultural conditioning and, as indicted earlier, none of us are immune from inheriting the biases, stereotypes, prejudices, and falsehoods of our society. This fact applies not only to White Americans, but to all people of color born and raised in the United States. Thus, it is possible for Latina/o Americans to harbor biases toward African Americans, Blacks against Asian Americans, and so on. Yet, people of color have remained relatively silent in dialoguing on these matters.

Ground Rules for Interracial/Interethnic Dialogues: "United We Stand, Divided We Fall"

To understand the reluctance and hesitation among people of color to engage in interracial/interethnic race talk, it is important to understand the history of groups of color, and their common struggle against discrimination from the larger society. During the civil rights movement of the 1950s and the ensuing Black, Brown, Yellow, and Red power movements of the 1960s and 1970s, oppressed groups banded together in their struggles against prejudice, discrimination, and oppression (Banks & Banks, 2004; Takaki, 1998). They shared a common sense of purpose and peoplehood derived from their experiences in an oppressive society. Because they were socially marginalized groups, few in numbers, and had little control over the political, economic, educational, and social levers of power, they banded together to confront a common enemy: a White, Western, European system that systematically deprived them of equal access and opportunity (Banks, 2004).

Even during the 1960s urban race riots in American cities, the coalition held together to lay bare the racial wounds of the society. The strength of the Third World movement came from its collective unity of mainly racial/ethnic minority groups: African Americans, Asian Americans, Latina/o Americans, and Native Americans. Anything that threatened the unity of the coalition was warded off, avoided, and deeply resisted. Many have credited this united front for the successes in obtaining political, economic, educational, social, and legal gains for people of color (Banks, 2004; National Advisory Commission on Civil Disorders, 1968).

Although the common enemy notion and the need to maintain unity have proven fruitful in combating many aspects of racism, they have also hindered people of color from addressing differences and conflicts between the groups. Indication of differences and the potential lack of harmony between groups of color that involve Latinas/os and African Americans has reared its ugly head in a number of communities in Durham, North Carolina, and in Los Angeles, where the struggle for political and economic dominance has been observed (*Economist*, 2007), and between African Americans and Koreans in the Los Angeles riots of 1992 (E. H. Kim, 1998). The media (newspaper reports, radio, and television coverage) has played an important role in these events by shaping the perceptions of White Americans and the perceptions of people of color toward one another. In the analysis of some scholars, the media has delighted in playing up interracial/interethnic conflicts leading to political consequences to the detriment of communities of color (E. H. Kim, 1998; Sue & Sue, 2013). Thus, reluctance to engage in race talk and the fears of disrupting unity between the groups are strong.

Ground Rules for Interracial/Interethnic Race Talk: "Don't Air Dirty Laundry in Public"

One of the greatest fears of people of color is that race talk will reveal to the public disagreements and differences that exist between them, thereby playing into the hands of those who would prefer to maintain the status quo (E. H. Kim, 1998). They are, therefore, admonished by their own groups "not to air dirty laundry in public" for four primary reasons.

- First, people of color fear that White Americans in power will use interracial/interethnic conflicts to assuage their own White guilt feelings, excuse their racism, and justify their passivity to making change— "People of color are equally racist, so why should I change when they can't even get along with one another?"
- Second, people of color are wary of the divide-and-conquer ploy that can be used to divide and diminish the strength of groups of color—"As long as people of color fight among themselves, they will be unable to form alliances against systemic forces of racism." This strategy is often employed when Asian Americans are held up to their African American counterparts as the model minority—"Why can't you people be more like Asian Americans who made it through hard work and good family values?"
- Third, people of color are concerned that honest discussion of interracial/interethnic conflicts will divert attention away from the injustices of society by defining racial problems as residing chiefly among racial/ethnic groups rather than the broader society.
- The fourth reason is more difficult and confusing to comprehend by most Whites and even many people of color. As discussed earlier, filmmaker Spike Lee, an African American, is known for taking the position that only Whites can be racist and people of color cannot be racist toward Whites nor toward one another. Such a position infuriates many, who believe that racism is a two-way process. In keeping with J. M. Jones's definition of racism (1997) and that of the APA Presidential Task Force (2012), however, this position holds great validity. It is true that people of color can be biased and prejudiced toward Whites and one another, but to define it as racism ignores the power dimension of oppression. It is important to understand that prejudice by people of color occurs under an umbrella of White racial superiority and supremacy. Raised in the United States, they are equally prone to inherit the stereotypes and biases of the society. Although people of color can be prejudiced and discriminate, they do not have the power to oppress on a large-scale basis (Spradlin & Parsons, 2008; Sue, 2003). In other words, they may be able to hurt one another on an individual basis, but they possess little power to cause systemic harm

to White Americans (education, employment, and health care). Further, many people of color believe that interracial/interethnic prejudice serves only to benefit Whites while disadvantaging their own groups.

Thus, while the politeness protocol, the academic protocol, and the color-blind protocol serve as ground rules that prevent race talk by Whites, the commandments (a) "Thou shall not air dirty laundry in public" and (b) "Thou shall not speak ill of one another and destroy group unity" are equally powerful forces preventing people of color from honestly dialoguing about their thoughts and feelings toward one another.

Although cognizant of the dangers of honest race talk between groups of color, recognition of the unquestioned merit of openly addressing racial issues is long overdue. People of color have always known that they, too, harbor prejudicial and detrimental beliefs about one another and about their White brothers and sisters. It is important, however, to understand the wider social context of race talk between groups of color when exploring the biases, prejudices, and conflicts that may be uncovered lest we lose sight of their political ramifications and unjustly blame the victims.

Sources of Conflict Between People of Color

Interracial/interethnic conflict is "the perceived and/or actual incompatibility of values, expectations, processes, or outcomes between two or more parties...over substantive and/or relational issues" (Ting-Toomey, 1994, p. 360). Substantive issues involve the *content* of conflicts such as fighting over limited resources (jobs), while *relational issues* refer to the cultural styles of expressing and resolving conflicts like those described in Chapter 7. This definition includes the term *perceived incompatibility*, which is an important distinction because it entertains the notion that perceptions may be false or mistaken (stereotypes, biases, and prejudices) and not based on fact. An illustrative example involving the converging of these factors that opened the door to interracial/interethnic differences occurred in the 1992 Los Angeles riots that involved the Korean/Korean American, African American, and to a lesser extent, the Latina/o communities.

The 1992 Los Angeles Riots

Following the acquittal of police officers in the videotaped beating of a Black man (Rodney King), South Central Los Angeles exploded in what was described as the largest race riot since the 1960s and resulted in an even greater death toll. Over a 6-day period, a series of riots, lootings, arsons, beatings, and homicides occurred right after the verdict; many believed the freeing of the officers accused of police brutality sparked the outrage that engulfed the Black community. Fifty-three people were killed, approximately 2,000 were injured, and an estimated damage to property ranged from $800 million to $1 billion (Wikipedia, 2014). The aftermath of the riots resulted in much soul searching by the nation, especially the city of Los Angeles and law enforcement agencies (Orbe et al., 2013). The outcome was that the officers accused of beating Rodney King were retried; the L.A. Police Department increased people of color in its force; the police chief resigned; the mayor lost community support; new guidelines were developed to prevent the use of excessive force; and numerous urban studies concluded that the tinder-box atmosphere of political and economic inequality in minority communities (in addition to the Rodney King verdict) was major contributing culprit to the conflagration.

The rest of the story: Although it was obvious that anger was directed at an unfair criminal justice system controlled by White Americans, and although this could be seen as a Black–White conflict, the riot contagion spread like wildfire to engulf the Korean/Korean American community as well (E. H. Kim, 1998; Yoon, 1997). Of the 4,500 stores that were looted and burned, 2,300 were Korean owned (Yoon, 1997). On the second day of the riots, Korean Americans saw the police retreat from protecting Koreatown due to the heavy and violent assaults by the roaming mobs. Korean shopkeepers wanting to protect their businesses issued a call to arms from their community, and many Koreans along with shopkeepers armed themselves with shotguns, handguns, and M1 carbines (Kivisto & Rundblad, 2000). Open warfare broke out between the primarily looting mobs and Koreans/Korean Americans as they exchanged gunfire that resulted in a retreat of the looters. All this was played out on national television, and the scene and events have seared into the minds of many, fairly or unfairly, the hard feelings that exist between Asians and Blacks (Bates, 2012). These events also evoked much sympathy from White Americans for the hard-working and "innocent Koreans," which further placed a wedge between the African American and Korean American communities.

But as in nearly all events, the misunderstanding and conflicts between the two groups were more complicated than a riot that accidentally spilled over to the Korean community, but actually began years before the 1992 riots (Jo, 1992). Tensions between the two groups were evident as Koreans established residences in a section of the Black community, purchased and took over Black businesses, opened many mom and pop stores, and displaced many older Black residents. Blacks complained that the Korean shop keepers were arrogant and rude, overcharged them, were cliquish, siphoned money out of the community, and did not contribute back to the community (Jo, 1992). More importantly, Korean Americans were perceived by their Black counterparts as prejudiced and biased against them; they were no different than Whites who exploited them.

This belief was reinforced when in March 16, 1991, female storekeeper Soon Ja Du shot and killed 15-year-old Latasha Harlins, an African American high school student, 2 weeks after the beating of Rodney King. The timing is important because some believe that the riots that engulfed Koreatown were sparked and exacerbated by this incident, and not due solely to the Rodney King beating/acquittal. Similar to the later killing of Trayvon Martin by George Zimmerman, Harlins was shot in the back of the head after a scuffle broke out between her and the Korean shopkeeper, who believed she was shoplifting. After slamming the bottle of juice down on the counter that she was accused of attempting to steal, Harlin turned to leave, and was then shot by Du.

A security tape obtained from the store revealed that Harlin was still clutching the $2 bill in her hand intended for the purchase of the juice. Although Du was convicted of involuntary manslaughter, she was sentenced to only 5 years' probation, a $500 fine, and 400 hours of community service. No jail time was served. The outrage and sense of betrayal were great among African Americans, numerous demonstrations in front of the store occurred, an unsuccessful recall effort for the judge was instigated, and intense lobbying to bring civil rights charges was attempted (J. Williams, 2012). During the following 1992 riots, multiple attempts to burn down the store, which had become a symbol of Korean racial prejudice, were rebuffed by the Korean residents.

Interracial/Interethnic Prejudice and Bias

Although speculative, one can surmise that the Korean shopkeeper might have harbored stereotypes of African Americans that led her to conclude that Harlin was shoplifting and up to no good, just as George Zimmerman believed Trayvon Martin to be a suspicious person. In both cases, these stereotypes and fears may have resulted in the unfortunate and sad deaths of two African Americans. For people of color, it is disturbing to know that it was an Asian (Korean) and Latino who killed the two innocent victims. Thus, while ugly and painful, we must ask the question: How prevalent are stereotypes that groups of color have of one another? The answer seems to be that it is quite widespread among people of color. Not only do groups of color hold stereotypes of one another, but they differ in how they perceive the manifestation and impact of racism. These differences can lead to how they define problems and solutions. Several national surveys (J. M. Jones, 2013a, 2013b; National Conference of Christians and Jews, 1994; Pew Research Center, 2008, 2012) found the following:

- More than 40% of African Americans and Hispanics and one of every four Whites believe that Asian Americans are "unscrupulous, crafty, and devious in business."
- Nearly half the Hispanic Americans surveyed and 40% of African Americans and Whites believe Muslims "belong to a religion that condones or supports terrorism."
- Blacks think they are treated far worse than Whites and worse than other minority groups when it comes to getting equal treatment in applying for mortgages, in the media, and in job promotions.
- Although an overwhelming number of people rate racial/ethnic relations between racial group combinations as positive, the most favorable ratings are Whites/Asians (80%) with Blacks/Hispanics in last place.
- Nearly 50% of African Americans believe Latino immigrants reduce job opportunities for them, while fewer than 40% of Latinos agree.
- Approximately 70% of Asian Americans rate their relations with Hispanics as good and 60% say that of Blacks. Interestingly and consistent with our earlier analysis, 50% of Korean Americans have negative views of their relationships with Blacks.
- Most Blacks and Latinos view their relationships positively, but Hispanics are less likely to say that the two groups get along well.
- Only 10% of African Americans—a staggeringly low number—believe the police treat them as fairly as other groups.
- African Americans believe that everyone else is treated with more equality and especially that Asian Americans are doing better.
- There is tremendous resentment of Whites by all minority groups.
- Two-thirds of minorities think Whites "believe they are superior and can boss people around," "are insensitive to other people," "control power and wealth in America," and "do not want to share it with non-Whites."

Three primary conclusions are noteworthy here: First, racial/ethnic groups experience considerable mistrust, envy, and misunderstandings toward one another as well. Surprisingly, African Americans and Latinos held stronger negative beliefs about Asian Americans than did White Americans (40% versus 25%). Second, and not surprisingly, people of color continue to hold beliefs and attitudes toward Whites that are very negative and filled with resentments, anger, and strong mistrust. Third, race talk between people of color must come out of the closet in order to make important and long-lasting progress toward mutual respect and understanding rather than one simply based on political convenience.

Historical Relationships Between Groups of Color

In this chapter, we have used a discussion of African American–Asian American relationships to illustrate interracial/interethnic misunderstandings, bias, and miscommunication. But difficulties in relationships extend to all group combinations. Space does not allow a thorough discussion of these differences, so we briefly touch upon some of them here. The following does not even present an adequate thumbnail sketch, but it serves a purpose in indicating how race talk may allow us to begin a journey of inquiry, understanding, and enlightenment.

African American and Asian American Relationships

The history and relationships between African Americans and Asian Americans did not begin with the Los Angeles riots of 1992, but their relationship remained relatively unspoken until then. This unknown history is part of how conflict and misunderstandings have occurred between Asians and Blacks (Takaki, 1998). Little doubt exists, however, that Asians harbor biases against Blacks and vice versa. In interviews right after the 1992 riots, Korean American business owners stereotyped Black customers as likely to steal or become violent; likewise, some Black American customers were reported to use overt racial slurs such as Chinaman or Chink when speaking to Koreans (Myers, 2001).

These inherited biases that have resulted in discriminatory behavior between the groups are often exaggerated and reinforced by cultural misunderstandings and a lack of knowledge of each other's life experiences and history. First, part of the misunderstanding between Korean American shopkeepers and Black customers was due to unspoken cultural differences.

It has been hypothesized that part of the so-called rudeness and the lack of exchanging pleasantries from Koreans was due to limited language facility; lack of hiring African American employees in their stores (cliquishness and discrimination) was because they could not afford to pay higher wages, and thus family members were employed; and the smile on the faces of Koreans during a disagreement was not gloating or arrogance, but embarrassment and the feeling of helplessness (a culturally dictated response; Jo, 1992; Orbe et al., 2013).

Second, the inability of many African American brothers and sisters to relate to Asian/Asian Americans as a group of color faced with severe oppression is relatively unknown as opposed to the model minority myth (Sue & Sue, 2013). The historical systematic harassment of early Chinese immigrants is well documented: being denied the rights of citizenship, having testimony in court ruled inadmissible, the passage of the Chinese Exclusion Act of 1882, and documented mass murders, physical attacks, and destruction of their property have all led to the phrase "not a Chinaman's chance," which alludes to these atrocities. The arrival of Japanese and their historical incarceration during World War II, being treated as spies, and having their homes and property taken away was part of the anti-Oriental movement that resulted in Asians being called the Yellow Peril. There is now widespread recognition that Chinatowns, Manilatowns, and Japantowns in New York and San Francisco represent ghetto areas behind the bright neon lights. And, as each new group of immigrants and refugees (Filipinos, Koreans, Laotian, Hmongs, etc.) arrived, they also encountered racism and bias that continues to today.

Third, in contrast to many groups of color, the contemporary image of Asian Americans is that of a highly successful minority that has made it in society. We have already cited statistics suggesting that the median income of Asian American families is higher, their educational attainment greater, and official rates of delinquency/mental illness much lower than the general population (B. S. K. Kim, 2011; Sue & Sue, 2013). A closer analysis of the status of Asian Americans reveals disturbing truths that contrast with popular views of their success story. First, in terms of economics, references to the higher median income of Asian Americans do not take into account (a) the higher percentage of Asian American families having more than one wage earner, (b) a higher prevalence of poverty despite the higher median income (14% versus 8% for the U.S. population), and (c) the discrepancy between education and income. For example, high rates of poverty exist among

Hmong, Guamanian, Indonesian, and Cambodian populations in the United States. In the area of education, Asian Americans show a disparate picture of extraordinarily high educational attainment and a large, undereducated mass. Among the Hmong, only 40% have completed high school, and fewer than 14% of Tongans, Cambodians, Laotians, and Hmongs 25 years and older have a bachelor's degree. When averaged out, this bimodal distribution indicates how misleading statistics can be. Additionally, figures suggesting low rates of delinquency and mental illness are due to cultural factors related to shame and stigma that prevent Asian American families from making it known that a member has become problematic.

On the other hand, many Asian American brothers and sisters have little understanding and appreciation for African Americans who have led the fight for civil rights in this country. The history of enslavement, historical and contemporary racism, discrimination directed at Black Americans, and the negative impact upon their psychological and physical well-being and standard of living are well documented in historical accounts and continuing social, economic, educational, and economic data (J. M. Jones, 1997). Other groups of color need to acknowledge the courage of Black America, and our indebtedness to them for what we have learned from their struggles. Although all groups can recount their own unique struggles for equal rights, African Americans have always been in the forefront in advocating for social justice. Many other groups of color (and other marginalized groups—women and LGBTQ [lesbian, gay, bisexual, transgender, and queer] individuals) have learned much from the Black movement, including the importance of group identity, and have profited from the work, struggle, and sacrifice of African American brothers and sisters.

Fairly or unfairly (because of the sociopolitical environment), African American brothers and sisters will always be placed in the forefront of combating racism. *Colorism*, a delicate and controversial concept in our society, will inevitably ensure that it will be African Americans who will be thrust into this lead role. Colorism has historically influenced not only between but *within* group perceptions of one another. Colorism is a touchy race talk topic for groups of color. For example, even within Latinas/os and Asian Americans, darker skin is associated with unfavorable traits and subject to greater discriminatory treatment. Those with lighter complexion are perceived more positively (intelligent, attractive, and desirable) than those with a darker complexion (unintelligent, unattractive, and undesirable; Kelly & Greene, 2010).

Thus, in some ways just being Black is to combat racism. The physical appearance of Black Americans, what they stand for, and their desire to be true to themselves force society to consider race, racial differences, and racism. Black Americans are a constant visible reminder to White America about the disparity between its values of equality (respect, inclusion, freedom, and civil rights) and its racist policies and practices (disrespect, exclusion, oppression, and White privilege). In many ways, the racial differences of Black Americans will always serve as the conscience of White America.

Asian and Latino/a Americans Relationships

The historical relationship between Asian Americans and Latino/a Americans is not discussed and is usually invisible in discussions of race (De Genova, 2006). However, there are several ways in which these two groups may share a sense of camaraderie with one another as well as experience divisive tension. Both groups share the experience of immigration; the majority of Asian Americans and Latino/a Americans are first- or second-generation Americans (De Genova, 2006; B. S. K. Kim, 2011). This shared history may lead to similar experiences of biculturalism (maintaining Asian or Latino/a American values), culture conflicts, similar linguistic concerns (bilingualism), and experiences of pursuing the American dream. One of the dominant similarities between these groups is their shared experience of being treated like foreigners in their own country (particularly when an individual was born and raised in the United States) and of being often left out of the Black–White racial paradigm debate. When issues or matters of race are discussed in the news media, for example, the dialogue is usually Black–White and seldom includes Asian Americans or Latino/a Americans. The invisibility as groups of color in the racial debate has often created hard feelings in these two groups toward African Americans as well.

Although this experience may be shared, it can also lead to competition between the groups. Because these groups may feel invisible, they may compete with each other in order to have their voices heard. Historically, this was present during the Chicano–Filipino United Farm Workers movement in the 1930s, in which Mexican and Filipino Americans worked cohesively for farm workers' rights in California, yet disbanded when the groups could not agree on common interests (Scharlin & Villanueva, 1994). Currently, this may be exemplified with U.S. politics in which Asian and Latino Americans may run against each other in local elections, instead of working harmoniously to form a unified alliance.

Latino/a Americans and Black Americans

The history between Latino/a Americans and Black Americans also has both solidarity and discord. Historically, there has been solidarity between the two groups, particularly in their quest for equality during the civil rights era (Behnken, 2011). Traditionally, both groups recognized each other as oppressed minority groups, understanding that the other may experience racism, is subjected to stereotyping, and may be denied equal access and opportunities given to White people. However, there are also points of contention between these two groups.

First, similar to the relationships between Asians and Latinos, there may be tension between Latinos and Blacks, as a result of fighting for the sociopolitical issues and needs for one's own group. In recent years, Latino/a Americans have overwhelmingly exceeded Black Americans in regard to population; this has led to Latinos gaining more visibility in politics and education (Wood, 2006). The rise of Latino/a demands has also created tension among Latinos and Blacks because they now find themselves competing for jobs, which has forced some Black Americans to oppose many Latino/a Americans in the immigration debate (Behnken, 2011). This has often resulted in problems related to a lack of alliance between the two groups, particularly when it comes to advocacy in government, education, and community organizing.

Second, it is important to recognize that racism within the Latino/a community has historical roots as a result of Spanish colonialism in Latin America. It is important to note that the term *Latino/a* is an ethnic designator and not a racial one. Thus, Latinos may be members of any racial grouping. As a result, they may range from phenotypically appearing Black to White, with many appearing to be somewhere in between (Bautista, 2003). However, because of colonial mentality, *mestizos*, or light-skinned Latinos, are valued more highly than darker-skinned Latinos, who may be viewed as inferior, unintelligent, or unattractive (Patrinos, 2000). This may lead to a hierarchy within the Latino/a community, in which light-skinned groups such as Argentineans, Colombians, or Cubans may view themselves as superior to darker-skinned groups such as Dominicans or Mexicans. This colonial mentality may transcend a Latino/a individual's view of a Black American; this is supported by studies that have shown that Latinos hold negative stereotypes of Black Americans as being lazy and untrustworthy, whereas Black Americans do not feel the same way about Latinos (McClain et al., 2006).

Native Americans and Black, Latino/a, and Asian Americans

The relationship between Native Americans and Black, Latino/a, and Asian Americans may not be discussed or known, due to the small numbers of Native Americans in the United States. Black Americans, Latinos, and Asians may have little interaction with Native Americans, which may lead to less obvious tension or dynamics between Native Americans and another racial group. In addition, because 40% of the Native American population may be of another race (U.S. Census Bureau, 2005), many Native Americans may physically look like members of other racial groups, causing others to perceive them and treat them in different ways. However, a Native American interacting with members of these racial groups may share similarities or experience tensions with individuals of other races, perhaps empathizing with a Black American's experiences of oppression or bonding with a Latino/a's or Asian's feelings of being an invisible minority. At the same time, a Black, Latino/a, or Asian individual who does not recognize the Native American's racial identity, realities, history, or experiences may cause the Native American to feel dismissed, ignored, or invalidated.

Table 10.1   Interracial/Interethnic Race Talk Issues: The Necessity of Dialogue

Difficult interracial/interethnic dialogues almost always have sociopolitical implications that make people of color wary about addressing these in public. As these various topics are discussed, it is important to acknowledge and understand the external social, political, and cultural forces affecting race talk between and within groups of color. None of these topics occur in isolation and are often a microcosm of wider race relations in the United States.

Interracial/interethnic bias and prejudice exist between groups of color. As discussed in the chapter, no groups or individuals are immune from inheriting them. This often creates major conflicts between groups.

The *Who's more oppressed?* game actually is related to perceiving which groups belong to the People of Color category discussed earlier in the chapter. Feelings of invisibility, rejection, and resentment often result when left out of the conversation.

Tentative political alliances involving shared and different goals often lead to economic and political competition for a small piece of the pie or desiring a seat at the table. At times, conflicts between groups have created hard feelings.

Immigration is a hot-button topic not only for White Americans, but for people of color as well. Some of the greatest sources of friction between African Americans and Latinos lie in the perception that immigration of the latter takes jobs away from the former.

(continued)

Table 10.1   (*Continued*)

Colorism is the practice of discrimination in which those with lighter skin tones are treated better than those with darker skin. Colorism occurs not only between groups, but within groups as well. Among almost all groups of color, those within the group with darker skin are often perceived and treated more negatively. This is an issue explored by Spike Lee in his film *School Daze* and creates within group friction.

Internalized racism is a concept referring to people of color internalizing racist attitudes and beliefs toward their own group and themselves. In this case, the positive reference group for a person of color becomes that of White Americans.

Being co-opted is a term used to indicate a person of color who is selling out to achieve the rewards of the larger White society. Derogatory terms such as *Uncle Tom* for Black Americans and the *Big Banana* (yellow outside, but White inside) for Asian Americans are used in reference to such individuals. Some believe, for example, that Supreme Court Justice Clarence Thomas is such an individual.

Interracial marriage and relationships are difficult dialogues to have for nearly all groups. As mentioned previously, Asian Americans have the largest out-group marriages of brides and some view this as greater acceptance by White society of Asian Americans. But many African American women feel great resentment toward African American men who marry outside of the group.

Male–female relationships within groups of color are also partially related to the feelings and reactions to interracial relationships and marriages. While Asian American women tend to out-marry in greater numbers than Asian American men, the reverse seems to be true about African Americans. The out-marriage of one gender over the other can create many hard feelings between the sexes.

Roles of men and women within a racial/cultural group can also create problems in a society that values egalitarian relationships. Among Latinos/as and Asians, for example, a patriarchal relationship is normative and can affect how men and women relate to one another.

Terrorism and relationships with MENA (Middle Eastern/North African) groups as perceived by people of color need to be openly discussed. Despite our conscious acknowledgment about Islam being a legitimate religion, many people of color continue to stereotype not only the religion, but also those who adhere to it as extremists/terrorists.

Externalizing blame to avoid personal or group responsibility means that not all bad things that happen to us individually and collectively are the result of racism. Sometimes it is easier to blame others than to face the truth that everyone has faults, limitations, and weaknesses, and that we must take responsibility for our own life situation.

Difficult Interracial/Interethnic Topical Race Dialogues

As you can see, race talk between and within groups of color is not only affected by the political ramifications of racial dialogues, but unmasks the biases, stereotypes, conflicts, and misunderstandings that occur between people of color. In no way has this chapter done justice to the complexity of interracial/interethnic dialogues, and I have used primarily an African American/Asian American framework to illustrate the politics of race talk and a few of the manifestations, dynamics, and impacts of issues confronting people of color. Numerous other hot-button topics need to be adequately addressed by people of color. Some of them are outlined in Table 10.1, but many more are present. How we, as people of color, deal with these race talk topics can either enhance our relationships or create disruptions in them.

CHAPTER ELEVEN

Race Talk and White Racial Identity Development: For Whites Only

I sometimes visualize the ongoing cycle of racism as a moving walkway at the airport. Active racist behavior is equivalent to walking fast on the conveyor belt. The person engaged in active racist behavior has identified with the ideology of White supremacy and is moving with it. Passive racist behavior is equivalent to standing still on the walkway. No overt effort is being made, but the conveyor belt moves the bystanders along to the same destination as those who are actively walking. Some of the bystanders may feel the motion of the conveyor belt, see the active racists ahead of them, and choose to turn around, unwilling to go to the same destination as the White supremacists. But unless they are walking actively in the opposite direction at a speed faster than the conveyor belt—unless they are actively antiracist—they will find themselves carried along with the others. (Tatum, 1997, pages 11–12)

Questions: What does this metaphor of racism tell about the difference between active and passive racism? What is the destination of the walkway? If it represents our society, can you describe what that destination looks like? What does the conveyor belt symbolize? Are you on the conveyor belt? Which direction are you traveling? Do you even feel the movement of the belt? What would it take for you to reverse directions? More importantly, how can you stop the movement of the conveyor belt? What changes would need to occur for you at the individual level to reverse directions? What changes would need to happen at the institutional and societal levels to stop or reverse the direction of the conveyor belt?

As repeatedly emphasized in earlier chapters, race talk must be seen through a larger prism of individual, institutional, and societal racism. All these elements conspire in such a manner as to avoid making the invisible visible and thus directly or indirectly discouraging race talk. Let us briefly return to the walkway metaphor provided by Tatum (1997) in her classic book, *Why Are All the Black Kids Sitting Together in the Cafeteria?*

First, the walkway metaphor is a strong and powerful statement of the continuous and insidious nature of racism; it is ever-present, dynamic, and oftentimes invisible as it takes us on a journey to White supremacist notions, attitudes, beliefs, and behaviors. The visible actions of White supremacists moving quickly on the belt represent our awareness of overt racism; these forms we consciously condemn. The conveyor belt represents the invisible forces of society or the biased institutional policies, practices, and structures that control our everyday lives. From the moment of birth, we are placed on the conveyor belt and culturally conditioned/socialized to believe that we are headed in the right direction. For many White people, the movement of the belt is barely noticeable, and its movement remains hidden from conscious awareness. This allows White people to remain naive and innocent about the harm their inaction imparts on people of color. Second, as indicated by Tatum (1997), one need not be actively racist in order to be racist. The pace by which one walks with the flow of the conveyor belt determines the degree to which one consciously or unconsciously harbors White supremacist notions: (a) *active racists* who are aware and deliberate in beliefs and actions move quickly; (b) those slowly strolling may be unintentional racists, unaware of their biases and the direction they are taking; and (c) *passive racists* may choose not to walk at all. Despite choosing not to walk in the direction of the walkway, passive racists are, nevertheless, being moved in a direction that allows for racism to thrive. On a personal level, despite beliefs of justice, equity, and fairness, inaction on the walkway ultimately means that these individuals are also responsible for the oppression of others. Race talk has potential to make White Americans aware of the conveyor belt movement and the ominous direction it is headed.

Third, most people of color are desperately trying to move or run in the opposite direction. Back talk from people of color is filled with attempts to make well-intentioned Whites aware of the direction they are taking and aware of the harm they are inflicting on people of color. But these people of color are hindered by many obstacles: well-intentioned White Americans who tell them they are going the wrong way (White talk); institutional policies and practices that put obstacles in their retreating path (institutional racism); and punishment from society for not obeying the traffic rules—a one-way street of bias and bigotry.

Fourth, despite limited success in battling the constant forces of racism, people of color are also slowly but surely being swept in a dangerous direction that has multiple implications for their psychological health, physical well-being, and standard of living. Walking at a fast pace and running in the opposite direction are never ending activities that are exhausting and energy depleting for people of color. Worst yet, they are being trampled by the large numbers of well-intentioned White Americans moving in the opposite direction. Giving up, or ultimately being swept to the end of the walkway, means a life of oppression and subordination.

Last, the questions being posed to us are challenging. How do we motivate White Americans to (a) notice the subtle movement of the walkway (making the invisible visible), (b) discern the ominous direction it is taking (White racial supremacy), (c) take action by moving in the opposite direction (antiracism), and (d) stop the conveyor belt and/or reverse its direction (institutional and societal change)?

Racial dialogues are one means by which we can impact the racial realities of Whites by making them racially/culturally aware, raise critical consciousness of the systemic forces of racism, and motivate them to consider changes at the individual, institutional, and societal levels. The unawareness of White Americans and the resistance to waking up are ingredients that manifest themselves in White talk that prevents the invisible from becoming visible. In the previous 10 chapters, I have outlined a number of obstacles to individual/personal change, and to institutional and societal changes. In this chapter I concentrate on personal changes that may be facilitated by race talk that result in greater comfort in discussing meaningful issues related to race, racism, Whiteness, and White privilege. On a personal level these goals include developing a *nonracist identity* and becoming *antiracist*. As mentioned previously, the former means listening to the voices of those most oppressed, self-reflection, and individual self-work; the later means breaking the silence of racism, taking personal and collective action to confront and end racism, and advocating for social justice in the policies, practices, and programs of our society.

DEVELOPING A NONRACIST AND ANTIRACIST RACIAL IDENTITY

Successful race talk is predicated on raising critical consciousness about race (Pasque et al., 2013) through cross-racial interactions (Valentine et al., 2012) and lived experience (Sue, 2013). For White Americans, successful racial dialogues allow them to grasp the significance of what it means to be White, and how Whiteness with its accompanying invisible norms and standards are entrenched into their everyday lives. This racial awakening and the development of a nonracist identity is intimately linked to racial identity development (Helms, 1990, 1995; Sue, 1995, 2013; Tatum, 1992, 1997). Thus, on a personal level, the question is, How do Whites develop a nonracist White identity and become antiracist—allies to people of color in the struggle for equal rights?

Over the past several decades, psychologists and educators have begun to emphasize the need for White Americans to deal with Whiteness as a sociodemographic racial category and to examine their own racism. They point out that most White Americans at some levels are willing to admit that persons of color are subjected to different experiences than majority group members. They are less willing, however, to admit that in many ways they have been unknowingly responsible for the oppression of others. Understanding these reactions and how they affect Whites is locked up in the process of White racial identity awakening. Further, psychologists and educators hypothesize that the comfort or discomfort experienced in race talk is related to the developmental level of the person's White racial identity (Helms, 1990; Tatum, 1992). Indeed, the emotive reactions of Whites during race talk seem correlated with their level of racial consciousness.

Studies, for example, have found that the level of White racial identity awareness was predictive of racism. The less aware Whites are of their racial identity, the more likely they were (a) to exhibit increased levels of racism, (b) to deny the racial reality of people of color, (c) to profess a color-blind approach to racial interactions, and (d) to find race talk uncomfortable, anxiety provoking, and threatening (Bell, 2003; Hardiman, 1982; Helms, 1990;

Pasque et al., 2013; Pope-Davis & Ottavi, 1994; Spanierman et al., 2006; Todd & Abrams, 2011). In some of these studies it was found that women tend to be less racist than men, probably because of women's greater experiences with discrimination and prejudice and a more enlightened sense of racial identity. Evidence also exists that multicultural competence (ability to communicate, understand the worldview of people of color, teach, manage, and supervise effectively in a pluralistic society) is correlated with White racial identity attitudes. Since developing multicultural sensitivity is a long-term developmental task, the work of many researchers has gradually converged toward a conceptualization of the process of racial/ethnic identity development for White Euro-Americans.

The process of healthy White identity development, according to psychologist Janet Helms (1990, 1995), involves a two-phase process: (1) the abandonment of White racism and (2) work to develop a nonracist White identity. Acceptance of this developmental process is based on several important assumptions that can be seen in resistance to race talk among White Americans. Entertaining their legitimacy is difficult for many White Americans because of the invisibility of Whiteness and racism, and their personal implications.

- First, racism is a basic and integral part of U.S. life and permeates all aspects of U.S. culture and institutions. This statement should be clear in light of our analysis of White supremacy, White privilege, and ethnocentric monoculturalism.
- Second, in keeping with previous assertions, everyone is socialized into U.S. society and, therefore, inherits the biases, stereotypes, and racist attitudes, beliefs, and behaviors of the society (some more and others less). Although an unpleasant conclusion for many, it is inescapable that Whites harbor racist beliefs whether knowingly or unknowingly.
- Third, the level of White racial identity development in an interracial encounter (working effectively with and understanding people of color) affects the process and outcome of relationships and how we talk about race to one another.
- Fourth, how Whites perceive themselves as racial/cultural beings seems to be strongly correlated with how they perceive and respond to racial stimuli. Consequently, their race-related realities often represent major differences between their view of the world and that of people of color.
- Fifth, White racial identity development seems to follow an identifiable sequence. That is, there is an assumption that White Americans who are

born and raised in the United States may move through levels of consciousness regarding their own identity as racial/cultural beings.

- Last, the most desirable development for White Americans is to not only accept their Whiteness, but also define it in a nondefensive and nonracist manner. This must be an active and constant ongoing process where Whites do so without guilt, but with a determined understanding that to deny the humanity of any one person is to deny the humanity of all.

The following developmental phases of White racial identity development are distilled from the work of a number of scholars (Hardiman, 1982; Helms, 1990; Ponterotto, Utsey & Pedersen, 2006; W. Rowe, Bennett, & Atkinson, 1994; Sue & Sue, 2013; Tatum, 1997). Considerable liberty has been taken to categorize, summarize, and condense their descriptive meanings.

Phase 1—Naïveté

While none of us enter this world as an empty slate, it is also clear that none of us are born with preconceived notions, stereotypes, racial bigotry, or hatred. As mentioned previously, our early childhoods are generally marked with a naive curiosity about race. There is a tendency to be innocent, open, and spontaneous regarding racial differences.

I remember one story an African American woman told me about a young White male child who had never before met a Black person in the flesh. She was interviewing for a job as a cook with a White couple, and was seated on their living room sofa. The young child played on the floor several feet away, but slowly but purposely rolled his truck closer and closer to her. When it rolled up against the woman's leg, he hastily retrieved it, but moved next to her. As the White couple and African American woman continued their conversation, the young child reached over, and with his right forefinger, rubbed it down her leg. He then looked at his finger, obviously interested in whether the black color would rub off on it. Needless to say, the White couple froze with horror at the actions of their son.

Examples like the above are not atypical for very young children. Other than the embarrassment and apprehensions of adults around the child, there is little discomfort associated with this behavior for the youngster. Young children notice differences, but the awareness of their social meaning attached to race and bias/prejudice are either absent or minimal. Such an open and naive orientation becomes less characteristic as the socialization process progresses.

Studies reveal that racial awareness and the burgeoning social meanings occur between the ages of 3 and 5 years (Aboud, 1988; APA Presidential Task Force, 2012; Hirschfield, 2001). The negative reactions of parents, relatives, friends, and peers toward issues of race, however, begin to convey mixed signals. This is reinforced by the educational system and mass media that instill racial biases in children and propel them into the Conformity developmental phase.

Phase 2—Conformity

The Naïveté phase ends quickly because of the social messages about race that bombard people from the moment of birth. Nevertheless, characteristics of this early developmental level are maintained throughout the Conformity phase. For example, people can continue to be very naive about the meaning and implications associated with race and racism. While there is increasing awareness of racial differences, there continues to be minimal awareness of being a White racial being and, subsequently, a strong belief in the universality of values and norms governing behavior.

Two major but diametrically opposed belief systems are being planted in people's psyche. First, they are taught about the virtues of democracy: that everyone was created equal, that the nation was built on the foundations of freedom, that equal access and opportunity are the building blocks of our society, and that prejudice, discrimination, and bigotry are not only distasteful, but evil. From this early schooling, they are told that racism is not only illegal, but also morally wrong. The good, decent, and moral citizen does not discriminate on the basis of race. These beliefs are deeply ingrained into their self-image and identity. To be accused of being a racist in our society is to malign their personal integrity. As mentioned throughout, this is one of the major impediments to race talk.

Yet, processes that are more insidious and powerful teach them that people of color are inferior and deserve their inferior treatment. The White parent who quickly locks the car doors while driving through a Latino neighborhood, the mother who discourages a child from playing with Black schoolmates, the young child who overhears racial epithets, and the negative portrayal of minorities in the media all lead to one damning conclusion: Persons of color are the dregs of our society and should be avoided. The Conformity phase is marked by acceptance of White superiority and minority inferiority. Consciously or unconsciously, Whites begin to believe that White culture is the most highly developed, and all others are primitive or inferior.

Contradictory beliefs can exist because of people's ability to compartmentalize attitudes, beliefs, and behaviors. On the one hand, they may believe that they are not racist, yet on the other hand they believe that minority inferiority justifies discriminatory and inferior treatment. Or they believe persons of color are different and deviant, yet believe that people are people and that differences are unimportant. The primary mechanisms operating here are denial and compartmentalization. For example, Whites deny that they belong to a race, which allows them to avoid personal responsibility for perpetuating a racist system. It is important to note that in general, people at this phase of development are unaware of these beliefs and operate as if others universally share them: "Differences are unimportant"; "People are people"; "We are all the same under the skin"; "We should treat everyone the same"; "Problems wouldn't exist if minorities would only assimilate"; and "Discrimination and prejudice are something that others do." During race talk, Whites at this level of consciousness profess color blindness and the belief that people are no different from one another regardless of race, gender, and so forth.

Because of naïveté and encapsulation, it is possible for two diametrically opposed belief systems to coexist in the mind of Whites: (1) There is an uncritical acceptance of White supremacist notions that relegate minorities into the inferior category with all the racial stereotypes, and (b) there is a belief that racial and cultural differences are considered unimportant. This allows Whites to avoid perceiving themselves as a dominant group member, or of having biases and prejudices. In her own White racial awakening, Peggy McIntosh (2002) stated,

> My schooling gave me no training in seeing myself as an oppressor, as an unfairly advantaged person, or as a participant in a damaged culture. I was taught to see myself as an individual whose moral state depended on her individual moral will. . . . Whites are taught to think of their lives as morally neutral, normative, and average, and also ideal, so that when we work to benefit others, this is seen as work which will allow "them" to be more like "us." (p. 99)

The primary mechanism used in encapsulation is denial—that people are different, that discrimination exists, and of your own prejudices. Instead, the locus of the problem is seen to reside in the minority individual or group. Minorities wouldn't encounter problems if they would assimilate and acculturate (melting pot), if they would value education, or if they would only work harder.

The Conformity stage is marked by conscious beliefs in the democratic ideal—that everyone has an equal opportunity to succeed in a free society and those who fail must bear the responsibility for their failure. White Euro-Americans become the social reference group and the socialization process consistently instills messages of White superiority and minority inferiority throughout one's upbringing. The underemployment, unemployment, and under education of marginalized groups in our society are seen as support that non-White groups are lesser than Whites. Because everyone has an equal opportunity to succeed, the lack of success of minority groups is seen as evidence of some negative personal or group characteristic (low intelligence, inadequate motivation, or biological/cultural deficits). Victim blaming is strong as the existence of oppression, discrimination, and racism are denied. While the Naïveté stage is brief in duration, the Conformity phase can last a lifetime.

Phase 3—Dissonance

In the Conformity phase of development, Whites are unlikely to recognize the polarities of democratic principles of equality and the unequal treatment of people of color. This is a major barrier to race talk. Such obliviousness may eventually break down when they become aware of inconsistencies. For example, a White person becomes conflicted over irresolvable racial moral dilemmas that are frequently perceived as polar opposites: believing they are nonracist, yet not wanting their son or daughter to marry outside of their race; believing that all men are created equal, yet seeing society treat people of color as second-class citizens; and not acknowledging the existence of oppression, yet witnessing it. Conflict between loyalty to one's group and those of humanistic ideals may manifest itself in various ways. Whites become increasingly conscious of their Whiteness and may experience dissonance, resulting in feelings of guilt, depression, helplessness, or anxiety. Statements such as "My grandfather is really prejudiced, but I try not to be" and "I'm personally not against interracial marriages, but I worry about the children" are representative of personal struggles occurring in the White person. This type of conflict is best exemplified in the following passage from Sara Winter (1977):

> When someone pushes racism into my awareness, I feel guilty (that I could be doing so much more); angry (I don't like to feel like I'm wrong); defensive (I already have two Black friends . . . I worry more about racism than most whites

do—isn't that enough); turned off (I have other priorities in my life with guilt about that thought); helpless (the problem is so big—what can I do?). I HATE TO FEEL THIS WAY. That is why I minimize race issues and let them fade from my awareness whenever possible. (p. 24)

Movement into the Dissonance phase occurs when Whites are forced to deal with the inconsistencies that have been compartmentalized or encounter information/experiences at odds with their denial. In most cases, they are forced to acknowledge their Whiteness at some level, to examine their own cultural values, and to see the conflict between upholding humanistic nonracist values and their contradictory behaviors. For example, they may consciously believe that all men are created equal and that they treat everyone the same but suddenly experience reservations about having African Americans move next door or having their son or daughter involved in an interracial relationship. These more personal experiences bring them face to face with their own prejudices and biases. In this situation, thoughts that "I am not prejudiced," "I treat everyone the same regardless of race, creed, or color," and "I do not discriminate" collide with their denial system.

Or, some major event (assassination of Martin Luther King, viewing the Rodney King beating, etc.) may force them to realize that racism is alive and well in the United States. The increasing realization that they are biased and that Euro-American society does play a part in oppressing people of color is an unpleasant one. Dissonance may make them feel guilty, shameful, angry, and depressed. Rationalizations may become the manner used to exonerate their own inactivity in combating perceived injustice or personal feelings of prejudice: "I'm only one person, what can I do" or "Everyone is prejudiced, even minorities." As these conflicts ensue, they may retreat into the protective confines of White culture (encapsulation of the previous stage) or move progressively toward insight and revelation (Resistance and Immersion stage).

Whether they regress is related to the strength of positive forces pushing them forward (support for challenging racism) or negative forces (fear of some loss) pushing them backward. For example, challenging the prevailing beliefs of the times may mean risking ostracism from other White relatives, friends, neighbors, and colleagues. Regardless of their choice, there are many uncomfortable feelings of guilt, shame, anger, and depression related to the realization of inconsistencies in their belief system. Guilt and shame is most likely related to the recognition of their role in perpetuating racism. Or, guilt may result from fear of speaking out on the issues or taking responsibility for their part in a current situation. For example, they may witness an act of racism, hear a racist comment, or be given preferential treatment over a person of color, but decide not to say anything for fear of violating racist White norms. Oftentimes, they may delude themselves with rationalizations: "I'm just one person. What can I do about it?" This approach is one frequently taken by many White people in which they rationalize their behaviors by the belief that they are powerless to make changes. There is a tendency to retreat into White culture. If, however, others (may include some family and friends) are supportive, encouraging, and accepting of truth seeking, forward movement is more likely.

Phase 4—Resistance and Immersion

This phase is marked by questioning and challenging one's own racism. For the first time, Whites may begin to realize the omnipresence of racism and achieve disturbing insights. Racism becomes noticeable in all facets of their daily lives (advertising, television, educational materials, interpersonal interactions, etc.). A major questioning of their racism and that of others marks this phase of development. In addition, increasing awareness of how racism operates and its pervasiveness in U.S. culture and institutions is the major hallmark at this level of development. It is as if Whites have awakened to the realities of oppression; see how educational materials, the mass media, advertising, and so on portray and perpetuate stereotypes; and recognize how being White has allowed them certain advantages denied to various groups of color. They are likely to experience considerable anger at family and friends, institutions, and larger societal values that are seen as having sold them a false bill of goods (democratic ideals) that were never practiced. Guilt is also felt for having been a part of the oppressive system. Strangely enough, the person is likely to undergo a form of racial self-hatred at this stage. Negative feelings about being White are present and the accompanying feelings of guilt, shame, and anger toward oneself and other Whites may develop.

The White liberal syndrome may develop and be manifested in two complementary styles: (1) the paternalistic protector role or (2) an overidentification with the minority group. In the former, they may devote energies in an almost paternalistic attempt to protect people of color from abuse. In extreme instances, people may actually even want to identify with a particular minority group (Asian, Black, etc.) in order to escape their own Whiteness. They will soon discover, however, that these roles are not appreciated by people of color and will experience rejection. Again, they may resolve this dilemma by moving back into the protective confines of White culture (Conformity), again experience conflict (Dissonance), or move directly to the Introspective phase. In many cases, they may develop a negative reaction toward their own group or culture. While these Whites may romanticize people of color, they cannot interact confidently with them because they fear making racist mistakes. This discomfort is best exemplified in a passage by Sara Winter (1977):

> We avoid Black people because their presence brings painful questions to mind. Is it okay to talk about watermelons or mention "black coffee"? Should we use Black slang and tell racial jokes? How about talking about our experiences in Harlem, or mentioning our Black lovers? Should we conceal the fact that our mother still employs a Black cleaning lady? . . . We're embarrassedly aware of trying to do our best but to "act natural" at the same time. No wonder we're more comfortable in all-White situations where these dilemmas don't arise. (p. 25)

The discomfort in realizing that they are White and that their group has engaged in oppression may propel them into the next phase of development.

Phase 5—Introspection

This phase is most likely a compromise of swinging from an extreme of unconditional acceptance of White identity to a rejection of the negative attributes of Whiteness. It is a state of relative quiescence, introspection, and reformulation of what it means to be White. Enlightened people realize and no longer deny that they have participated in oppression, that they benefit from White privilege, and that racism is an integral part of U.S. society. However, they become less motivated by guilt and defensiveness, accept their Whiteness, and seek to define their own identity and that of their social group. This acceptance, however, does not mean a less active role in combating oppression. The process may involve addressing these questions: What does it mean to be White? Who am I in relation to my Whiteness? Who am I as a racial/cultural being?

The feelings or affective elements may be existential in nature and involve feelings of lack of connectedness, isolation, confusion, and loss. In other words, they realize that they may never fully understand the minority experience but feel disconnected from their Euro-American group as well. In some ways, the Introspective phase is similar in dynamics to the Dissonance one in that both represent a transition from one perspective to another. The process used to answer the preceding questions and to deal with the ensuing feelings may involve a searching, observing, and questioning attitude. Answers to these questions involve dialoging and observing their own social group and actively creating and experiencing interactions with various groups of color as well.

Asking painful question of who they are in relation to their racial heritage; honestly confronting their biases and prejudices; and accepting responsibility for their Whiteness is the culminating outcome of the Introspective stage. New ways of defining their White Euro-American social group and membership in that group become important. The intense soul searching is most evident in Sara Winter's (1977) personal journey as she writes,

> In this sense we Whites are the victims of racism. Our victimization is different from that of Blacks, but it is real. We have been programmed into the oppressor roles we play, without our informed consent in the process. Our unawareness is part of the programming: None of us could tolerate the oppressor position, if we lived with a day-to-day emotional awareness of the pain inflicted on other humans through the instrument of our behavior.... We Whites benefit in concrete ways, year in and year out, from the present racial arrangements. All my life in White neighborhoods, White schools, White jobs and dealing with White police (to name only a few), I have experienced advantages that are systematically not available to Black people. It does not make sense for me to blame myself for the advantages that have come my way by virtue of my Whiteness. But absolving myself from guilt does not imply forgetting about racial injustice or taking it lightly (as my guilt pushes me to do). (p. 27)

There is realization that their Whiteness has been defined in opposition to people of color, by standards of White supremacy. By being able to step out of this racist paradigm and redefining what her Whiteness meant to her, Sara Winter is able to add meaning to developing a nonracist identity. The extremes of good/bad or positive/negative attachments to White and people of color begin to become more realistic. They no longer deny being White, honestly confront their racism, understand the concept of White privilege, and feel increased comfort in relating to persons of color.

Phase 6—Integrative Awareness

Reaching this level of development is most characterized as (a) understanding self as a racial/cultural being, (b) awareness of sociopolitical influences with respect to racism, (c) appreciation of racial/cultural diversity, and (d) rooting out buried and nested racial fears and emotions. The formation of a nonracist White Euro-American identity emerges and becomes internalized. Whites begin to value multiculturalism, are comfortable around members of culturally different groups, and feel a strong connectedness with members of many groups. Perhaps, most importantly, is their inner sense of security and strength, which needs to develop and which is needed to function in a society that is only marginally accepting of integratively aware White persons.

The Integrative Awareness stage is the result of forming a new social and personal identity. With the greater comfort in understanding themselves and the development of a nonracist White identity, social action becomes a primary goal. Whites begin to accept responsibility for effecting personal and social change without always relying on persons of color to lead the way.

> To end racism, Whites have to pay attention to it and continue to pay attention. Since avoidance is such a basic dynamic of racism, paying attention will not happen naturally. We Whites must learn how to hold racism realities in our attention. We must learn to take responsibility for this process ourselves, without waiting for Blacks' actions to remind us that the problem exists, and without depending on Black people to reassure us and forgive us for our racist sins. In my experience, the process is painful but it is a relief to shed the fears, stereotypes, immobilizing guilt we didn't want in the first place. (Winters, 1977, p. 28)

The racist-free identity, however, must be nurtured, validated, and supported in order to be sustained in a hostile environment. As in the metaphor of the moving walkway, integrative aware people will be constantly bombarded by attempts to resocialize them into the oppressive society. Increasing awareness of their own Whiteness, reduced feelings of guilt, acceptance of their role in perpetuating racism, and renewed determination to abandon White entitlement leads to an integrative status. Such people become increasingly knowledgeable about racial, ethnic, and cultural differences; value diversity; and are no longer fearful, intimated, or uncomfortable with the experiential reality of race. Development of a nonracist White identity becomes increasingly strong. Indeed, many begin to feel comfortable with their nonracist White identity, do not personalize attacks upon White supremacy, and can explore the issues of racism and personal responsibility without defensiveness. In other words, they can walk the talk and actively value and seek out interracial experiences. Characteristics of this stage can be found in the personal journey of Mark Kiselica (1998):

> I was deeply troubled as I witnessed on a daily basis the detrimental effects of institutional racism and oppression on ethnic-minority groups in this country. The latter encounters forced me to recognize my privileged position in our society because of my status as a so-called Anglo. It was upsetting to know that I, a member of White society, benefited from the hardships of others that were caused by a racist system. I was also disturbed by the painful realization that I was, in some ways, a racist. I had to come to grips with the fact that I had told and laughed at racist jokes and, through such behavior, had supported White racist attitudes. If I really wanted to become an effective, multicultural psychologist, extended and profound self-reckoning was in order. At times, I wanted to flee from this unpleasant process by merely participating superficially with the remaining task . . . while avoiding any substantive self-examination. (pp. 10–11)

This status is different from the previous one in two major ways: (1) It is marked by a shift in focus from trying to change people of color to changing the self and other Whites, and (2) it is marked with increasing experiential and affective understanding that were lacking in the previous developmental levels. This later process is extremely important. Indeed, Helms (1990) believes that a successful resolution of this stage requires an emotional catharsis or release that forces people to relive or reexperience previous emotions that were denied or distorted. The ability to achieve this affective/experiential upheaval leads to a euphoria or even a feeling of rebirth and is a necessary condition to developing a new nonracist White identity. Again, Sara Winter (1977) states,

> Let me explain this healing process in more detail. We must unearth all the words and memories we generally try not to think about, but which are inside us all the time: "nigger," "Uncle Tom," "jungle bunny," "Oreo"; lynching, cattle prods, castrations, rapists, "black pussy," and black men with their huge penises, and hundreds more. (I shudder as I write.) We need to review three different kinds of material: (1) all our personal memories connected with blackness and black people including everything we can recall hearing or reading; (2) all the racist images and stereotypes we've ever heard, particularly the grossest and most hurtful ones; (3) any race related things we ourselves said, did or omitted doing which we feel bad about today. . . . Most whites begin with a good deal of

amnesia. Eventually the memories crowd in, especially when several people pool recollections. Emotional release is a vital part of the process. Experiencing feelings seems to allow further recollections to come. I need persistent encouragement from my companions to continue. (p. 27)

While Sara Winter speaks primarily about the internally racist messages regarding African Americans, her process of healing is also applicable to all marginalized groups.

Phase 7—Commitment to Antiracist Action

Integrative Awareness is a major step in combating racism, but it is not enough. Phase 7 is most characterized by social action. If Whites reach this developmental phase, there is likely to be a consequent change in their behavior and an increased commitment toward eradicating oppression as well. It requires courage on their part to act in a manner that speaks to social justice. Seeing wrong and actively working to right it require moral fortitude and direct action. Objecting to racist jokes; trying to educate family, friends, neighbors, and coworkers about racial issues; and taking direct action to eradicate racism in the schools, workplace, and social policy often put them in direct conflict with other Whites.

They will, however, become increasingly immunized to social pressures for conformance because their reference group begins to change. In addition to family and friends, they will begin to actively form alliances with persons of color and other liberated Whites. They will become a second family to liberated Whites, giving them validation and encouraging them to continue the struggle against individual, institutional, and societal racism: stopping the conveyor belt. Some antiracist actions associated with Phase 7 include

- Searching out valid information on race and racism.
- Actively seeking out interracial relationships and experiences.
- Being open to discussing racial issues with acquaintances of color.
- Expressing positive racial messages to family members, friends, and coworkers.
- Standing against racist comments and jokes.
- Joining or forming community or professional groups that work on behalf of multiculturalism, diversity, and antiracism.
- Planning, coordinating, conducting, or attending antiracism forums with other interested parties.

- Voting for candidates who share your vision of multiculturalism and antiracism.
- Supporting public policies that allow for equal access and opportunity.
- Advocate for a multicultural curriculum in schools.

WHITE RACIAL IDENTITY DEVELOPMENT AND RACE TALK

It would be naive to believe that race talk alone could result in the development of a nonracist White racial identity. But, knowledge of White racial identity development, especially by educators and those hoping to facilitate racial dialogues, is extremely helpful in understanding the cognitive, emotional, and behavioral reactions manifested during race talk (Bell, 2002, 2003; Pasque et al., 2013; Sue, 2013). In most cases, these reactions provide clues as to the most likely resistances associated with each level of developmental consciousness. Further, by anticipating the resistances and challenges posed by White participants in a dialogue, it may allow educators to devise intervention strategies or techniques to overcome them. Here is a brief summary of the most likely reactions associated with each level of White racial consciousness.

Naïveté—Because this phase is marked by *innocence* and a lack of associating racial/ethnic differences with the dominant stereotypes and biases of society, it applies mainly to children. *Openness, curiosity, and a nondefensive attitude* toward differences are the norm. The implications for educational interventions are prevention and developing activities to combat associating differences with inferiority, deviancy, and otherness. This has major implications for how parents raise their children and for our educational systems, especially in the curriculum of pre-K through 12 schools. If our schools were truly multicultural in how they teach and educate, it would allow us to prevent the formation of biases and bigotry. Race talk, especially how we model talking about race to one another and how we talk to children about race, will determine whether they develop firmly ingrained biases or become immunized to them.

Conformity—Individuals at this level of consciousness are unaware of themselves as racial beings, hold contradictory beliefs and attitudes about minority inferiority, and believe in the universality of the human condition (people are people and differences don't matter). *Compartmentalization* of these contradictory beliefs and attitudes allows them to be held at odds with one another. In race talk, such individuals on a conscious level are likely to express themes of meritocracy, equal access and opportunity, assimilation and acculturation, and color blindness. Beneath this exterior, however, are deeply embedded beliefs and feelings of White racial superiority and minority inferiority. The challenge for educators is how to get Whites to recognize these inconsistencies in their beliefs, attitudes, and behaviors. For educators it may mean overcoming the primary mechanism by which disparate attitudes are kept from confronting one another, the mechanism of *denial*.

Dissonance—Race talk forces Whites to confront the hypocrisy of their incongruent attitudes and beliefs: "I am not racist, but I do not want my son/daughter to marry a person of color." This phase of White development is likely to be evident by pronounced expressions of intense feelings: *anger* and *defensiveness* toward the confronter, *anxiety* about the meaning of these inconsistencies, and *fears* about recognizing one's own racism. Most educators who attempt to facilitate difficult dialogues on race will recognize this phase as the most characteristic in classroom racial dialogues. The Dissonance phase symbolizes the potential breakdown in the invisibility of racism, and opens the gateways to confronting the other fears outlined in previous chapters: (a) fear of appearing racist, (b) fear of realizing one's racism, (c) fear of confronting White privilege, and (d) fear of taking responsibility to end racism. Devising strategies and techniques to handle these nested or embedded emotions and resistances in race talk is important for a successful dialogue.

Resistance and Immersion—This phase is the result of realizing the meaning of inconsistences from the previous one. Resisting the cultural conditioning of a racist society and attempting to immerse oneself into understanding other groups of color become goals. Here the White person becomes extremely aware of inequities in society and the prevalence of racism in significant others and in the mass media. Racism in oneself, others, and society can no longer be denied. With it comes a sense of *anger* toward being sold a "false bill of goods" and these feelings may externalize toward family, significant others, and institutional entities. Becoming aware of one's complicity in the perpetuation of racism (albeit unknowingly) may also be accompanied by *guilt* and *shame*. Being ashamed of one's Whiteness or experiencing discomfort in being White may result in an attempt to escape one's identity as a White person and with attempts to overidentify with people of color. In facilitative race talk, this phase is most aided by helping Whites to realize that no one was born wanting to be racist, that guilt is nonproductive in making changes, and that they were socialized into oppressor roles, and then getting them to take action in defining their own Whiteness and what it means.

Introspection—In race talk, this phase is most characterized by an acceptance of one's own racism, and while some residual guilt may exist, there continues to be questioning of one's own Whiteness and what it means. Issues of White privilege and the meaning of White entitlement are now conscious to the person. Feelings are often *existential* in nature because the person seems to exist on the margins of multiple group identities and/or has difficulty with resolving conflicting issues. This phase of identity may prove a very uncomfortable one for White Americans; there are feelings of *disconnection* from other Whites (a sense of *loss* and ensuing *sadness*), *isolation* (lack of a supportive reference group), *hypocrisy* (rejection of White privilege, but benefiting from it), *confusion* about one's personal identity as a White person, and *awkwardness* and *discomfort* around groups of color, despite wanting intimate contact with them. Thus there is *confusion* about what to do and *helplessness* in realizing the vastness of the problem. The person exists in a never-never land and is most helped by race talk assignments that involve personal and group reflections and lived experience activities with people of color.

Integrative Awareness and Commitment to Antiracist Action—Both of these developmental phases represent two sides of the same coin and must be expressed together to have social justice implications. We combine them here because the following chapters address in more detail how to maintain a nonracist identity and to become antiracist. In both phases, the issues of isolation, disconnection, and loneliness are resolved as Whites become comfortable with defining their White identity in a nondefensive and nonracist manner. They are likely to be *comfortable* around many groups (Whites and people of color), advocate White self-reflection and action rather than attempting to change people of color, and feel *less fear and intimidation* over racial interactions. More importantly, in race talk, these individuals become valuable allies in educating their own White brothers and sisters. It is important to note, however, that Integrative Awareness does not necessarily lead to action on behalf of combating racism. As mentioned earlier in the conveyor belt analogy, becoming nonracist does not mean becoming antiracist. And, as our earlier research findings suggest, considerable *courage* and *determination* are required to stand against the toxicity of racism. Educational experiences and activities aimed at maintaining a nonracist and antiracist stance are of paramount importance, especially in a society that constantly attempts to resocialize liberated Whites back into the mainstream. We will address this important point in the following chapters.

In summary, race talk can help start the process of developing a healthy White racial identity. Successful racial dialogues can make use of White racial identity development processes to address the four important goals of race talk. First, race talk places Whites in new and oftentimes uncomfortable situations, impels them to question themselves as racial/cultural beings, and increases awareness of racial issues, especially racism. Second, race talk can help create conditions that impel change in the form of new insights, attitudes, and behaviors that lead Whites to a realization of their roles in the perpetuation of racism. Third, race talk that stresses the development and maintenance of a healthy White racial identity (nonracist) is of utmost to success. Last, race talk will hopefully facilitate the lived experience of White Americans, increase their understanding and comfort in relating to groups of color, and motivate them to take personal and social action in eradicating racism (antiracist).

Guidelines, Conditions, and Solutions for Having Honest Racial Dialogues

CHAPTER TWELVE

Being an Agent of Change: Guidelines for Educators, Parents, and Trainers

Recently after interviewing a potential nanny, I asked my daughter Chloe, 4, what she thought. "I don't like her brown skin?" my daughter replied, phrasing it like a question in that hesitant way she does when she knows she's testing. I was shocked—and horrified. She'd never mentioned skin color before, despite having good friends of different ethnicities, and I naively believed she was colorblind. Now, faced with the fear that I had inadvertently raised a pint-size racist, I biffed it. "That's not a nice thing to say," I scolded her. And then, unsure of what else to say, I said nothing at all. (Emmons, 2013)

As an Asian mother, how do I console my 6-year-old daughter who wants so much to be White, like all the other children in her class? June came home crying yesterday about kids teasing her over the shape of her eyes and other physical features. I told her she was beautiful, although different from the other kids, but it didn't seem to help. I remember going through the same thing, but I can't remember what my own mother told me. I suffered in silence, wishing to be like my other classmates. I don't want June to suffer in silence, but what can I say? How do I tell her there is nothing wrong with being

Chinese? Should I just ignore it and hope she will eventually understand? (Anonymous workshop participant's story)

It happens in every class. We're discussing a text, a publication, a current event, a poem. The content doesn't matter. It's the phrase that counts. A student comments and uses the phrase "African American" or even "black people." The reaction of the class—almost all white—is swift. As if chore-ographed, all eyes turn to the one student of color. The spotlight of eyes shines down and he or she blinks back as if staring into the sun. The teacher should use this moment to open a discussion. But let's talk first about what some teachers do: Nothing. In many cases, for many reasons, we miss this teachable moment by ignoring it. (Cytrynbaum, 2011)

Educators at all levels would benefit from experience and training in facil-itating difficult dialogues on race. A common and recurrent theme [among White educators] . . . was that successful and unsuccessful dialogues on race depended heavily on the racial sensitivities and skills of the teacher . . . most . . . were ineffective facilitators; most were "frozen or paralyzed" when a diffi-cult dialogue ensued, were "obviously uncomfortable and anxious," seemed as "confused as their students." (Sue, Lin, et al., 2009, p. 7)

Questions: In all four examples, how did parents and teachers respond to racial incidents or topics when presented to their children and students? What lessons are being taught to our young people by the adults most important in their lives? If you were the mother of Chloe, what would you say to her? If you were the Asian American mother, what would you say to the daughter? If you are a teacher and race-related issues arise in class, are you prepared to handle the situation? If these situations represent "teach-able moments," what would make them learning experiences? How should parents talk to their children about race and racism? How do teachers facil-itate a difficult dialogue on race among students?

All four examples represent how most parents and educators handle topics on race and racism: They ignore them, do nothing about them, or feel para-lyzed with anxiety and indecision (APA Presidential Task Force, 2012; Bryan, Wilson, Lewis, & Wills, 2012; Gomez, Overbey, Jones, & Beckrich, 2007; Sue, 2003). When one considers that parents and teachers are two of the most signif-icant others in the lives of our young, it becomes all too clear why race talk is so difficult. How adults view, react to, and talk about race and racism are passed on from generation to generation. Let us briefly explore the lessons embedded in these four examples.

First, the failure to adequately talk about race comfortably and honestly, to combat the misinformation and negative associations attributed to it, and to intervene in the continued victimization of children of color is unconscionable. We can clearly see the burgeoning psychological harm it is having on June, but there is also harm and victimization of Chloe as a White youngster as well. Both kids have little choice in how they view race and in the roles they play, because they are being raised in a society that teaches them that some groups are better than others and that it is best not to talk about it! For June it may mean a life combating low self-esteem and constantly dealing with the forces of prejudice and discrimination. For Chloe it means being socialized into an oppressor role, inheriting false beliefs and assumptions, desensitizing oneself to the pain and suffering of others, and having to remain oblivious to the harmful impact of racism. Avoidance of educational race talk, as we have seen, can damage the psyche of both children.

Second, the first two examples drive home the importance of early experiences in developing a nonracist identity as parents occupy a critical role in helping children first recognize the meaning of differences (APA Presidential Task Force, 2012; Rogin, 2013a). As mentioned previously, around ages 3 to 4, children become curious about the world around them, notice differences, view things through eyes of openness, and are receptive to parental interpretations of what these differences mean (Rogin, 2013b). Around ages 5 to 6, they begin to associate differences with what they hear from peers, the media and significant others. In most cases, these differences are associated with what the dominant society considers to be desirable and undesirable (Kashef, 2014). Both Chloe and June are encountering these associations, but with different effects on their racial identities. Unfortunately for both, the parents are at a loss regarding how best to deal with these situations. Thus, they avoid the topic, let it slip through the cracks, perpetuate the myth of color blindness, communicate that talking about race is taboo, and pass on the fears and apprehensions about race to their children. Thus, when Chloe and June become parents themselves, they are equally likely to pass on to their own sons and daughters the confusions, apprehensions, and fears of their mothers.

Third, it may be surmised that teachers are second to parents in the early influence they exert over young children. They are in a unique position to teach children and young adults about issues of race, diversity, and multiculturalism

(Bolgatz, 2005). They have the ability to determine the curriculum (monocultural or multicultural), to teach about life events (lived realities of race, gender, and sexual orientation), and to facilitate difficult dialogues on race in the classroom when they arise (teachable moments). Like parents, they have the ability to influence and convey their own hopes, fears, and perspectives about race and racism to their students. When educators lack critical consciousness about race/racism, have not adequately dealt with their own racial hang-ups, and are uncomfortable and unprepared to deal with difficult dialogues on race, they become part of the race talk problem (Bell, 2003; Pollock, 2004). Instead of teaching children how to address and talk openly and honestly about issues of race, they model behavior similar to their parental counterparts: Race is a taboo topic and should be avoided or ignored.

Fourth, it is clear that prevention is better than remediation. Unfortunately, most adults have already gone through a flawed socialization process and have inherited the biases and fears about race taught by significant others, the mass media, an educational curriculum deficient in addressing race matters, and biased institutional policies and practices (APA Presidential Task Force, 2012; Bolgatz, 2005; J. M. Jones, 1997). Without adequate intervention by enlightened parents and teachers during the pre-K through 12 years, our young will internalize the prejudices of society. Thus, as adults, our biases are already invisible and embedded in our identities; we fear exploring the topic of race. Unlearning our prejudices and becoming aware of them through exercises that confront our biases and fears must be *remedial* in nature; a task much more difficult than if we were to *prevent* them from forming in the first place. If children in the pre-K through 12 levels were truly exposed to a multicultural curriculum that was antiracist in nature, we could prevent these biases from taking hold by countering the prejudicial messages of society. Thus, multicultural education that has a strong antiracist orientation is of utmost importance in helping children to develop a nonracist identity.

Last, it is clear that most parents and teachers recognize some of the racial dilemmas faced by their sons, daughters, and students, but are paralyzed by indecision and not knowing what to do. As a White parent, how does Chloe's mother teach her daughter about race and racism? As a parent of color, how does June's mother help her child to understand the sting and stigma of racism? When a difficult dialogue on race arises in the classroom, how do teachers make it a teachable moment for all students? There is much that parents and teachers can do. They must not become paralyzed by these difficult racial questions and observations, because they only foster inaction by giving people an excuse not to challenge others and themselves. While the battle against prejudice and discrimination must be a systemic national effort, there is much that can be done on an individual basis, especially as a parent or teacher. Race talk as a means to make the invisible visible; to confront biases, prejudices, and fears; and to help one another understand ourselves as racial/cultural beings opens the educational gateways to self-reflection and positive change. Developing race talk skills is crucial for parents and teachers if they desire to help themselves and young people.

Talking to Children About Race and Racism

> An unenlightened person cannot enlighten others. All he or she can do is spread ignorance and misinformation.

This is a statement I frequently make to teachers and parents who ask what they should say or do with their students or children when confronted with racial incidents such as those described in the four narratives. Most teachers and parents are quick to ask for techniques and strategies to deal with racial situations or topics that they realize should be addressed, but they are paralyzed in deciding what type of action to take. Providing them with specific race talk skills can be very effective if they are enlightened about issues of race, have done the necessary hard and painful task of understanding their own biases and prejudices (Kiselica, 1998, 1999), and are comfortable in their relationships with people of color (APA Presidential Task Force, 2012; Bolgatz, 2005). If unenlightened, however, providing strategies of race talk will do little good without knowledge and understanding of the racial issues and goals they hope to achieve. Attempts to do so may only lead to misinformation, ignorance, and a perpetuation of the fears associated with race dialogues. Becoming culturally competent in facilitating difficult dialogues on race presupposes that parents and teachers must first do the necessary work of confronting their own biases, prejudices, and assumptions about human behavior. Self-healing must come before other healing. Developing a healthy racial identity means becoming liberated from one's racist social conditioning and developing the ability to truly understand the meaning and implications of racism. To attain these goals, parents and their children, and teachers and their students must all learn through lived experience, and not just through situations and contexts removed from the people they hope to understand. Research supports the belief that racial awakening is most likely to occur when people encounter situations, events, and/or experiences that challenge their preconceived notions, beliefs, or values (Bryan et al., 2012; Pasque et al., 2013; Sue, Lin, et al., 2009).

GUIDELINES FOR TAKING PERSONAL RESPONSIBILITY FOR CHANGE

Taking responsibility for change means overcoming the inertia and feeling of powerlessness on a personal level. People can grow and change if they are personally willing to confront and unlearn their racist conditioning (Kiselica, 1999; Sue, 2003; Winter, 1977). To accomplish this task, people must unlearn racist misinformation on a cognitive level (factual), as well as misinformation that has been glued together by painful emotions and behaviors. More importantly, they must begin to accept the responsibility for the pain and suffering they may have personally caused others.

Unlearning hidden biases means acquiring accurate information and experiences. Much of how people come to know about other cultures is through the media, what family and friends convey to them, and through public education texts (President's Initiative on Race, 1998, 1999). These sources cannot be counted on to give an accurate picture because they can be filled with stereotypes, misinformation, and deficit portrayals (Sue, 2003). Five commonsense guidelines seem to hold promise in obtaining a more accurate picture of culturally diverse groups in the United States (Gomez et al., 2007; Kashef, 2014; President's Initiative on Race, 1998, 1999; Rogin, 2013a, 2013b; Sue, 2003).

Guideline 1—Learn About People of Color From Sources Within the Group

First, parents and children, and teachers and students, must experience and learn from as many sources as possible (not just the media or what neighbors, peers, and significant others may say) in order to check out the validity of their assumptions and understanding. Especially important is information that originates from the groups people hope to understand. If White Americans want to understand racism, for example, information from other Whites may not be the most insightful or accurate sources. Sources that come directly from communities of color and from people of color act as a counterbalance to the worldview expressed by White society about culturally diverse groups. Acquiring information from minority-run or minority-edited radio and TV stations or publications may allow others to more accurately understand the thoughts, hopes, fears, and aspirations from the perspective of people of color.

For the average citizen, for example, reading fiction, poetry, or attending plays about the culture is one way to develop knowledge of it. Educators and teachers should try to avoid narratives that reinforce negative attitudes and stereotypes by selecting those works written by a person from within the culture. Read literature written by or for persons of the culture. This applies to both fiction and nonfiction. While the professional and nonprofessional literature often portrays minorities in stereotypic ways, writings from individuals of that group may provide richness based on experiential reality. For example, there are many books (many have been on the *New York Times* best-seller list) written by minority authors about nearly every racial or ethnic group; about their history, culture, family relationships; and about topics such as prejudice and racism. Reading such literature makes it possible to enter the cultural world of minorities in a safe and nonthreatening way. Time and space do not permit recommending specific texts, nor outlining how they might be used to aid our own growth and development, or that of children and young adults. But, with a little work, these can be identified quickly and easily. Here are three examples of the racial/cultural themes that are ripe for discussion with older students and children. These have become classics.

1. *The House on Mango Street* by Sandra Cisneros (1994) is a compelling and insightful story of Esperanza's life in a Latino neighborhood of Chicago. It is told in a series of short vignettes that are a commentary on race relations and cultural differences.

   Those who don't know any better come into our neighborhood scared. They think we're dangerous. They think we will attack them with shiny knives. They are stupid people who are lost and got here by mistake.... All brown all around, we are safe. But watch us drive into a neighborhood of another color and our knees go shakityshake and our car windows get rolled up tight and our eyes look straight ahead. Yeah. That is how it goes and goes. (p. 12)

2. The following passage comes from *Shadowman's Way* by Paul Pitts (1992) that describes the contemporary life of a Navaho adolescent. In his description of differences between a White student and himself, he says,

   He seemed to be working to keep the conversation going. In class, I have noticed that it's important to the white kids to keep talking. It's different with Navajos, we like silence. If there's a pause in the talking, it's not uncomfortable for us.

3. This passage comes from *A Lesson Before Dying* by Earnest Gaines (1997). It is the story about an educated Black man's struggle to maintain his personal dignity in the face of racism and marginalization.

> I had come through the back door against my will, and it seemed that he and the sheriff were doing everything they could to humiliate me even more by making me wait on them. I had to put up with that because of those in the quarter, but I damned sure would not add hurt to injury by eating at his kitchen table. I tried to decide how I should respond to them. Whether I should act like the teacher that I was, or like the nigger that I was supposed to be.... To show too much intelligence would have been an insult to them. To show a lack of intelligence would have been a greater insult to me. (p. 172)

In the first passage, the main character speaks to the irrational fears people may experience when they enter a minority neighborhood, but it is muted with understanding that people of color also experience similar fears; the second passage speaks to differences in communication and learning styles between Whites and Native Americans; and the last passage speaks to the humiliation of racism and the struggle to maintain personal dignity in the face of forced compliance. Such readings contain so many nuggets of truth concerning race relations and cultural differences that they are excellent tools to generate discussions of racial issues.

Another safe and enjoyable way to learn about minority experiences is to attend a play, movie, musical, dance, or entertainment event put on by ethnic minority group members. In many respects, you will be amazed by the many universal themes they portray about life, but also cultural and race-related themes that deal with their own cultures, struggles, and ethnic celebrations. *12 Years a Slave*, written by Solomon Northrup (1853) and adapted into a film, the 2013 Oscar winner for best picture, is a powerful picture depicting the travesty of slavery (past and present) and the dehumanizing impact on both Blacks and Whites. Amy Tan's *The Joy Luck Club* (1989) is one of the best novels (made into a film in 1993) that explores Chinese American relationships between mothers and daughters and provides insights into the unique cultural struggles of Asian Americans in U.S. society. Those of my generation cannot forget the major impact that the television miniseries *Roots* by Alex Haley (1974) had on many viewers. It traced the history of a Black man, kidnapped from Africa and enslaved in the South, and the evolution of his family, friends, and generations that followed. For those who have never seen the series, the entire dozen or so tapes are available at almost all video rental stores and school libraries. Even if seen before, sharing them with family and friends can generate much race talk. Another very rich source of information often comes from PBS (Public Broadcasting System). Not too long ago, they produced a series of films shown on television that revolved around their race initiative. The films continue to be available for everyone to access.

In summary, literary narratives, entertainment, and educational events have been used throughout human history to explore, entertain, and reveal truths about the human condition. They are powerful means to enhance the empathic response of readers, explore issues of tolerance and understanding of different lifestyles and worldviews, and increase sensitivity, knowledge, and awareness of culturally different groups in our society. These sources can be used to facilitate race talk by allowing children, young adults, and adults to discuss race issues from a safe vantage point. As seen in the next chapter, a skilled race talk facilitator can help readers and viewers move the dialogue to a more personal level and encourage self-exploration through the reactions and feelings generated from the audience.

Guideline 2—Learn From Healthy and Strong People of the Culture

A balanced picture of people of color requires spending time with healthy and strong individuals of that culture. The mass media and our educational texts (usually written from the perspectives of Euro-Americans) frequently portray groups of color as uncivilized, pathological, criminals, or delinquents. Little wonder the images people acquire are primarily negative. Parents and teachers must make an effort to fight such negative conditioning and ask, "What are the desirable aspects of the culture, the history, and the group?" This can only come about if Whites have contact with healthy representatives of that community. Since Whites seldom spend much intimate time with persons of color, they are likely to believe the societal projection of minorities as being law breakers, unintelligent, prone to violence, unmotivated, and uninterested in relating to the larger society.

Social psychological studies suggest that contact with people of color is a necessary condition to dispel stereotypes and fears (Allport, 1954; APA Presidential Task Force, 2012; J. M. Jones, 1997). Ironically, White Americans are most likely to have contact with people of color who represent only a narrow spectrum of the group—those who have gotten into trouble with society or who need special help. Thus, contacts are usually with the homeless, antisocial indigents, and the mentally troubled. A social worker, for example, is unlikely to work with clients who are problem free, well adjusted, successful, and have a strong family upbringing. Rather, they see dysfunctional families, homeless people, those in poverty, and those who have problems functioning independently without aid. Although White social workers also work primarily with disturbed White clients as well, their relationships with their own White communities place them in contact with others who represent healthy friends, neighbors, and coworkers. An absence of contact with the multitude of healthy, autonomous, successful, and well-adjusted families and individuals in minority communities provides an unbalanced or lopsided picture of people of color.

Overcoming personal racial fears and discomfort around people of color is not an easy task. It requires trying out new behaviors and changing people's pattern of relationships. It is hard enough to meet and become comfortable with people of one's own group, but becomes harder with people of another race or culture. Here are some everyday examples of what can be done to increase healthy contact with people of color and their communities.

- Frequent minority-owned businesses and get to know the proprietors.
- Attend services at a variety of churches, synagogues, temples, and other places of worship to learn about different faiths and meet church leaders.
- Invite colleagues, coworkers, neighbors, or students of color home for dinner or a holiday.
- Live in an integrated or culturally diverse neighborhood and attend neighborhood organizational meetings and/or attend/throw block parties.
- Form a community organization on valuing diversity and invite local artists, authors, entertainers, politicians, and leaders of color to address your group.
- Attend street fairs, educational forums, and events put on by the community.

Although it may sound easy, preparing for and learning from these activities are challenging. Furthermore, Whites must engage in these activities out of sincere motivation and in a manner respectful of the community. Acting out a White liberal guilt trip or being a political tourist may only create resentment among people of color to what they see as an intrusion into their lives. They may view the presence of such individuals in their neighborhoods as visitors at a zoo (their communities) taking a peek at how the animals (people of color) live. As a result, Whites are likely to be viewed with suspicion, hostility, and resentment. Rather than being welcomed, they are likely to be seen as intruders with suspect motives. Under such circumstances, their presence may only lead to greater misunderstanding on both sides. Naive good intentions can get people into great trouble, and potentially pose personal dangers.

> Several years ago, while teaching a racism awareness course in California, I had presented to a group of graduate students on counseling about the need to become acquainted with the people they hope to serve. Most of the students were White, and I challenged them to get to know the communities of color to enhance their multicultural knowledge. They were to keep a journal of their interracial interactions with people of color. One White student took up the challenge and decided to attend a Chinese Baptist Church and a Black Baptist Church in Oakland, California.
>
> Needless to say, his experiences left him even more entrenched in his fears and apprehensions about people of color. At both churches, he felt open hostility directed toward him. When he tried to speak with the parishioners after the service, they ignored and avoided him. He felt isolated, uncomfortable, and frightened. After the service at the Black church, as he walked to his car, he spotted a group of Black youths standing on the corner. He recalls experiencing a panicky feeling as he quickly fumbled for his keys, dropped them on the ground, and had difficulty unlocking his door. The Black youngsters seemed to read his fears and appeared amused as he quickly drove off. (Author's personal recollection)

This example is a case study in failure. First, no one should enter a minority neighborhood or any unfamiliar neighborhood without an understanding or some knowledge of it. Second, people should not enter as uninvited strangers who may be seen as interlopers. Third, reciprocity is important: In what ways are Whites willing to give back or help those they hope to understand? People of color are very sensitive to being used as a guinea pig to fulfill the purposes of White needs (in this case, to fulfill a class assignment). To be received favorably by persons of color and the community requires several conditions. The parent or teacher must be genuine in wanting to know people of color. The interactions and relationships must not be transitory and a one-shot thing. It has to be an ongoing process. For example, just to attend the Black church on a one-time basis does not immerse the individual in the community and results in only cursory acquisition of knowledge. Whites must introduce themselves to the community and people of color in a nonhurried manner. But, how can that be done?

Guideline 3—Learn From Experiential Reality

While readings, attending theater, and going to museums are helpful to increase understanding, people must supplement their factual understanding with the experiential reality of the groups they hope to understand. These experiences, however, must be something carefully planned to be successful. As with the White student attending ethnic minority churches, some form of personal connection can be most valuable in allowing entry into the benefits of interracial encounters. It may be helpful to identify a cultural guide; someone willing to help the person understand his or her racial/cultural group; someone willing to introduce the person to new experiences; someone willing to help process one's thoughts, feelings, and behaviors. This allows one to more easily obtain valid information on race and racism issues. But, where does one find cultural guides who will aid in the desire to understand people of color? Anyone who is racially or culturally different can act as a cultural guide. To do so means that one must make a concerted effort to meet and interact with visible racial/ethnic individuals. A potential cultural guide may be found in a neighbor, coworker, fellow student, or acquaintance at the local gym, community committee, or interest group. Opportunities abound everywhere, but the challenge is to reach out and form a friendship with that person of color.

The White student, for example, might have overcome the suspicions of the community if he had relied on an acquaintance or friend of color who could serve as a liaison to the pastor or some other elder of the church. Making friends or having someone of color attend with the White person goes a long way in the White person's perceived legitimacy among the congregation. Often, attending with a partner or family member, especially children, will be a good way to break the ice with other parishioners. Or, the person could contact the pastor and explain his or her motivations and reasons for wanting to attend. In many cases, the pastor might suggest that individuals first make themselves known by volunteering for services in their soup kitchen, singing in the choir, and so on to increase their visibility. Such things also are powerful statements to the congregation and community that the person is not a political tourist and is willing to give back to the community. The important point is that these solutions or suggestions may sound easy but are complex and fraught with difficulties. These actions require humility, courage, the willingness to be vulnerable, perseverance in the face of discomfort, and the willingness to learn, to listen, and to be open.

Cultural understanding and sensitivity cannot occur without lived experience. Thus, everyone must make an effort to attend cultural events, meetings, and activities of the groups they hope to understand. This allows people to view the people of color interacting in their community and observe their values in action. Hearing from church leaders, attending open community forums, and attending community celebrations allow the parent, child, teacher, and students to sense the strengths of the community, observe leadership in action, and personalize their understanding, and allow them to identify potential guides and advisers. The journey to overcome fears and biases has to be a step-by-step process. Immersing oneself with people who differ in race, culture, and ethnicity without adequate preparation may only result in a hardening of prejudices.

Guideline 4—Learn From Constant Vigilance of Your Biases and Fears

The lives of White Americans must become a "have to" in being constantly vigilant to manifestations of bias in themselves and the people around them. Learn how to ask sensitive racial questions and learn from friends of color, associates, and acquaintances. Persons subjected to racism seldom get a chance to engage in honest race talk with nondefensive and nonguilty persons from the majority group. White Americans, for example, often avoid mentioning race even with close friends of color. Most people of color are more than willing to respond, to enlighten, and to share, *if they sense the questions and concerns are sincere and motivated by a desire to learn and serve the group.* When Whites listen nondefensively, for example, to a Latino American speak about racism both parties gain.

Let me provide an example of a lost race talk opportunity:

Some years back, in the State of California, anti-affirmative action legislation was being strongly debated in nearly every community. The legislation would make it illegal to use race as a criterion for admission into institutions of higher education and for awarding state contracts. Feelings ran very high because the author of the legislation was a Black man who sat on the Regents of the University of California. The proposition found instantaneous support from many Whites who quickly claimed the author as an ally. Needless to say, many persons of color perceived the Black man as being a front for the conservative elements of California and of being co-opted by the system. Indeed, among certain groups, he was, unfortunately, labeled an Uncle Tom or an Oreo [reference to being black outside (chocolate wafers), but white inside (crème filling)].

I recall being at a reception held after a debate about the merits of the proposition. Most of those who attended were White folks from the community, with very few people of color. I observed a group of Whites gathered together, sipping wine, and engaged in conversation about the merits of the debate. They were very animated and freely spoke about their admiration for the author of the legislation and referred to him as "a credit to his race." Someone in the group remarked that he wished other minorities would have the courage to take a stand against special privileges like the Black author. He could not understand why the ethnic minority community refused to claim him as one of their own. Another person said it would be a good idea to ask African Americans about this matter.

Shortly after this reference, one of the hosts brought a Black woman attendee over to introduce her to the other guests. While the group was cordial and polite to the woman, there was obvious discomfort among the group. When the Black woman apologized for interrupting their conversation and told them to please carry on, there was a moment of silent awkwardness. Then, someone stated, "Oh, we were just introducing ourselves to one another."

For the rest of the evening, the conversation dealt with comments and questions about the type of work people did and other more superficial comments regarding the evening debate. Never did the conversation ever return to the topic of affirmative action, or the earlier conversation concerning their admiration for the author of the proposition. Indeed, the situation can be likened to the elephant in the middle of the room analogy. That is, people are well aware of the presence of the elephant, but do not acknowledge or mention it. It became obvious that speaking about race or racial issues in the presence of a Black person created extreme discomfort for the group. Yet, it was equally uncomfortable not to mention it at all! A valuable opportunity to learn from one another was lost in that situation. (Author's personal recollection)

We have already spent considerable time dissecting the reasons for the barriers to race talk and can easily apply them to the preceding situation. But, the point being made is that situations like this occur frequently with similar outcomes. They are pregnant with opportunities to learn from one another and more importantly about the fears, apprehensions, and biases one may possess. When around people of color or when race-related issues or racial situations present themselves, it is important to ask, "Where are the feelings of uneasiness, differentness, or outright fear coming from?" They may reveal or say something about one's biases and prejudices. What makes it difficult to talk about issues of race around people of color? Why do you cross the street when you see minority youngsters approaching you? Do you do it when Whites approach you? Why do you tense up and clutch your purse more securely when a minority person enters your space? Don't make excuses for these thoughts and feelings, dismiss them, or avoid attaching some meaning to them. Only if we confront them directly can they be unlearned or dealt with in a realistic manner.

Guideline 5—Learn From Being Committed to Personal Action Against Racism

Dealing with racism means a personal commitment to action. It means interrupting other White Americans when they make racist remarks or jokes or engage in racist actions, even if this is embarrassing or frightening. It means noticing the possibility for direct action against bias and discrimination in everyday life: in the family, at work, and in the community. It means taking initiative to make sure that minority candidates are fairly considered in places of employment, advocating to teachers of your children to include multicultural material in the curriculum, volunteering in community organizations to have them consider multicultural issues, and contributing and working for campaigns of political candidates who will advocate for social justice.

For persons of color, dealing with bias and prejudice is a day-to-day occurrence. If Whites are to be helpful, their lives must also be a constant "have to" in dealing with racism. The American Psychological Association has advocated 10 very useful commonsense suggestions that parents, educators, and all concerned citizens can utilize.

1. **Be Honest:** You must develop an ability to recognize your own biases through open discussion with others. Examine your own prejudices, stereotypes, and values. Be willing and open to exploring your own experiences of being hurt by prejudice, but also be willing to explore the ways you have benefited from discrimination. Don't get defensive. Be open to hearing from people of color.

2. **Be a Partner:** Volunteer to work on projects with groups different from your own. It has been found that working alongside a person of color as an equal does more to destroy prejudices and stereotypes. Opportunities abound, especially if you are involved in groups or organizations whose agendas deal with issues of diversity and multiculturalism. There are generally community

organizations or groups that sponsor educational forums related to improving race relations or trying to instill a multicultural curriculum in the schools.

3. **Be an Antiracist Parent:** You must begin to raise your children to understand concepts such as prejudice, discrimination, and racism. Be active in introducing your children to interacting and learning from children of color. Do it before prejudices become hardened. Take them to school-sponsored events on multiculturalism, don't discourage them from interacting with children of color, and make topics of inclusion, democracy, and antiracism a part of your everyday vocabulary.

4. **Be a Role Model:** Whether you want to or not, parents serve as models for their children. So, being vocal in opposing racist views and practices is very important for your son and daughter to witness. Invite neighbors, colleagues, and other acquaintances of color to your home. Have children witness you, as a role model, interacting, laughing, talking, and enjoying relationships with persons of color.

5. **Be an Ally:** You must reach out and become an ally of persons of color. Support victims of discrimination, be willing to join them in advocating for fair treatment, and be willing to serve as a mentor to people of color. Speak out if you see racial discrimination. When serving on committees with persons of color, help in allowing their voices to be heard.

6. **Be an Activist:** When you see racial injustice, speak out and object. Be willing to challenge your family, friends, and neighbors when they make racial jokes or slurs, or act in ways that indicate bias. Be vigilant not only with family and friends, but in your workplace, church, and other organizations to which you belong. Work to make sure that your school district and place of employment treat groups of color fairly. Serve on groups and committees that have a multicultural agenda.

7. **Be a Member:** Are you a member of the numerous organizations that stand for social justice and antidiscrimination? Join groups and organizations that stand for equality of opportunity, social justice, antidiscrimination, and antiracism. For example, explore the possibility of membership in the Anti-Defamation League, Human Rights Campaign, National Asian Pacific American Legal Consortium, National Association for the Advancement of Colored People, National Council of La Raza, National Organization for Women, and Southern Poverty Law Center.

8. **Be a Teacher:** As a coworker, parent, neighbor, or teacher, you can teach others to value diversity and multiculturalism. The Southern Poverty Law

Center, for example, can give you many examples of what ordinary citizens can do to combat hatred and bigotry. Their *Teaching Tolerance* magazine contains many good ideas and pages of references. Volunteer to be a Sunday school teacher and make sure racial equality is part of the curriculum.

9. **Be a Student:** You must realize that antiracism education is a constant and ongoing process. You must educate yourself and others on a continuing and ongoing basis. Reading books, seeing movies, and going to hear minority speakers are all intended to enlighten, educate, and free us from our bigotry. Attend workshops and the many educational events on racial understanding put on by local colleges and universities, neighborhood organizations, and other groups.

10. **Be Secure:** Don't be ashamed of your cultural heritage. It means, however, recognizing both positive and negative aspects of your group. Know your strengths and limitations. Understanding yourself as a racial/cultural being does much to reduce defensiveness and build bonds of mutual trust with others. Take an active part in defining your Whiteness in a nonracist manner and live by these newly found tenets. If you define your racial identity in such a manner, you will no longer respond with defensiveness or guilt when racism becomes an issue.

Following these guidelines will hopefully serve to enlighten and increase awareness and comfort in talking about race issues by educators, parents, and their students and children. In the next chapter we provide specific suggestions of how best educators can effectively facilitate difficult dialogues on race.

CHAPTER THIRTEEN

Helping People Talk About Race: Facilitation Skills for Educators and Trainers

I [Author] was conducting a workshop on antiracism for a group of teachers in a school district. I remember one particular session where the topic was on past discrimination and oppression against people of color. As I traced the history of enslavement of Blacks and the taking away of land from Native Americans, I noticed that one female teacher seemed agitated about the topic. As I pressed forward with how Whites historically have oppressed these groups, the teacher raised her hand. I could tell from her facial expression and body language that she seemed upset. When I called on her, she forcefully and angrily stated that women were an oppressed minority group as well, and wondered why I was not talking about sexism and the detrimental impact on women. She implied that by ignoring the plight of women, I was guilty of a gender microaggression by making her feel invalidated. The following represents how, in my early days, I would handle the situation.

Unsuccessful Racial Dialogue

Female Trainee (stating her thoughts angrily): Why aren't we also addressing issues like sexism? We women are an oppressed minority group as well! I always feel training like this makes women invisible and that our needs are ignored. Women are paid less than men, the Equal Rights Amendment was never passed, and we are treated like sex objects.... I mean, everything is about race and racism, but what about us...what about our situation?

Me: Yes, I can understand that, but we can't cover every single group that has been oppressed, and this training is about the oppression of people of color and the harm they experience from oppression. [Attempting to deal with the challenge intellectually and losing control of the process.]

Trainee (raising voice): Women are harmed too...why does it have to be like that anyway? Why use an arbitrary decision in deciding which group to address? I just don't believe you can relate to my situation as a woman!

Me (becoming slightly defensive, and attempting to calm and appease the trainee): Okay, let's talk about the plight of women as an oppressed group. It's not my intent to ignore discrimination against women. In fact, many of our studies on discrimination have dealt with gender microaggressions like sexual objectification.

Since those early days, I have come to understand that this was *a potential trap* that could serve to (a) deflect the conversation away from race to some other sociodemographic identities such as gender, (b) dilute the importance and impact of racism by equating it with all the other "isms" of the world, (c) create defensiveness in me, and (d) allow participants to escape from exploring their own racial biases and responsibilities. In the past I would have taken the bait (as I did in this example) and tried to explain why I was covering racism only and not sexism, argued how racism and sexism were different forms of oppression, and/or become defensive in the implied accusation. I would have interacted with the trainee on an intellectual/cognitive content level. Although my factual arguments were solid and accurate, it seldom seemed to have a desirable resolution. The debate usually resulted in a very poor outcome in that the lesson I was trying to convey would be lost, and the discussion between the trainee and me would only result in both of us staking out our positions. Both of us would feel unheard and resentful. The interaction would then be debated on a content (cognitive) level with the underlying strong feelings unrecognized.

Since that time, I have learned that to facilitate a difficult dialogue on race, I need to understand not only the content of the communication but also the process resulting from the interpersonal dynamics. I have learned that race talk is often not about the substance of an argument, but a cover for what is actually happening. In the preceding example, I was responding to the content of the argument, trying to present my case in a logical fashion, and trying to placate her strong feelings. But the substance of the trainee's argument really had little to do with why she reacted in such an angry way. In essence, I had lost control of the process, become defensive, and failed to understand what the strong reactions of the trainee really meant.

The following is an example of a more enlightened intervention, which led to a discussion of the trainee's strong reactions and what they meant.

Successful Racial Dialogue

Female Trainee (stating her thoughts angrily): Why aren't we also addressing issues like sexism? We women are an oppressed minority group as well! I always feel training like this makes women invisible and that our needs are ignored. Women are paid less than men, the Equal Rights Amendment was never passed, and we are treated like sex objects. . . . I mean, everything is about race and racism, but what about us . . . what about our situation?

Me: I'm glad you brought that up. You make excellent points. Yes, women are definitely an oppressed group, and we can talk about that as well. Before we do that, however, I'm picking up on lots of strong feelings behind your statement and wonder where they are coming from. [In this response, the trainer controls the process by refocusing exploration on the trainee.]

Trainee: What do you mean?

Me: You seem angry at something I've said or done.

Trainee: No, I'm not . . . just upset that women get short shafted.

Me: I can understand that, but the intensity by which you expressed yourself made me feel that my points on racism were being dismissed and that issues of racism were unimportant to you. Being a woman, I know you understand prejudice and discrimination. Can you use the experience of having been oppressed to better understand the experience of people of color?

Trainee: I guess so.... I ... I guess racism is important.

Me: You don't seem very sure to me ... you still seem upset. What is happening now? Can you get into those feelings and share with us what's going on?

Trainee: Nothing is going on ... it's just that, you know, it's a hot topic. I guess, talking about racism, it seems like you are blaming me. And, I don't like to feel wrong or at fault or responsible.

Me: Tell me about feeling blamed. In what ways do you feel blamed?

Trainee: Well, maybe there are feelings of guilt, although I'm not to blame for slavery or things of the past.

Me: Good, let's *all* (referring to entire workshop group) talk about that. Now we are getting somewhere. (Turning to entire group of teachers who have been transfixed by the interaction) I wonder if some of you can tell me what you see happening here. Do any of you feel the same way? What sense do you make of the dialogue we just had here?

Questions: What do you see happening between the facilitator and the trainee? What do you think the real issue is? Can you distinguish between the *content* of what is being discussed and the *process* of the discussion? What feelings are being expressed by the trainee? What is behind them and what meaning do they have for her? What is different in how the facilitator handled the matter in the first situation and that of the second? Why is the second approach considered by the facilitator to be more successful? Can you outline the reasons? Given your understanding of the situation, how else might you facilitate the dialogue? Can you provide a rationale for the actions you would take?

Welcome to difficult dialogues on race! As educators and facilitators involved in racial conversations, we are often confronted in our teaching or training with challenges about how to make them teachable moments rather than failed exercises. Difficult dialogues on race can happen spontaneously or be expected or planned by facilitators. Most teachers, for example, may encounter race talk in their normal day-to-day teaching activities whether due to the content of the day's lesson or remarks by students, which represent microaggressions to students of color. Thus, teachers need to be able to recognize and be equipped to facilitate race talk discussions in a productive manner. Facilitators who conduct training or workshops on raising critical consciousness of race, racism, Whiteness, and White privilege must also contain in their training armament tools, techniques, and strategies to help trainees work through the intense and oftentimes explosive interactions that occur in race talk.

As mentioned throughout this text, dialogues on race are usually clashes between the racial realities of one group (people of color) and another (generally Whites). The conflicts and their hidden meanings between racial groups are most likely manifested in race talk. The opening example is representative of the characteristics of race talk and the dilemma that often teachers face in classrooms and that facilitators encounter in workshops on racism and antiracism. In this chapter, we concentrate on providing effective facilitation strategies for educators and trainers to conduct positive race talk outcomes. These suggestions and strategies, however, are based on the assumption that facilitators are enlightened individuals who have done the necessary personal work to develop nonracist and antiracist identities (Helms, 1990; Spanierman et al., 2006; Sue, 2013; Tatum, 1997). It is important to note that these suggestions are based on and derived from research findings, scholarly deconstruction of linguistic meanings, and social psychological/ sociopolitical analysis of race talk provided in each of the previous 12 chapters.

INEFFECTIVE STRATEGIES: FIVE THINGS NOT TO DO

It may seem strange to begin this section with a discussion of ineffective strategies, but our studies indicate that they are widespread among teachers and facilitators who have not developed a good sense of who they are as racial/cultural beings. These behaviors generally lead to negative outcomes in race talk, but contain the lessons for what not to do and suggest possible solutions (Sue, Lin, et al., 2009; Sue, Rivera, et al., 2010; Sue, Rivera, et al., 2011; Sue, Torino, et al., 2009). These responses by teachers/facilitators have been identified by participants as highly ineffective in race talk, and may result in greater misunderstanding among racial groups, hardening of biased racial beliefs, increased anger and tension toward one another, and lost opportunities to increase awareness and understanding (teachable moments).

All of the following behaviors have several things in common: They are behaviors that (a) are characterized by inactivity, (b) allow the discussion to be deflected away from the problematic area, and (c) generate defensiveness on the part of the trainer, as evidenced in our opening scenario.

1. Do Nothing

In the face of a difficult dialogue on race, many facilitators remain silent as heated race talk occurs between participants. In classrooms, for example, they allow the students to take over the conversation, and they exhibit not only behavioral but emotional passivity in their own reactions. They offer little if any guidance to students about the conflicting conversations and make few attempts to bridge the differences being discussed. This does not mean, however, that teachers or facilitators are uncaring, unconcerned, or unfeeling. In general, our studies suggest that they are experiencing powerful emotions and fears when a dialogue on race occurs (Sue, Torino, et al., 2009), but they attempt to conceal them for fear of appearing lost and inept. Many educators in the study were unable to critically ascertain what was happening, and they felt confused about what to do. They became concerned about being perceived as incompetent, of losing control of classroom dynamics, of being biased, and of being inadequately prepared to handle the situation. Their perception of the problematic situation became constricted due to anxiety, as they became more focused on themselves (self-protection) rather than being concerned with understanding and helping their students. They expressed feeling paralyzed, a lack of critical racial consciousness, and confusion as to how best to effectively intervene (Valentine et al., 2012). In general, the inactivity and feelings of impotence by facilitators and teachers led to a deep and personal sense of failure and disappointment in them; more problematic is that their actions or lack of actions model to students and participants that race talk should be avoided.

2. Sidetrack the Conversation

In the opening vignette, we have a prime example of a White female trainee attempting to sidetrack the conversation from the topic of race to gender. In classroom settings, race talk is often uncomfortable for students and teachers alike. In the first intervention scenario, the discomfort and avoidance of talking about race or racism are clear for the participant as she tries to sidetrack the conversation to something more safe for her (gender) and less anxiety provoking. The trainer may unintentionally collude with the participant in avoiding race talk for many reasons (being unaware of how to handle the situation, taking the bait, or becoming defensive), but the ultimate result is to be diverted from discussing the real issue. Trainers have to be cognizant of the many defensive strategies used by participants to avoid race talk in order to anticipate and overcome them. More problematic, however, is when sidetracking the conversation comes from the facilitator's own discomfort and fears about racial conversations. In class, a racial dialogue may ensue with the teacher being unprepared to handle it. He or she may be sufficiently uncomfortable with the topic and allow the topic to be changed. These maneuvers are often very visible to students or trainees in a racial dialogue. Their use often diminishes the credibility of facilitators and makes them even less effective in teaching and training.

> Race comes up, you know, the faculty person is uncomfortable, they change the subject, they get support from some students in the classroom to change the subject, and then we're all sitting there. It's a big elephant in the middle of the room. The ignoring it is a feeling for many students of color and some White students of complete invalidation. (Sue, Torino, et al., 2009, p. 1105)

3. Appease the Participants

Appeasement is a strategy often used by facilitators to avoid a disagreement on a race issue with participants. In many cases, appeasement is the result of anxiety over the ability of the facilitator to handle challenging situations associated with race talk and the discomfort that comes from confronting participants about their personal biases and prejudices. To avoid conflict or a potential heated exchange with participants, to maintain the involvement and goodwill of an audience, and to not lose credibility or influence, appeasement becomes the goal. Usually, the trainer is uncomfortable with the expression of powerful emotions in race talk that may prove divisive.

Appeasement may take many forms:

- Allowing the conversation to be sidetracked.
- Avoiding confrontation with the points being made by the participant.
- Stressing commonalities and avoiding differences.
- Discussing superficial issues without exploring deeper personal meanings.

Many teachers, for example, avoid deep discussions of race in order to maintain what they perceive as classroom harmony and the fostering of positive feelings. They are sensitive to how the workshop or class is perceived by the school, college, or organization and attempt to elicit positive feelings and opinions of participants or students. The problem with the maintenance of harmony is that it negates deeper explorations of biases, stereotypes, and nested emotions associated with race and racism. The teachable moment is lost.

4. Terminate the Discussion

When facilitators are concerned that a racial dialogue threatens to get out of control and are unable to determine how best to handle the situation, one of the most common techniques is to terminate the dialogue using several strategies.

- First, conditions may be placed on how the dialogue should be discussed or conducted. A professor may, for example, make it known that the topic is not relevant to the content of the course, that opinions or feelings are not facts, and that issues should be discussed with respect. In many cases, such a tactic dictates avoidance of emotions or feelings, which are considered irrelevant to classroom dialogues.
- Second, the facilitator may simply table the discussion, in essence ending any further race talk. Some teachers may say that they will return to this issue in the future, but never carry through on the promise.
- Third, a facilitator may ask the parties involved to discuss the matter with him or her individually outside of the workshop or class. This action compartmentalizes the dialogue and removes it from the larger public arena.
- Fourth, the facilitator may stress that the parties involved should calm down, respect one another, and discuss the topic in a rational manner.

There are several downsides to these strategies. Usually, the facilitator fails to realize that race talk between several individuals does not occur in isolation from other observers or students; although other participants may not have actively engaged in the dialogue, they are usually vicariously involved. By shutting down the communication between two individuals, it shuts down the entire group process. Further, the ground rules being imposed by the facilitator may be culturally and educationally biased (objectivity is valued over subjectivity and emotion is antagonistically opposed to reason).

5. Become Defensive

Although facilitators/teachers may be White or people of color, defensiveness or having one's buttons pushed is a very common phenomenon. When dealing with difficult racial conversations, feeling blamed or accused of wrongdoing (being racist) is a common reaction of race talk, especially among White trainees. These feelings of defensiveness may be conscious, but generally occur outside the level of awareness. Race talk between trainer and trainee operates on the principle of reciprocity as evidenced by our opening vignette. When trainees feel accused of being biased, they engage in self-protective behavior in the form of righteous indignation or innocent victimhood. That is the reaction and hidden meaning of the female trainee's reaction in our opening scenario; she felt wrongly accused and closed her mind to information being presented by the trainer. In order to deflect the perceived criticism, trainees may directly or indirectly attack the content of the communication (message) and/or the credibility of the communicator. When confronted with a defensive challenge by trainees, facilitators of race talk may also become defensive when they find that their message is being invalidated or that their credibility is being assailed. A White trainer, for example, may be indirectly accused as being a bleeding heart liberal or a sellout. Faculty of color in our studies reported implicit and explicit microaggressions they received from White students who challenged their authority or expertise (Sue, Rivera, et al., 2011). In these situations, facilitators often report becoming defensive, going into a self-protective mode, becoming angry, shutting down two-way communication, and themselves becoming contentious. In these cases, both trainers and trainees feel unheard, misunderstood, invalidated, frustrated, angry, and resentful (the precise characteristics of an unsuccessful dialogue on race).

SUCCESSFUL STRATEGIES: ELEVEN POTENTIALLY POSITIVE ACTIONS

Having critical racial consciousness formed from a nonracist and antiracist orientation is a necessity to the development and use of successful race talk strategies. Most of the ineffective reactions just outlined provide us with clues about what facilitative conditions need to exist and the type of interventions most likely to help trainees move from racial obliviousness to becoming racially conscious of themselves and one another. A most important lesson is that inaction or passivity on the part of the facilitator, trainer, or teacher leads to negative outcomes (Sue, Torino, et al., 2009). Some requirements and suggestions for effective intervention are provided next. They are directly derived from the psychology of racial dialogues presented in the first 12 chapters of this book: (a) understanding the dynamics and characteristics of race talk; (b) being knowledgeable of the ground rules that hinder open discussions of topics on race, racism, Whiteness, and White privilege; (c) anticipating and being able to deconstruct the clash of racial realities between different groups; (d) being cognizant of how race talk is embedded in the larger sociopolitical system and influenced by it; (e) being aware and nonjudgmental about communication style differences; (f) understanding White and people-of-color fears about engaging in racial conversations; and (g) having knowledge of racial/cultural identity development.

1. Understand One's Racial/Cultural Identity

First and foremost, teachers, trainers, and facilitators must understand themselves as racial/cultural beings by making the invisible visible. Unless they are well grounded and comfortable about who they are, a lack of insight and awareness only perpetuates ignorance in the students or participants they hope to help. They cannot be effective facilitators unless they are aware of their own worldview—their values, biases, prejudices, and assumptions about human behavior. For, example, what does being White, Black/African American, Asian American/Pacific Islander, Latino/Hispanic American, or Native American mean to them? How does their racial identity impact the way they view others and the way they view you? There are three aspects that are important in this goal:

1. Understanding oneself as a racial/cultural being inevitably goes hand in hand with how well grounded and secure one will be in a racial dialogue. Self-protection of self-esteem will be minimized resulting in low defensive reactions.
2. Awareness of differences in worldviews of participants will allow for empathic understanding and help facilitators deconstruct worldview differences. They are thus able to help trainees more realistically understand the differences in racial realities.
3. Awareness of one's racial identity will allow facilitators to anticipate how their own race will impact racial dialogues and take effective educational actions to facilitate a difficult dialogue.

2. Acknowledge and Be Open to Admitting One's Racial Biases

On an intellectual/cognitive level, teachers and trainers must be able and willing to acknowledge and accept the fact that they are products of the cultural conditioning of this society, and as such, they have inherited the biases, fears, and stereotypes of the society. When facilitating a difficult dialogue on race, most trainers or teachers are wary about communicating their own prejudices and will respond in a cautious fashion that may be less than honest. I would suggest that covering up, refusing to self-disclose, or playing it cautiously may actually hinder race talk and may only model to trainees the very behaviors that obstruct honest dialogue. But publicly and honestly acknowledging their personal biases and weaknesses (to self and to others) may have several positive consequences:

- It frees them from the constant guardedness and vigilance exercised in denying their own racism or other biases.
- They can model truthfulness, openness, and honesty to students or participants about race and racism.
- They communicate their courage in making themselves vulnerable by taking a risk to share with students their own biases, limitations, and attempts to deal with their own racism.
- It may encourage others in the group to approach the dialogue with honesty, because their own teachers/trainers are equally flawed.

3. Be Comfortable and Open to Discussing Topics of Race and Racism

On an emotional level, it is best if trainers are comfortable in discussing issues of race and racism, and are open to, honest about, and vulnerable in exploring their own biases and those of trainees. If students, for example, sense the teacher is uncomfortable, it will only add fuel to their own discomfort and defensiveness. One of the goals of a teacher or facilitator is to become comfortable and open to race talk. Attaining comfort means practice outside of the classroom or training situation. Remember, addressing one's own personal biases is more than an intellectual exercise of reading books or going to workshops. Attaining comfort and understanding comes from lived reality experiences that require continued and frequent interaction with people who differ from them in race, culture, and ethnicity. In Chapter 12 we provided numerous examples of such experiential activities and learning situations.

4. Understand the Meaning of Emotions

For both trainers and trainees, deconstructing the symbolic meaning of emotions in race talk is an essential ingredient for successful dialogue. Because few of us can have experiences with all groups who differ from us in worldviews, discomfort and confusion when diversity/multicultural issues arise are normal. These feelings should not be denied, avoided, or suppressed. Rather, the effective facilitator should help others to make sense of them—what do they mean and say about the person? This is a two-prong approach that involves the ability to monitor and attribute meaning to one's own feelings and those of the trainees. Remember, I have repeatedly stressed that nested or embedded emotions are frequently expressed in race talk—although they may not be acknowledged or understood by those initially engaged in such conversations. The skilled facilitator helps others make sense of these feelings and frees the individual from being controlled by them. As long as feelings remain unnamed and unacknowledged, they represent emotional roadblocks to having a successful dialogue. The most common feelings and their hidden meanings derived from earlier chapters are the following:

- *I feel guilty*: "I could be doing more."
- *I feel angry*: "I don't like to feel I'm wrong."
- *I feel defensive*: "Why blame me? I do enough already and am not responsible."
- *I feel turned off*: "I have other priorities in life."
- *I feel helpless*: "The problem is too big. What can I do?"
- *I feel afraid*: "I'm going to lose something." "I don't know what will happen."

If the teacher or trainer experiences these feelings, it is important to acknowledge them even if it does not make immediate sense. By doing so, anxiety or confusion is lessoned. Teaching and encouraging trainees to do so likewise allows further exploration of the feelings, as in the example of the effective intervention given in the opening scenario.

5. Validate and Facilitate Discussion of Feelings

This is a primary goal in race talk. In the previous suggestion, I note how important it is to understand the meaning of feelings and what they symbolize. In this situation, the facilitator or teacher must create conditions that make the expression and presence of feelings a valid and legitimate focus of experience and discussion. As we have seen, the academic protocol works against the discussion of feelings in classroom settings, and the belief that emotion is antagonistic to reason places restrictive ground rules for race talk in many other training venues. In our studies in classroom settings, nearly all students indicate

- The importance of allowing space for the strong expression of feelings.
- That it was okay to have them.
- That talking about their anxieties or anger helped them understand themselves and others better.
- That it was important to create conditions that allowed for openness and receptivity to strong emotions.

They especially appreciated instructors who were unafraid to recognize and name the racial tension and the feelings emanating from the discussion because it helped them demystify its source and meaning. One participant provided a specific example of what he found helpful: "A here and now discussion with a facilitator who knows when to let it happen and when to interject ... have the facilitator say, 'how are you feeling right now talking or being confronted by this Black person?' and going off on real feelings rather than trying to rationalize it or make it cognitive" (Sue, Rivera, et al., 2010, p. 210).

6. Control the Process and Not the Content of Race Talk

When a heated dialogue occurs on race, the duel between participants of different races is nearly always on the substance or content level. But the hidden and less visible levels are where the true dialogue is taking place (White talk vs. back talk). When referring to dreams, Freud took the stance that the manifest content (what one recalls about the dream) is not the real or latent content of the unconscious. What one remembers about their dreams is only the tip of the iceberg that contains hidden fears and meanings. Again, it is important to note that race talk, especially White talk, has hidden meanings, and that using process observations or interventions ultimately helps in unmasking the beliefs and attitudes (biases and prejudices) of the communicants. Some common statements (content level) when White talk occurs are

- "So what, we women are oppressed, too."
- "My family didn't own slaves! I had nothing to do with the incarceration of Japanese Americans."

- "Excuse me sir, but prejudice and oppression were and are part of every society in the world ad infinitum, not just the U.S."
- "We Italians [or Irish] experienced severe discrimination when we arrived here. Did my family harp on the prejudice? We excelled despite the prejudice. Why? Because the basic founding principles of this country made it possible!"
- "I resent you calling me White. You are equally guilty of stereotyping. We are all human beings or we are unique."

The substance of these assertions has great validity, but to deal with them strictly on the content level will only result in having race talk sidetracked, diluted, diminished, or ignored. There is a time to discuss these issues, but understanding the hidden transcript that generates these statements is important for both the facilitator and trainees to deconstruct. In our opening scenario, we indicated how the facilitator made process observations (the strong feelings behind the woman trainee's statements) that allowed the conversation to focus on the strong feelings and their meanings. He controlled the process and not the content of the dialogue. An important educational exercise would be to practice analyzing these statements from both the content and process levels.

7. Unmask the Difficult Dialogue Through Process Observations and Interventions

Strategies 6 and 7 are intimately related to one another. The goal here is to use an understanding of group process to unmask the meaning of the difficult dialogue occurring between two parties by (a) acknowledging the accuracy of statements (when appropriate), (b) intervening in the process rather than the content, (c) helping participants see the difference between intention and impact, and (d) moving to the feeling tone level of the communication.

a. While all the statements in item 6 are to most extent true, they can hinder a successful dialogue by covering up the real one. As in the opening scenario, by agreeing with the accuracy of the statement, it no longer becomes the distraction (argument) and allows the facilitator to focus on the real issues, feelings, and conflicts in worldviews.
b. Do not get sucked into the argumentative dialogue by taking sides in the debate of content. Rather, intervene in the process by directing students and participants to examine their own reactions and feelings. Encourage them to explore how their feelings may be saying something about them.

c. The blame game creates monologues. Help participants differentiate between their intention and impact. When the female trainee says, "So what, we women are oppressed as well!" have her explore the intention behind the statement and the impact. In most cases, trainees will state that they only had the best of intentions—to point out the oppression of others or to indicate they had also experienced discrimination. Get them to understand that it might have been their intention, but the statement itself tended to dilute, diminish, and negate the racism examples. This type of statement serves only to create a chasm, rather than bridge an understanding. How else could they have responded, for example, to bridge mutual understanding rather than separate and divide?

d. Refocus the dialogue on feelings: "I wonder if you can tell me how and what you are feeling." For example, the teacher might say, "John (Black student) has just agreed with you that women are an oppressed group. Does that make you feel better? [Usually the student says no.] No. I wonder why not." Try to help the student to explore why the feelings are still there. If there is continued difficulty, enlist speculation from other members in the group. The last option is for the facilitator to make the interpretation or speculation.

8. Do Not Allow a Difficult Dialogue to Be Brewed in Silence

When a difficult dialogue occurs and an impasse seems to have been reached, do not allow it to be brewed in silence. Resolving issues and making race talk a teachable moment may require time to understand what has happened. Likewise, many facilitators also need time to reflect upon a particular situation and are not equipped to deal with it in the immediacy of the moment. Ignoring it and not addressing the impasse only creates the elephant in the room that will continue to hold power over participants throughout the workshop or class. Several strategies may prove helpful in unlocking the blockage and allowing some resolution:

- When in a classroom situation or continuing workshop, the facilitator can make note of the impasse and instruct the group to process their thoughts and feelings about the situation, informing them that they will take it up at the next meeting. The important lesson here is that solutions and understanding require time and that the facilitator and group do not intend to avoid the challenge.
- Although it is nearly always better to have participants work through their conflicts, the facilitator may, in some situations, choose to personally

intervene by using any number of relationship models to help participants listen, observe, reflect, or paraphrase back to one another. Sometimes an impasse is due primarily to participants engaging in monologues rather than a true dialogue. We have not really discussed communication-skills training, but facilitators should consider familiarizing themselves with these various techniques so that they are armed with communication tools to help participants work through a difficult dialogue on race (Ivey, Ivey, & Zalaquett, 2014).

- As indicated in our second intervention strategy of the opening scenario, facilitators may enlist the aid of class or workshop members in helping to overcome the race talk barrier. This latter technique is very useful because it actively involves other members by simply asking, "What do you see happening here?" or "What do you see happening between John and Mary?" This strategy opens up multiple channels of communication and ensures a diversity of perspectives.

9. Understand Differences in Communication Styles

Differences in communication styles often present difficulties in race talk because different culture-bound conversation conventions may lead to increased misunderstandings. Race and gender are powerful determinates of how people communicate with one another. In Chapter 7, for example, we noted that African Americans, Asian Americans, and White Americans communicate in ways that may lead to misinterpretations or may trigger fears and biases associated with stereotypes. The stereotypes of the angry Black man or woman; the passive, unfeeling, and uncaring Asian; or the sterile, objective White may be triggered by the styles of African Americans (speaking with passion and emotion), Asian Americans (being reserved and relatively nonverbal), and Whites (task orientation). A skilled facilitator may use his or her knowledge of these styles to advance effective dialogue in several ways.

- First, it is important for the facilitator to be aware of his or her own communication style and the possible impact it has on the group when race talk occurs. A White facilitator may have a different social impact on participants than an African American or Asian American. This is also compounded by the race/style of the facilitator with either the race or style of participants.
- Second, differences in communication styles that have race implications commonly occur among the participants as well. Getting people to be

cognizant of these differences and mistaken interpretations aids successful race talk.

• Last, as indicated earlier, differences in communication styles often reflect
unconscious biases or fears held by participants in race talk. Being able to
acknowledge and deconstruct them are important elements of successful
race talk.

10. Forewarn, Plan, and Purposefully Instigate Race Talk

One of the most valuable techniques for facilitating race talk is to prepare students or workshop participants for difficult dialogues that will likely occur.
For example,

> This is a workshop (or class) on race and racism awareness. We are going to have
> some difficult, emotional, and uncomfortable moments in this group, but I hope
> you will have the courage to be honest with one another. When we talk about
> racism it touches hot buttons in all of us, including me. Being honest and authentic
> takes guts. But if we do it and stick it out, we can learn much from each other. Are
> you willing to take a risk so that we can have that experience together?

Even in classes or other forums where the topic is not specifically on racial
topics, race talk can be instigated in a purposeful, educational, and meaningful manner. For example, sometimes instigating a difficult dialogue through
an exercise, assignment, or role play can preempt resistances by introducing
the concepts of prejudice and bias in a step-by-step fashion. Watching a video
or film on racism allows participants to discuss the topic in a safer and distant
manner. The trainer then helps participants move to a more personal discussion through facilitation techniques or other activities (role plays) that personalize race talk issues. One of the great advantages of preplanning a difficult
dialogue is that it allows the facilitator to immediately control the process
rather than having a dialogue arise by happenstance. There are many videos,
such as *The Color of Fear* and *A Class Divided*; contemporary films such as *12
Years a Slave*; simulation and gaming activities/exercises; and role plays that
are excellent resources to raise racial issues and generate meaningful race talk.
In my teaching, for example, I often plan exercises or assignments for my students that place them in situations that expose them to events that question
their racial reality. I have them visit minority communities, make home visits,
and/or do internships in agencies where racial/ethnic minorities comprise the
majority of clients. Only recently, however, have I come to the realization that

if the eradication of racism is dependent on the courses or workshops we offer, then we have lost the battle. Only if teachers and parents are willing to create their own learning experiences will they have any hope of becoming helpful in race talk situations.

11. Validate, Encourage, and Express Admiration and Appreciation to Participants Who Speak When It Is Unsafe to Do So

Engaging in race talk is often a threatening situation for participants. Although many of my colleagues often talk about creating a safe space for race talk, I have begun to believe that what is safe for one group (Whites) may not be safe for another (people of color). In an earlier chapter, I mentioned that what White Euro-Americans consider safe is often based on White conversation conventions and White definitions of respect; these conditions may inherently be unsafe for people of color. Thus, I prefer to encourage, validate, and express admiration for those individuals willing to speak when it is unsafe to do so. Courage, I tell them, is to be honest when it is unsafe to speak their true thoughts and feelings. It takes little courage to express one's point of view when they feel safe. Thus, I am constantly seeking opportunities to express appreciation and validation to members of the group who take a risk and show courage, openness, and willingness to participate in a difficult dialogue. This can be done throughout a dialogue:

- "Mary, I know this has been a very emotional experience for you, but I value your courage in sharing with the group your personal thoughts and feelings. I hope I can be equally brave when topics of sexism or homophobia are brought up in this class."
- "As a group, we have just experienced a difficult dialogue. I admire you all for not 'running away' but facing it squarely. I hope you all will continue to feel free about bringing up these topics. Real courage is being honest and risking offending others when the situation is not safe. Today, that is what I saw happen with several of you and for that, the group should be grateful."

These 11 suggestions represent only a few of the important ones that educators and facilitators may find helpful in aiding others to grow from healthy race talk. There are many other strategies that are helpful in facilitating difficult dialogues on race, too numerous to cover in one chapter. Furthermore, it is important to realize that facilitating difficult dialogues may be more an art than a science. There are very few places where we can open a book with clear suggestions and directions about how to handle and facilitate a difficult racial dialogue. Trial and error, experience, an ability to understand oneself as a racial/cultural being, understanding and feeling comfortable with the worldview of others, and developing appropriate intervention skills are crucial to becoming an effective facilitator. Finally, becoming culturally skilled and competent in facilitating difficult race talk is a constant lifelong journey. Understanding that everyone commits racial blunders or makes insensitive remarks is a given. As one of my colleagues once said, "It is how one recovers, not how you cover up that matters."

Although this book is on the psychology of race talk, it is really more than that. The attitudes, beliefs, and fears inherent in race talk symbolize our society's resistance to unmasking the embedded inequities and basic unfairness imposed on citizens of color. We avoid honest racial dialogues, but innocence and naïveté can no longer serve as excuses for inaction. Courage, risk, and vulnerability have been a constant theme stressed in our race talk analysis. Race talk potentially makes the invisible visible and opens possibilities to view the world of oppression through realistic eyes. The final question I pose to readers, therefore, is this: As a nation, will you choose the path we have always traveled, a journey of silence that has benefited only a select group and oppressed others, or will you choose the road less traveled, a journey of racial reality that may be full of discomfort and pain, but offers benefits to all groups in our society? It would be unfortunate, indeed, to look back one day and echo the words of poet John Greenleaf Whittier, who wrote, "For of all sad words of tongue or pen, the saddest are these: It might have been!"

References

Aboud, F. E. (1988). *Children and prejudice*. Cambridge, MA: Basil Blackwell.

Accapadi, M. M. (2007). When White women cry: How White women's tears oppress women of color. *College Student Affairs Journal, 26,* 208–215.

Allport, G. W. (1954). *The nature of prejudice*. Reading, MA: Addison-Wesley.

American Psychological Association Presidential Task Force on Preventing Discrimination and Promoting Diversity. (2012). *Dual pathways to a better America: Preventing discrimination and promoting diversity*. Washington, DC: American Psychological Association.

Anderson, S. H., & Middleton, V. A. (2011). *Explorations in diversity*. Belmont, CA: Cengage.

Apfelbaum, E. P., Pauker, K., Sommers, S. R., & Ambady, N. (2011). In blind pursuit of racial equality? *Psychological Science, 21,* 1587–1592.

Apfelbaum, E. P., Sommers, S. R., & Norton, M. I. (2008). Seeing race and seeming racist: Evaluating strategic colorblindness in social interaction. *Journal of Personality and Social Psychology, 95,* 918–932.

Astor, C. (1997). Gallup poll: Progress in Black/White relations, but race is still an issue. *U.S. Society & Values, 2,* 1–3.

Babbington, C. (2008). *Poll shows gap between blacks and whites over racial discrimination*. Retrieved from http://www.assatashakur.org/forum/open-forum/33612-blacks -whites-over-racial-discrimination.html

Banks, J. A. (2004). Race, knowledge construction, and education in the United States. In J. A. Banks & C. A. Banks (Eds.), *Handbook of research on multicultural education* (pp. 3–39). Hoboken, NJ: Wiley.

Banks, J. A., & Banks, C. A. (1993). *Multicultural education*. Boston, MA: Allyn & Bacon.

Banks, J. A., & Banks, C. A. (2004). *Handbook of research on multicultural education*. Hoboken, NJ: Wiley.

Baron, A. A., & Banaji, M. R. (2006). The development of implicit attitudes. *Psychological Science, 17*, 53–58.

Barongan, C., Bernal, G., Comas-Diaz, L., Iijima Hall, C. C., Nagayama Hall, G. C., LaDue, R. A., ... Root, M. P. P. (1997). Misunderstandings of multiculturalism: Shouting fire in crowded theaters. *American Psychologist, 52*, 654–655.

Bates, K. G. (2012, April 27). *How Koreatown rose from the ashes of L. A. riots.* NPR. Retrieved from http://www.npr.org/2012/04/27/151524921/how-koreatown-rose -from-the-ashes-of-l-a-riots

Bautista, E. M. (2003). The impact of context, phenotype, and other identifiers on Latina/o adolescent ethnic identity and acculturation. *Dissertation Abstracts International: Section B: The Sciences and Engineering, 63*(7B), 3464.

Bell, L. A. (2002). Sincere fictions: The pedagogical challenges of preparing white teachers for multicultural classrooms. *Equity and Excellence in Education, 35*, 236–244.

Bell, L. A. (2003). Telling tales: What stories can teach us about racism. *Race, Ethnicity and Education, 6*, 3–28.

Behnken, B. D. (2011). *Fighting their own battles: Mexican Americans, African Americans, and the struggle for civil rights in Texas.* Charlotte: University of North Carolina Press.

Berbrier, M. (1999). Impression management for the thinking racist: A case study of intellectualization as stigma transformation in contemporary white supremacist discourse. *Sociological Quarterly, 40*, 411–433.

Bolgatz, J. (2005). *Talking race in the classroom.* New York, NY: Educators College Press.

Bolino, M. C., & Turnley, W. H. (1999). Measuring impression management in organizations: A scale development based on the Jones and Pittman taxonomy. *Organizational Research Methods, 2*, 187–206.

Bolino, M. C., & Turnley, W. H. (2003). More than one way to make an impression: Exploring profiles of impression management. *Journal of Management, 29*, 141–160.

Bonilla-Silva, E. (2006). *Racism without racists: Color-blind racism and the persistence of racial inequality in the United States.* Lanham, MD: Rowman & Littlefield.

Boyd-Franklin, N. (2003). *Black families in therapy.* New York, NY: Guilford Press.

Boyd-Franklin, N. (2010). Black families. *Counseling Psychologist, 38*, 976–100.

Boysen, G. A. (2010). Integrating implicit bias into counselor education. *Counselor Education and Supervision, 49*, 210–226.

Boysen, G. A., & Vogel, D. L. (2008). The relationship between level of training, implicit bias, and multicultural competency among counselor trainees. *Training and Education in Professional Psychology, 2*, 103–110.

Bryan, M. L., Wilson, B. S., Lewis, A. A., & Wills, L. E. (2012). Exploring the impact of "race talk" in the education classroom: Doctoral student reflections. *Journal of Diversity in Higher Education, 5*, 123–137.

Capodilupo, C. M., & Kim, S. (2013, November 4). Gender and race matter: The importance of considering intersections in black women's body image. *Journal of Counseling Psychology. Advance online publication.* doi:10.1037/a0034597.

Cassidy, K. D., Quinn, K. A., & Humphreys, G. W. (2011). The influence of ingroup/outgroup categorization on same- and other-race face processing: The moderating role of inter- versus intra-racial context. *Journal of Experimental Social Psychology, 47,* 811–817.

Children Now. (1998). *A different world: Children's perceptions of race and class in the media.* New York, NY: Author.

Choney, S. K., Berryhill-Paake, E., & Robbins, R. R. (1995). The acculturation of American Indians: Developing frameworks for research and practice. In J. G. Ponterotto, J. M. Casas, L. A. Suzuki, & C. M. Alexander (Eds.), *Handbook of multicultural counseling* (pp. 73–92). Thousand Oaks, CA: Sage.

Cisneros, S. (1994). *The house on Mango Street.* New York, NY: Perfection Learning.

Clark, R., Anderson, N. B., Clark, V. R., & Williams, D. R. (1999). Racism as a stressor for African Americans. *American Psychologist, 54,* 805–816.

CNN Staff. (2014, August 15). *Five things to know about Michael Brown's shooting.* Retrieved from http://www.cnn.com/2014/08/14/us/ferguson-michael-brown-shooting-5-things/index.html

Condon, J. C., & Yousef, F. (1975). *An introduction to intercultural communication.* New York, NY: Bobbs-Merrill.

Correll, J. (2009, May 5). Racial bias in the decision to shoot? *The Police Chief, LXXVI.* Alexandria, VA: International Association of Chiefs of Police.

Correll, J., Park, B., Judd, C. M., & Wittenbrink, B. (2007). The influence of stereotypes on decisions to shoot. *European Journal of Social Psychology, 37,* 1102–1117.

Cortes, C. E. (2008). Knowledge construction and popular culture: The media as multicultural educator. In J. A. Banks & C. A. McGee Banks (Eds.), *Handbook of research on multicultural education* (pp. 211–227). San Francisco, CA: Jossey-Bass.

Cose, E. (1997). *Color-blind: Seeing beyond race in a race-obsessed world.* New York, NY: HarperCollins.

Cytrynbaum, P. (2011, August 12). Race talk when diversity equals one. *Teaching Tolerance.* Retrieved from http://www.tolerance.org/blog/race-talk-when-diversity-equals-one

De Genova, N. (2006). *Racial transformations: Latinos and Asians remaking the United States.* Durham, NC: Duke University Press.

DePaulo, B. M. (1992). Nonverbal behavior and self-presentation. *Psychological Bulletin, 111,* 203–243.

Devine, P. G. (1989). Stereotypes and prejudice: Their automatic and controlled components. *Journal of Personality and Social Psychology, 56,* 5–18.

DeVos, T., & Banaji, M. R. (2005). American = White? *Journal of Personality and Social Psychology, 88*, 447–466.

Dovidio, J. F., & Gaertner, S. L. (2000). Aversive racism and selective decisions: 1989–1999. *Psychological Science, 11*, 315–319.

Dovidio, J. F., Gaertner, S. L., Kawakami, K., & Hodson, G. (2002). Why can't we all just get along? Interpersonal biases and interracial distrust. *Cultural Diversity and Ethnic Minority Psychology, 8*, 88–102.

Dunham, Y., Baron, A. S., & Banaji, M. R. (2008). The development of implicit intergroup cognition. *Trends in Cognitive Sciences, 12*, 248–253.

Duran, E. (2006). *Healing the soul wound.* New York, NY: Teachers College Press.

Dyer, R. (2002). The matter of whiteness. In P. S. Rothenberg (Ed.), *White privilege* (pp. 9–14). New York, NY: Worth.

Eberhardt, J. L., Davis, P. G., Purdie-Vaughns, V., & Johnson, S. L. (2006). Looking death-worthy. *Psychological Science, 17*, 383–386.

Economist. (2007, August 2). Where black and brown collide (pp. 1–3).

Eligon, J. (2013, July 17). Florida case spurs painful talks between Black parents and their children. *New York Times.* Retrieved from http://www.nytimes.com/2013/07/18/us/florida-case-spurs-painful-talks-between-black-parents-and-their-children.html

Ellison, R. (1972). *Invisible man.* New York, NY: Random House.

Emmons, S. (2013). 5 tips for talking about racism with kids. Retrieved November 1 from http://www.parenting.com/article/5-tips-for-talking-about-racism-with-kids

Feagin, J. R. (2001). *Racist America: Roots, current realities, and future reparations.* New York, NY: Routledge.

Feagin, J. R., & Vera, H. (1992). Confronting one's own racism. In P. S. Rothenberg (Ed.), *White privilege* (pp. 121–125). New York, NY: Worth.

Ford, K. A. (2012). Shifting white ideological scripts: The educational benefits of inter- and intraracial curricular dialogues on the experiences of White college students. *Journal of Diversity in Higher Education, 5*, 138–158.

Frankenberg, R. (1997). *Displacing Whiteness: Essays in social and cultural criticisms.* Durham, NC: Duke University Press.

Freire, P. (1970). *Pedagogy of the oppressed.* New York, NY: Continuum.

Gaertner, S. L., & Dovidio, J. F. (2005). Understanding and addressing contemporary racism: From aversive racism to the common ingroup identity model. *Journal of social Issues, 61*, 615–639.

Gaines, E. J. (1997). *A lesson before dying.* New York, NY: Vintage.

Garrett, M. T., & Portman, T. A. A. (2011). *Counseling Native Americans.* Belmont, CA: Cengage.

Goffman, E. (1959). *The presentation of self in everyday life.* Garden City, NY: Doubleday.

Gomez, F., Overbey, M., Jones, J., & Beckrich, A. (2007). *Race, are we so different? A family guide to talking about race.* Washington, DC: American Anthropological Association.

Gone, J. P. (2009). A community-based treatment for Native American historical trauma: Prospects for evidence-based practice. *Journal of Consulting and Clinical Psychology, 17*, 751–762.

Gone, J. P. (2010). Psychotherapy and traditional healing for American Indians: Exploring the prospects for therapeutic integration. *Counseling Psychologist, 38*, 166–235.

Goodman, D. J. (2001). *Promoting diversity and social justice: Educating people from privileged groups.* Thousand Oaks, CA: Sage.

Goodwin, C. J. (2003). *Research in psychology.* Hoboken, NJ: Wiley.

Goodwin, S. A., Williams, D. D., & Carter-Sowell, A. R. (2010). The psychological sting of stigma: The costs of attributing ostracism to racism. *Journal of Experimental Social Psychology, 46*, 612–618.

Greenwald, A. G., McGhee, D. E., & Schwartz, J. L. K. (1998). Measuring individual differences in implicit cognition: The implicit association task. *Journal of Personality and Social Psychology, 74*, 1464–1480.

Grier, W., & Cobbs, P. (1968). *Black rage.* New York, NY: Basic Books.

Grier, W., & Cobbs, P. (1971). *The Jesus bag.* San Francisco, CA: McGraw-Hill.

Grutter v. Bollinger, 539 U. S. 306 (2003).

Gurin, P., Dey, E. L., Hurtado, S., & Gurin, G. (2002). Diversity and higher education: Theory and impact on educational outcomes. *Harvard Educational Review, 72*, 330–366.

Guthrie, R. V. (1997). *Even the rat was White: A historical view of psychology* (2nd ed.). New York, NY: Oxford University Press.

Haley, A. (1974). *Roots: The saga of an American family.* New York, NY: Vanguard Press.

Hall, E. T. (1959). *The silent language.* Greenwich, CT: Premier Books.

Hall, E. T. (1969). *The hidden dimension.* Garden City, NY: Doubleday.

Hall, E. T. (1974). *Handbook for proxemics research.* Washington, DC: Society for the Ontology of Visual Communications.

Hall, E. T. (1976). *Beyond culture.* New York, NY: Anchor Press.

Hanna, F. J., Talley, W. B., & Guindon, M. H. (2000). The power of perception: Toward a model of cultural oppression and liberation. *Journal of Counseling and Development, 78*, 430–441.

Hansen, J. C., Stevic, R. R., & Warner, R. W. (1982). *Counseling: Theory and process.* Toronto, Canada: Allyn & Bacon.

Hardiman, R. (1982). White identity development: A process oriented model for describing the racial consciousness of White Americans. *Dissertation Abstracts International, 43*, 104A. University Microfilms No. 82-10330.

Harlow, R. (2003). "Race doesn't matter, but . . .": The effects of race on professors' experiences and emotion management in the undergraduate college classroom. *Social Psychology Quarterly, 66*, 348–363.

Harris, A. (1993). Whiteness as property. *Harvard Law Review, 106*, 1707–1791.

Harris Poll. (1994). *Minority mistrust and perceptions*. National Conference of Christians and Jews.

Helms, J. E. (1984). Toward a theoretical explanation of the effects of race on counseling: A Black and White model. *Counseling Psychologist, 12*, 153–165.

Helms, J. E. (1990). *Black and White racial identity: Theory, research, and practice*. New York, NY: Greenwood Press.

Helms, J. E. (1992). *A race is a nice thing to have: A guide to being a White person or understanding the White persons in your life*. Topeka, KS: Content Communications.

Helms, J. E. (1995). An update of Helms's White and people of color racial identity models. In J. G. Ponterotto, J. M. Casas, L. A. Suzuki, & C. M. Alexander (Eds.), *Handbook of multicultural counseling* (pp. 181–191). Thousand Oaks, CA: Sage.

Heppner, P. P., Wampold, B. E., & Kivlighan, D. M. (2008). *Research in counseling psychology*. Belmont, CA: Brooks/Cole.

Highlen, P. S. (1996). MCT theory and implications for organizations/systems. In D. W. Sue, A. L. Ivey, & P. D. Pedersen (Eds.), *A theory of multicultural counseling and therapy* (pp. 65–85). Pacific Grove, CA: Brooks/Cole.

Hirschfield, L. A. (2001). On a folk theory of society: Children, evolution, and mental representations of social groups. *Personality and Social Psychology Review, 5*, 107–117.

hooks, b. (1994). *Teaching to transgress*. New York, NY: Routledge.

Hwang, W. C., & Goto, S. (2009). The impact of perceived racial discrimination on the mental health of Asian Americans and Latino college students. *Asian American Journal of Psychology, 1*, 15–28.

Irvine, J. J., & York, D. E. (1995). Learning styles and culturally diverse students: A literature review. In J. A. Banks & C. A. M. Banks (Eds.), *Handbook of research on multicultural education* (pp. 484–497). New York, NY: Macmillan.

Ito, T. A., & Urland, G. R. (2003). Race and gender on the brain: Electrocortical measures of attention to race and gender multiple categorical individuals. *Journal of Personality and Social Psychology, 85*, 616–626.

Ivey, A. E., Ivey, M. B., & Zalaquett, C. P. (2014). *Intentional interviewing and counseling*. Belmont, CA: Cengage.

Jayakumar, U. M. (2008). Can higher education meet the needs of an increasingly diverse and global society? Campus diversity and cross-cultural workforce competencies. *Harvard Educational Review, 78*, 615–651.

Jenkins, A. H. (1982). *The psychology of the Afro-American*. New York, NY: Pergamon Press.

Jensen, J. V. (1985). Perspective on nonverbal intercultural communication. In L. A. Samovar & R. E. Porter (Eds.), *Intercultural communication: A reader* (pp. 256–272). Belmont, CA: Wadsworth.

Jensen, R. (2002). White privilege shapes the U.S. In P. S. Rothenberg (Ed.), *White privilege* (pp. 103–106). New York, NY: Worth.

Jo, M. H. (1992). Korean merchants in the Black community: Prejudice among the victims of prejudice. *Ethnic and Racial Studies, 15*, 395–411.

Johnson-Cartee, K. S. (2010). Impression management. In R. A. Couto (Ed.), *Political and civic leadership* (pp. 838–848). Thousand Oaks, CA: Sage.

Jones, C., & Shorter-Goodwin, K. (2003). *Shifting: The double lives of Black women in America*. New York, NY: HarperCollins.

Jones, E. E. (1964). *Ingratiation*. New York, NY: Appleton-Century-Crofts.

Jones, J. M. (1997). *Prejudice and racism* (2nd ed.). Washington, DC: McGraw-Hill.

Jones, J. M. (2013a, July 17). *Americans rate racial and ethnic relations in U.S. positively*. Retrieved from http://www.gallup.com/poll/163535/americans-rate-racial-ethnic-relations-positively.aspx

Jones, J. M. (2013b, August 2). Race always matters! *Diversity Us*. Retrieved from http://sites.udel.edu/csd/

Kashef, Z. (2014). *How to talk to your child about race*. Retrieved from http://www.baby center.com/0_how-to-talk-to-your-child-about-race_3657097.bc

Katz, J. (1985). The sociopolitical nature of counseling. *Counseling Psychologist, 13*, 615–624.

Kawakami, K., Dunn, E., Karmali, F., & Dovidio, J. F. (2009). Mispredicting affective and behavioral responses to racism. *Science, 223*, 276–278.

Keita, G. (2013). *After the acquittal: The need for honest dialogue about racial prejudice and stereotyping*. Retrieved from http://www.apa.org/pubs/newsletters/access/2013/07-24/racial-prejudice.aspx

Kelly, J. F., & Greene, B. (2010). Diversity within African American, female therapists: Variability in clients' expectations and assumptions about the therapist. *Psychotherapy: Theory, Research, Practice and Training, 47*, 186–197.

Kim, B. S. K. (2011). *Counseling Asian Americans*. Belmont, CA: Cengage.

Kim, E. H. (1998). "At least you're not Black": Asian Americans in U. S. race relations. *Social Justice, 25*, 1–6.

Kiselica, M. S. (1998). Preparing Anglos for the challenges and joys of multiculturalism. *Counseling Psychologist, 26*, 5–21.

Kiselica, M. S. (1999). Confronting my own ethnocentrism and racism: A process of pain and growth. *Journal of Counseling and Development, 77*, 14–17.

Kivisto, P., & Rundblad, G. (Eds.). (2000). *Multiculturalism in the United States: Current issues, contemporary voices*. Thousand Oaks, CA: Pine Forge Press.

Kochman, T. (1981). *Black and White styles in conflict*. Chicago, IL: University of Chicago Press.

Lass, N. J., Mertz, P. J., & Kimmel, K. (1978). The effect of temporal speech alterations on speaker race and sex identification. *Language and Speech, 21*, 279–190.

Lee, T. (2009, August 10). Here's a tip: Think before you insult. *Star Tribune*.

Leong, F. T. L., Wagner, N. S., & Tata, S. P. (1995). Racial and ethnic variations in help-seeking attitudes. In J. G. Ponterotto, J. M. Casas, L. A. Suzuki, & C. M.

Alexander (Eds.), *Handbook of multicultural counseling* (pp. 415–438). Thousand Oaks, CA: Sage.

Martinez, M., & Gutierrez, T. (2010). 11 Tucson teachers sue Arizona over new "anti-Hispanic" schools law. Retrieved from http://www.cnn.com/2010/US/10/19/arizona.ethnic.studies.lawsuit/

McClain, P. D., Carter, N., DeFrancesco Soto, V., Lyle, M., Grynaviski, J. D., Nunnally, S. C., . . . Cotton, K. D. (2006). Racial distancing in a southern city: Latino immigrants' views of Black Americans. *Journal of Politics, 68*, 3–23.

McIntosh, P. (2002). White privilege: Unpacking the invisible knapsack. In P. S. Rothenberg (Ed.), *White privilege* (pp. 97–101). New York, NY: Worth.

Miller, J. B. (1986). *Toward a psychology of women*. Boston, MA: Beacon Press.

Mindess, A. (1999). *Reading between the signs*. Yarmouth, ME: Intercultural Press.

Minow, M., Shweder, R. A., & Markus, H. (2008). *Just schools*. New York, NY: Russell Sage Foundation.

Montepare, J. M., & Opeyo, A. (2002). The relative salience of physiognomic cues in differentiating faces: A methodological tool. *Journal of Nonverbal Behavior, 26*, 43–59.

MTV. (2014, March). *MTV Bias Survey Final Results*. Retrieved from http://research.lookdifferent.org

Myers, E. R. (2001). African-American perceptions of Asian-American merchants: An exploratory study. In E. R. Myers (Ed.), *Challenges of a changing America: Perspectives on immigration and multiculturalism in the United States* (pp. 171–179). San Francisco, CA: Caddo Gap Press.

National Advisory Commission on Civil Disorders. (1968). *Report of the National Advisory Commission on Civil Disorders* (2 vols.). Washington, DC: National Academy Press.

National Conference of Christians and Jews. (1994). *Taking American's pulse: A summary report of the national survey report of intergroup relations*. New York, NY: Author.

National Journal Staff. (2013, July 19). Full Text: President Obama's Remarks on Trayvon Martin. Retrieved from http://www.nationaljournal.com/whitehouse/full-text-president-obama-s-remarks-on-trayvon-martin-20130719

Neville, H., Awad, G. H., Brooks, J. E., Flores, M. P., & Bluemel, J. (2013). Color-blind racial ideology. *American Psychologist, 68*, 455–466.

Neville, H., Lilly, R. L., Duran, G., Lee, R. M., & Browne, L. (2000). Construction and initial validation of the Color-Blind Racial Attitudes Scale (CoBRAS). *Journal of Counseling Psychology, 47*, 59–70.

Neville, H., Spanierman, L., & Doan, B. (2006). Exploring the association between color-blind racial ideology and multicultural counseling competence. *Cultural Diversity and Ethnic Minority Psychology, 12*, 275–290.

Northrup, S. (1853). *12 years a slave*. Auburn, NY: Derby Miller.

Norton, M. I., Sommers, S. R., Apfelbaum, E. P., Pura, N., & Ariely, D. (2006). Colorblindness and interracial interaction: Playing the "political correctness game." *Psychological Science, 17*, 949–953.

Nydell, M. K. (1996). *Understanding Arabs: A guide for westerners.* Yarmouth, ME: Intercultural Press.

Obama, B. (2013, July 19). *Remarks from the President on Trayvon Martin.* Retrieved from http://www.whitehouse.gov/the-press-office/2013/07/19/remarks-president-trayvon-martin

Oetzel, J. G., & Ting-Toomey, S. (2013). *Handbook of conflict communication.* Thousand Oaks, CA: Sage.

Ong, A. D., Burrow, A. L., Fuller-Rowell, T. E., Ja, N., & Sue, D. W. (2013). Racial microaggressions and daily well-being among Asian Americans. *Journal of Counseling Psychology, 60*, 188–199.

Orbe, M. P., Everett, M., & Putman, A. L. (2013). Interracial and interethnic conflict and communication in the United States. In J. G. Oetzel & S. Ting-Toomey (Eds.), *The Sage handbook of conflict communication* (pp. 661–687). Thousand Oaks, CA: Sage.

Orwell, G. (1945). *Animal farm: A fairy tale.* London, England: Secker & Warburg.

Palmer, P. J. (2007). *The courage to teach.* Hoboken, NJ: Wiley.

Parham, T., Ajamu, A., & White, J. L. (2011). *The psychology of Blacks: Centering our perspectives in the African consciousness.* Boston, MA: Prentice-Hall.

Pasque, P. A., Chesler, M. A., Charbeneau, J., & Carlson, C. (2013). Pedagogical approaches to student racial conflict in the classroom. *Journal of Diversity in Higher Education, 6*, 1–16.

Patrinos, H. A. (2000). The cost of discrimination in Latin America. *Studies in Comparative International Development, 35*, 3–17.

Pearson, J. C. (1985). *Gender and communication.* Dubuque, IA: W. C. Brown.

Pettigrew, T. F., & Tropp, L. R. (2006). A meta-analytic test of intergroup contact theory. *Journal of Personality and Social Psychology, 90*, 751–783.

Pew Research Center. (2007). *Blacks see growing values gap between poor and middle class.* Washington, DC: Author.

Pew Research Center. (2008). *Do Blacks and Hispanics get along?* Washington, DC: Author.

Pew Research Center. (2012). *The rise of Asian Americans.* Washington, DC: Author.

Pierce, C. (1995). Stress analogs of racism and sexism: Terrorism, torture and disaster. In C. Willie, P. Rieker, B. Kramer, & B. Brown (Eds.), *Mental health, racism, and sexism* (pp. 277–293). Pittsburgh, PA: University of Pittsburgh Press.

Pin, E. J., & Turndorg, J. (2009). Staging one's ideal self. In D. Brissett & C. Edgley (Eds.), *Life as theater: A dramaturgical sourcebook* (pp. 163–181). New York, NY: Aldine.

Pitts, P. (1992). *The shadowman's way.* New York, NY: Avon.

Plaut, V. C., Thomas, K. M., & Goren, M. J. (2009). Is multiculturalism or color blindness better for minorities? *Psychological Science, 20*, 444–446.

Pollock, M. (2004). *Colormute: Race talk dilemmas in an American high school*. Princeton, NJ: Princeton University Press.

Ponterotto, J. G., Utsey, S. O., & Pedersen, P. B. (2006). *Preventing prejudice: A guide for counselors, educators, and parents*. Thousand Oaks, CA: Sage.

Pope-Davis, D. B., & Ottavi, T. M. (1994). Examining the association between self-reported multicultural counseling compencies and demographic and educational variables among counselors. *Journal of Counseling and Development, 72*, 651–654.

President's Initiative on Race. (1998). *One America in the 21st century*. Washington, DC: U.S. Government Printing Office.

President's Initiative on Race. (1999). *Pathways to one America in the 21st century*. Washington, DC: U.S. Government Printing Office.

Purdie-Vaughns, V., Steele, C. M., Davies, P. G., Ditlmann, R., & Crosby, J. R. (2008). Social identity contingencies: How diversity cues signal threat or safety for African Americans in mainstream institutions. *Journal of Personality and Social Psychology, 94*, 615–630.

Rabow, J., Venieris, P. Y., & Dhillon, M. (2014). *Ending racism in America: One microaggression at a time*. Dubuque, IA: Kendall Hunt.

Ramsey, S., & Birk, J. (1983). Preparation of North Americans for interaction with Japanese: Considerations of language and communication style. In D. Landis & R. W. Brislin (Eds.), *Handbook of intercultural training* (Vol. 3, pp. 227–259). New York, NY: Pergamon Press.

Rasinski, H. M., & Czopp, A. M. (2010). The effect of target status on witnesses' reactions to confrontation of bias. *Basic and Applied Social Psychology, 32*, 8–16.

Richeson, J. A., & Nussbaum, R. J. (2004). The impact of multiculturalism versus color-blindness on racial bias. *Journal of Experimental Social Psychology, 40*, 417–423.

Richeson, J. A., & Shelton, N. J. (2007). Negotiating interracial interactions: Costs, consequences, and possibilities. *Current Directions in Psychological Science, 16*, 316–320.

Richeson, J. A., Trawalter, S., & Shelton, J. N. (2005). African Americans' implicit racial attitudes and the depletion of executive function after interracial interactions. *Social Cognition, 23*, 934–947.

Ridley, C. R. (2005). *Overcoming unintentional racism in counseling and therapy*. Thousand Oaks, CA: Sage.

Roberts, L. M. (2005). Changing faces: Professional image construction in diverse organizational settings. *Academy of Management Review, 30*, 685–711.

Robinson, G. (2013, July 19). Chris Matthews shows us how to talk about race. *The Washington Post*.

Rogin, M. (2013a, June 6). How do you talk to kids about race? This guide can help. *Good*. Retrieved from http://magazine.good.is/articles/how-do-you-talk-to-kids-about -race-this-guide-can-help

Rogin, M. (2013b, October 13). *How I talk to my kindergarten classroom about race.* Retrieved from http://www.incultureparent.com/2013/10/how-i-talk-to-my-kindergarten-classroom-about-race

Rosenfeld, P. R., Giacalone, R. A., & Riordan, C. A. (1995). *Impression management in organizations: Theory, measurement and practice.* New York, NY: Routledge.

Rowe, M. P. (1990). Barriers in inequality: The power of subtle discrimination to maintain unequal opportunity. *Employer Responsibilities and Rights Journal, 3,* 153–163.

Rowe, W., Bennett, S., & Atkinson, D. R. (1994). White racial identity models: A critique and alternative proposal. *Counseling Psychologist, 22,* 120–146.

Roy, B. (1999). *Bitters in the honey: Tales of hope and disappointment across divides of race and time.* Fayetteville: University of Arkansas Press.

Saguy, T., Dovidio, J. F., & Pratto, F. (2008). Beyond contact: Intergroup contact in the context of power relations. *Personality and Social Psychology, 34,* 432–445.

Scharlin, C., & Villanueva, L. V. (1994). *Philip Vera Cruz: A personal history of Filipino immigrants and the farmworkers movement.* Seattle: University of Washington Press.

Scott, J. C. (1990). *Domination and the arts of resistance: Hidden transcripts.* New Haven, CT: Yale University Press.

Shade, B. J., & New, C. A. (1993). Cultural influences on learning: Teaching implications. In J. A. Banks & C. A. Banks (Eds.), *Multicultural education* (pp. 317–331). Boston, MA: Allyn & Bacon.

Shakespeare, W. (1623). *As you like it.*

Shelton, J. N., Richeson, J. A., Salvatore, J., & Trawalter, S. (2005). Ironic effects of racial bias during interracial interactions. *Psychological Science, 16,* 397–402.

Shih, M., Young, M. J., & Bucher, A. (2013). Working to reduce the effects of discrimination: Identity management strategies in organizations. *American Psychologist, 68,* 145–157.

Shutts, K., Banaji, M. R., & Spelke, E. S. (2010). Social categories guide young children's preferences for novel objects. *Developmental Science, 13,* 599–610.

Singelis, T. (1994). Nonverbal communication in intercultural interactions. In R. W. Brislin & T. Yoshida (Eds.), *Improving intercultural interactions* (pp. 268–294). Thousand Oaks, CA: Sage.

Smith, E. J. (1981). Cultural and historical perspectives in counseling Blacks. In D. W. Sue (Ed.), *Counseling the culturally different: Theory and practice* (pp. 141–185). New York, NY: Wiley.

Solórzano, D., Ceja, M., & Yosso, T. (2000). Critical race theory, racial microaggressions, and campus racial climate: The experiences of African American college students. *Journal of Negro Education, 69*(1/2), 60–73.

Sorensen, N., Nagda, B. A., Gurin, P., & Maxwell, K. E. (2009). Taking a "hands on" approach to diversity in higher education: A critical-dialogic model for effective intergroup interactions. *Analysis of Social Issues and Public Policy, 9,* 3–35.

Spanierman, L. B., Poteat, V. P., Beer, A. M., & Armstrong, P. I. (2006). Psychosocial costs of racism to Whites: Exploring patterns through cluster analysis. *Journal of Counseling Psychology, 53*, 434–441.

Spanierman, L. B., Todd, N. R., & Anderson, C. J. (2009). Psychosocial costs of racism to Whites: Understanding patterns among university students. *Journal of Counseling Psychology, 56*, 239–252.

Spradlin, I. K., & Parsons, R. D. (2008). *Diversity matters.* Belmont, CA: Thompson Wadsworth.

Stanback, H. M., & Pearce, W. B. (1985). Talking to "the man": Some communication strategies used by members of "subordinate" social groups. In L. A. Samovar & R. E. Porter (Eds.), *Intercultural communication: A reader* (pp. 236–253). Belmont, CA: Wadsworth.

Stanley, C. A. (2006). Coloring the academic landscape. *American Educational Research Journal, 43*, 701–736.

Steele, C. M., Spencer, S. J. & Aronson, J. (2002). Contending with group image: The psychology of stereotype and social identity threat. In M. Zanna (Ed.), *Advances in experimental social psychology* (Vol. 34, pp. 379–440). San Diego, CA: Academic Press.

Sternberg, R. J. (Ed.). (1990). *Wisdom: Its nature, origins and development.* New York, NY: Cambridge University Press.

Stevens, F. G., Plaut, V. C., & Sanchez-Burks, J. (2008). Unlocking the benefits of diversity. *Journal of Applied Behavioral Science, 44*, 116–133.

Sue, D. W. (1995). Multicultural organizational development: Implications for the counseling profession. In J. G. Ponterotto, J. M. Casas, L. A. Suzuki, & C. M. Alexander (Eds.), *Handbook of multicultural counseling* (pp. 474–492). Thousand Oaks, CA: Sage.

Sue, D. W. (2003). *Overcoming our racism: The journey to liberation.* San Francisco, CA: Jossey-Bass.

Sue, D. W. (2004). Whiteness and ethnocentric monoculturalism: Making the "invisible" visible. *American Psychologist, 59*, 759–769.

Sue, D. W. (2005). Racism and the conspiracy of silence. *Counseling Psychologist, 33*(1), 100–114.

Sue, D. W. (2008). Multicultural organizational consultation: A social justice perspective. *Consulting Psychology Journal: Practice and Research, 60*, 157–169.

Sue, D. W. (2010). *Microaggressions in everyday life: Race, gender and sexual orientation.* Hoboken, NJ: Wiley.

Sue, D. W. (2013). Race talk: The psychology of racial dialogues. *American Psychologist, 68*, 663–672.

Sue, D. W., Capodilupo, C. M., & Holder, A. M. B. (2008). Racial microaggressions in the life experience of Black Americans. *Professional Psychology: Research and Practice, 39*, 329–336.

Sue, D. W., Capodilupo, C. M., Torino, G. C., Bucceri, J. M., Holder, A. M. B., Nadal, K. L., & Esquilin, M. E. (2007). Racial microaggressions in everyday life: Implications for clinical practice. *American Psychologist, 62,* 271–286.

Sue, D. W., Lin, A. I., Torino, G. C., Capodilupo, C. M., & Rivera, D. P. (2009). Racial microaggressions and difficult dialogues on race in the classroom. *Cultural Diversity and Ethnic Minority Psychology, 15,* 183–190.

Sue, D. W., Nadal, K. L., Capodilupo, C. M., Lin, A. I., Torino, G. C., & Rivera, D. P. (2008). Racial microaggressions against Black Americans: Implications for counseling. *Journal of Counseling and Development, 86,* 330–338.

Sue, D. W., Rivera, D. P., Capodilupo, C. M., Lin, A. I., & Torino, G. C. (2010). Racial dialogues and White trainee fears: Implications for education and training. *Cultural Diversity and Ethnic Minority Psychology, 16,* 206–214.

Sue, D. W., Rivera, D. P., Watkins, N. L., Kim, R. H., Kim, S., & Williams, C. D. (2011). Racial dialogues: Challenges faculty of color face in the classroom. *Cultural Diversity and Ethnic Minority Psychology, 17,* 331–340.

Sue, D. W., & Sue, D. (2013). *Counseling the culturally diverse: Theory and practice.* Hoboken, NJ: Wiley.

Sue, D. W., Torino, G. C., Capodilupo, C. M., Rivera, D. P., & Lin, A. I. (2009). How White faculty perceive and react to classroom dialogues on race: Implications for education and training. *Counseling Psychologist, 37,* 1090–1115.

Takaki, R. (1998). *Strangers from a distant shore.* Boston, MA: Little, Brown.

Tan, A. (1989). *The joy luck club.* New York, NY: Penguin Books.

Tatum, B. D. (1992). Talking about race, learning about racism: The application of racial identity development theory in the classroom. *Harvard Educational Review, 62,* 1–24.

Tatum, B. D. (1997). *Why are all the Black kids sitting together in the cafeteria?* New York, NY: Basic Books.

Tatum, B. D. (2002). Breaking the silence. In P. S. Rothenberg (Ed.), *White privilege* (pp. 115–120). New York, NY: Worth.

Terry, R. (1972). *For whites only.* Grand Rapids, MI: Eerdmans.

Thomas, A., & Sillen, S. (1972). *Racism and psychiatry.* New York, NY: Brunner/Mazel.

Ting-Toomey, S. (1994). Managing intercultural conflicts effectively. In L. A. Samovar & R. E. Porter (Eds.), *Intercultural communication: A reader* (pp. 360–372). Belmont, CA: Wadsworth.

Todd, N. R., & Abrams, E. M. (2011). White dialectics: A new framework for theory, research and practice with White students. *Counseling Psychologist, 39,* 353–395.

Trawalter, S., & Richeson, J. A. (2008). Let's talk about race, baby! When Whites' and Blacks' interracial contact experiences diverge. *Journal of Experimental Social Psychology, 44,* 1214–1217.

Turner, C. S. V., Gonzalez, J. C., & Wood, J. L. (2008). Faculty of color in academe: What 20 years of literature tells us. *Journal of Diversity in Higher Education, 1,* 139–168.

Tynes, B. M., & Markoe, S. (2010). The role of color-blind racial attitudes in reactions to racial discrimination in social network sites. *Journal of Diversity in Higher Education, 3*, 1–13.

U.S. Census Bureau. (2005). *Statistical abstract of the United States: 2004–2005. The national data book.* American Indian, Alaska Native tables. Retrieved from http://www.census.gov/statab/www/sa04aian.pdf

Utsey, S. O., Gernat, C. A., & Hammar, L. (2005). Examining White counselor trainees' reactions to racial issues in counseling and supervision dyads. *Counseling Psychologist, 33*, 449–478.

Valentine, K., Prentice, M., Torres, M. F., & Arellano, E. (2012). The importance of student cross-racial interactions as part of college education: Perceptions of faculty. *Journal of Diversity in Higher Education, 5*, 191–206.

van Dijk, T. A. (1992). Discourse and the denial of racism. *Discourse and Society, 3*, 87–118.

van Dijk, T. A. (1993). *Elite discourse and racism.* Newbury Park, CA: Sage.

van Dijk, T. A. (1999). Discourse analysis as ideology analysis. In C. Schaeffer and A. Wenden (Eds.), *Language and peace* (pp. 17–33). Amsterdam: Harwood Academic Press.

Vorauer, J. S., & Kumhyr, S. M. (2001). Is this about you or me? Self- versus other-directed judgments and feelings in response to intergroup interactions. *Journal of Personality and Social Psychology, 87*, 384–399.

Vorauer, J. S., & Turpie, C. (2004). Disruptive effects of vigilance on dominant group members' treatment of outgroup members: Choking vs. shining under pressure. *Journal of Personality and Social Psychology, 87*, 384–399.

Walsh, R., & Shapiro, S. L. (2006). The meeting of meditative disciplines and Western psychology. *American Psychologist, 61*, 227–239.

Warren, J. W. (2000). Masters in the field: White talk, White privilege, White biases. In F. W. Twine & J. W. Warren (Eds.), *Racing research, researching race: Methodological dilemmas in critical race studies* (pp. 135–164). New York, NY: New York University Press.

Watt, S. K. (2007). Difficult dialogues and social justice: Uses of the privileged identity exploration (PIE) model in student affairs practice. *College Student Affairs Journal, 26*, 114–125.

Weber, S. N. (1985). The need to be: The sociocultural significance of Black language. In L. A. Samovar & R. E. Porter (Eds.), *Intercultural communication: A reader* (pp. 244–253). Belmont, CA: Wadsworth.

Wehrly, B. (1995). *Pathways to multicultural counseling competence.* Pacific Grove, CA: Brooks/Cole.

Wikipedia. (2014). *The 1992 Los Angeles riots.* Retrieved from http://en.wikipedia.org/wiki/1992_Los_Angeles_riots

Williams, J. (2012, May 7). *Remembering the L. A. riots, remembering Latasha Harlins*. Retrieved from http://msmagazine.com/blog/2012/05/07/remembering-the-l-a-riots-remembering-latasha-harlins

Williams, K. (2011, January/February). The pain of exclusion. *Scientific American Journal, 34*–39.

Willow, R. A. (2008). Lived experience of interracial dialogue on race: Proclivity to participate. *Journal of Multicultural Counseling and Development, 36*, 40–51.

Winter, S. (1977). Rooting out racism. *Issues in Radical Therapy, 17*, 24–30.

Wise, T. (2002). Membership has its privileges: Thoughts on acknowledging and challenging Whiteness. In P. S. Rothenberg (Ed.), *White privilege* (pp. 107–110). New York, NY: Worth.

Wolfgang, A. (1985). The function and importance of nonverbal behavior in intercultural counseling. In P. Pedersen (Ed.), *Handbook of cross-cultural counseling and therapy* (pp. 99–105). Westport, CT: Greenwood Press.

Wood, D. B. (2006, May 25). Rising Black-Latino clash on jobs. *Christian Science Monitor*. Retrieved from http://www.csmonitor.com/2006/0525/p01s03-ussc.html

Yankah, E. (2013, July 15). *The truth about Trayvon*. Retrieved from http://www.nytimes.com/2013/07/16/opinion/the-truth-about-trayvon.html

Yoon, I. (1997). *On my own: Korean business and race relations in America*. Chicago, IL: University of Chicago Press.

Young, G. (2003). Dealing with difficult classroom dialogues. In P. Bronstein & K. Quina (Eds.), *Teaching gender and multicultural awareness* (pp. 437–360). Washington, DC: American Psychological Association.

Young, G., & Davis-Russell, E. (2002). The vicissitudes of cultural competence: Dealing with difficult classroom dialogue. In E. Davis-Russell (Ed.), *The California School of Professional Psychology handbook of multicultural education, research, intervention, and training* (pp. 37–53). San Francisco, CA: Jossey-Bass.

Zetzer, H. A. (2011). White out: Privilege and its problems. In S. H. Anderson & V. A. Middleton (Eds.), *Explorations in diversity: Examining privilege and oppression in a multicultural society* (pp. 11–24). Belmont, CA: Cengage.

Zou, L. X., & Dickter, C. L. (2013). Perceptions of racial confrontation: The role of color blindness and comment ambiguity. *Cultural Diversity and Ethnic Minority Psychology, 19*, 92–96.

Author Index

Subject Index